I0138599

Academic. Analytical. Articulate. Dr. Joel Muddamalle tackles questions surrounding spiritual warfare head-on with a steady hand and a scholar's heart. *The Unseen Battle* offers a thoughtful framework for readers who want to better understand spiritual warfare through a biblical lens. Keep this ready nearby!

—Louie Giglio, pastor of Passion City Church, founder of Passion Conferences, author of *Don't Give the Enemy a Seat at Your Table*

There is no one I trust more to give me theological wisdom regarding my questions about Scriptures than my dear friend and brilliant theologian Dr. Joel. He helps make biblical truth accessible and better understood by readers. His latest work, *The Unseen Battle*, is one of Joel's most important and highly anticipated resources. This book is a must-read for anyone who wants solid teaching on the topic of spiritual warfare.

—Lysa TerKeurst, #1 *New York Times* bestselling author and president of Proverbs 31 Ministries

If you've ever wondered why the world seems so broken, why evil appears so organized, or what your role is in the cosmic story, *The Unseen Battle* provides answers rooted deeply in Scripture. This is the book I'll be recommending to everyone who wants to understand not just what we believe but what we're actually up against and, more importantly, the victory that's already ours in Christ.

—Luke Rodgers, *Blurry Creatures* podcast

Dr. Joel Muddamalle is remarkable for bringing theology to life in a way that is both faithful to the text and incredibly practical. With scholarly precision and livable truth, he shows us that where the enemy offers counterfeit, Jesus offers clarity. In a culture looking to vibes and spiritual fads, this book is sure to point you to the unchanging truth of Scripture.

—Levi Lusko, author of *Blessed Are the Spiraling*

In an age suspicious of the supernatural, Muddamalle restores the Bible's vision of a world where the seen and unseen are inseparably joined. With clarity and insight, he pulls back the curtain on the unseen battle, tackles hard questions, and connects the story's details into a bigger picture.

—Patrick Schreiner, associate professor of New Testament and biblical theology at Midwestern Baptist Theological Seminary

Most of us don't know what to do with the stranger passages of Scripture, so we tend to ignore them. Joel doesn't. He does the hard work for us, showing how they all fit into the bigger story. *The Unseen Battle* is such a gift to the church.

—Zach Windahl, author of *The Bible, Simplified*

The Unseen Battle will help you strap up, think deeply, and stand firmly with fresh clarity and grounding in God's Word regarding the spiritual realm. You'll finish with the confidence that in Christ the dark powers of this world are stripped, disarmed, and defeated, and the light has already won.

—Dr. Megan Fate Marshman, DMin, author of *Relaxed*, speaker and Bible teacher

In this timely book, Dr. Joel Muddamalle paints a holistic picture and a thoughtful theological frame of the supernatural realm that we live among today. I believe his work will bring clarity and vision in the midst of so much confusion.

—Jon Tyson, Church of the City New York

With exquisite scholarship and studious attention to the biblical text, Muddamalle peals back the curtain on the spiritual battle that is integral to the story of Scripture. If you want to gain a fuller understanding of the biblical drama of salvation, *The Unseen Battle* is a must-read!

—Preston Sprinkle, PhD, host of *Theology in the Raw* and president of the Center for Faith, Sexuality, and Gender

Pushing against both an unhealthy obsession with the supernatural and a desupernaturalized reading of Scripture, Joel Muddamalle invites us to look closer at what the Bible says about angels and demons. If you've wondered about "divine council theory" or what the Bible means when it speaks of God's family or the heavenly royal court, this book will provide a clear and helpful introduction. Highly recommended!

—Gavin Ortlund, president of Truth Unites, visiting professor of historical theology, Phoenix Seminary

Dr. Joel Muddamalle has delivered a biblically balanced approach to the cosmic supernatural reality of our lives. He beautifully avoids both excessive obsession and severe neglect of the supernatural. We live in an enchanted world, and *The Unseen Battle* calls us to take the supernatural realm seriously.

—Matt Chandler, lead pastor of the Village Church

Joel finds the middle path between ignorance and obsession toward the spiritual realm and guides the reader down a biblical path toward awareness and confidence. A necessary work delivered in perfect timing.

—Dr. Brian McCormack, author, speaker, Bible teacher, and executive director of Breakaway

THE
UNSEEN
BATTLE

**SPIRITUAL WARFARE,
THE THREE REBELLIONS,
AND CHRIST'S VICTORY
OVER DARK POWERS**

JOEL MUDDAMALLE

ZONDERVAN
REFLECTIVE

ZONDERVAN REFLECTIVE

The Unseen Battle
Copyright © 2025 by Joel Muddamalle

Published by Zondervan, 3950 Sparks Drive SE, Suite 101, Grand Rapids, MI 49546, USA.
Zondervan is a registered trademark of The Zondervan Corporation, L.L.C., a wholly owned
subsidiary of HarperCollins Christian Publishing, Inc.

Requests for information should be addressed to customercare@harpercollins.com.

Zondervan titles may be purchased in bulk for educational, business, fundraising, or sales promo-
tional use. For information, please email SpecialMarkets@Zondervan.com.

ISBN 978-0-310-17764-7 (audio)

Library of Congress Cataloging-in-Publication Data

Names: Muddamalle, Joel author
Title: The unseen battle : spiritual warfare, the three rebellions, and Christ's victory over dark
    powers / Joel J. Muddamalle.
Description: Grand Rapids, MI : Zondervan Aademic, [2025] | Includes bibliographical references
    and index.
Identifiers: LCCN 2025041837 (print) | LCCN 2025041838 (ebook) | ISBN 9780310177623
    paperback | ISBN 9780310177630 ebook
Subjects: LCSH: Spiritual warfare
Classification: LCC BV4509.5 .M826 2025 (print) | LCC BV4509.5 (ebook)
LC record available at https://lccn.loc.gov/2025041837
LC ebook record available at https://lccn.loc.gov/2025041838

Unless otherwise noted, Scripture quotations are taken from the Christian Standard Bible®,
Copyright © 2017 by Holman Bible Publishers. Used by permission. Christian Standard Bible®
and CSB®, are federally registered trademarks of Holman Bible Publishers. · Scripture quotations marked ESV are taken from the ESV® Bible (The Holy Bible, English Standard Version®).
Copyright © 2001 by Crossway, a publishing ministry of Good News Publishers. Used by permis-
sion. All rights reserved. · Scripture quotations marked NIV are taken from the Holy Bible, New
International Version®, NIV®. Copyright © 1973, 1978, 1984, 2011 by Biblica, Inc.® Used by
permission of Zondervan. All rights reserved worldwide. www.Zondervan.com. The "NIV" and
"New International Version" are trademarks registered in the United States Patent and Trademark
Office by Biblica, Inc.® · Scripture quotations marked RSV are taken from the Revised Standard
Version of the Bible. Copyright © 1946, 1952, and 1971 National Council of the Churches of Christ
in the United States of America. Used by permission. All rights reserved.

Any internet addresses (websites, blogs, etc.) and telephone numbers in this book are offered as a
resource. They are not intended in any way to be or imply an endorsement by Zondervan, nor does
Zondervan vouch for the content of these sites and numbers for the life of this book.

All rights reserved. No part of this publication may be reproduced, stored in a retrieval system, or
transmitted in any form or by any means—electronic, mechanical, photocopy, recording, or any
other—except for brief quotations in printed reviews, without the prior permission of the publisher.

Published in association with the literary agency of Brock, Inc., P.O. Box 384, Matthews, NC
28105.

Without limiting the exclusive rights of any author, contributor or the publisher of this publication,
any unauthorized use of this publication to train generative artificial intelligence (AI) technologies
is expressly prohibited. HarperCollins also exercise their rights under Article 4(3) of the Digital
Single Market Directive 2019/790 and expressly reserve this publication from the text and data
mining exception.

HarperCollins Publishers, Macken House, 39/40 Mayor Street Upper,
Dublin 1, D01 C9W8, Ireland (https://www.harpercollins.com)

Cover design: Studio Gearbox
Cover art: Morphart Creation / Shutterstock
Interior design: Sara Colley

Printed in the United States of America

25 26 27 28 29 LBC 5 4 3 2 1

CONTENTS

*Dedicated to my friend, mentor,
and Doktorvater, Dr. Mike Heiser*

*Mike, you always said your biblical worldview shifted
when you encountered Psalm 82. Well, mine shifted
when I met you. This book stands on the shoulders
of your lifetime of research. Praying this one makes
you proud, and I apologize ahead of time for my
bibliography not being "beefy enough" for you.*

See you in the divine council, my friend.

FOREWORD

I can still remember the day I received the phone call. On the other end of the line was the author of this book, Dr. Joel Muddamalle, trying his best to contain his excitement. He began sharing about a new book he was writing and how he wanted to honor his mentor, my late husband, Dr. Michael Heiser. I absorbed his enthusiasm and loved the flavor of the book he described—you've seen the title, right? But then he surprised me, asking if I would consider writing the foreword. I wasn't expecting that. Since you are reading this, you know I said yes, but as soon as I hung up it hit me. Mike should be the one writing this. He should be the one here with us, reading Joel's manuscript and telling you why you should read it.

As many of you know, my husband went home to his eternal reward on February 20, 2023, after a two-year battle with pancreatic cancer. Some say he was taken too soon. Most times, I agree with that. But I know we serve a gracious, loving, and sovereign God, and he wanted Mike. Still, one of Mike's greatest fears was the uncertainty of not knowing who would pick up where he had left off. I'm telling you, he agonized over this, and I had my doubts as well.

Those doubts were put to rest when one day I happened to be listening to a *Blurry Creatures* podcast featuring Joel. The conversation was all about his dissertation (the same one this book is based upon) as they recalled stories about Mike and his influence on Joel, as well as some of the editorial comments he had made as Joel's dissertation advisor. Listening to that podcast, I said to myself, "Mike, this is the guy!" I sensed that Joel had that same contagious enthusiasm for the topics Mike had spent the last fifteen years of his life working on. And I knew right then and there that Mike's legacy would continue with Joel in his court. Though he isn't here to write this foreword, I have no doubt he would have endorsed it wholeheartedly, proud and honored to see someone taking up the mantle of his research and going beyond what he would have been able to accomplish alone.

Now although they share a similar love for scholarly research of the Bible there are also some very noticeable differences between them. Mike's humor was understated and a bit dry; Joel's is loud and proud. Joel is a fast talker, while Mike was more measured. Joel loves him some basketball; Mike couldn't stand the game. Despite these differences, Mike and Joel were buds, both friends and colleagues.

I first met Joel when we were living in the Pacific Northwest where Mike was working at Logos Bible Software as a scholar-in-residence. Joel and his wife, Brittany, and their young son had just moved to Lynden, Washington, where Joel had started a new job at Logos. We were acquainted with their family through mutual social gatherings and company functions, and it was immediately apparent that Joel was a devoted husband, father, and son of God. His excitement for life, his love for this family, and his hunger to gain a greater understanding of the Scriptures were clearly evident, leaving a deep impression on both me and Mike. I am still impressed every time I listen to Joel talk about theology, hear him on podcasts, see him on social media, or learn about the books he is writing.

The book you are about to read is an attempt to take the best of Joel's dissertation and make it accessible to a popular audience. It still has lots of Greek and Hebrew, and I know Mike would have been thrilled to see the vast number of footnotes, not just those citing Mike, but so many other scholars and great thinkers. This book is a deep dive into the context of the biblical world and the text of the Bible, and I know the work and research in this book would have blessed Mike and encouraged him, as it does me.

As you read *The Unseen Battle*, I hope that you will experience, as I have, the unique way Joel expounds on several of the same topics that Mike wrote about, though in a fresh and new way, with even more clarity and color. I am grateful to Joel for fulfilling one of Mike's biggest dreams: having a kindred brother come along beside him in the mission of opening up those confusing passages of the Bible so we can fall in love with the message of Scripture all over again. Thank you as well to Zondervan Reflective for daring to publish a cutting-edge theology book that may challenge some accepted understandings of the ancient texts.

Joel, I believe I am authorized to thank you on behalf of my late husband, Dr. Mike Heiser, for the work you have done. He would be so proud of you.

Best regards and blessings to you all,
Drenna Heiser-Hollander

INTRODUCTION

C. S. Lewis once said, "There are two equal and opposite errors into which our race can fall about the devils. One is to disbelieve in their existence. The other is to believe and to feel an excessive and unhealthy interest in them. They themselves are equally pleased by both errors and hail a materialist or a magician with the same delight."[1] Lewis's observations apply not only to his context but to our current culture. At times there can be an overwhelming obsession with spiritual beings, and other times there can be severe neglect. We see evidence of the obsession at work with the meteoric rise of shows like *Ancient Aliens, Roswell,* and various documentaries that explore the world of conspiracy theories related to aliens and government cover-ups. But this is all the tip of the iceberg. Books like *Harry Potter* and *Game of Thrones* lead readers into the enchanting world of magic, dragons, and the supernatural.

On the other side of this paradigm is a worldview approach that can be categorized as "de-mythologizing," an intentional attempt to strip our world of anything supernatural or cosmic.[2]

---

1. C. S. Lewis, *The Screwtape Letters* (San Francisco: HarperOne, 2001), ix.
2. Throughout this book I will use the terms "supernatural" and "cosmic"

We need a return to a biblically balanced approach regarding the cosmic reality of our world that protects us from obsession yet does not reject what is explicit in the Scriptures.

To make this point let's do a quick thought experiment. Please identify what is *not* supernatural in the next statement:

> As Christians, we believe Jesus is the Son of God, who in the incarnation and through the virgin birth entered humanity, taking upon human flesh without losing an ounce of his divinity. He lived a perfect life on earth, literally died by being hung on a Roman cross, after three days defeated death through death, and then rose to sit at the right hand of the Father in his ascension.

If you are struggling to identify what is *not* supernatural in this statement, it's because it is *all* supernatural. All of this is cosmic. And this is a statement summarizing the foundational beliefs we have as followers of Jesus.

For many of us, the supernatural reality of the Jesus story has been normalized so we don't even blink an eye when we hear it. And yet this is all interconnected with a supernatural, cosmic understanding of reality and is integral to the gospel message. If we took out one part of this statement, we would lose the fabric of the gospel, the good news of

interchangeably. There are some challenges with the term "supernatural" as it can suggest an unhelpful separation of the earthly and cosmic. The language of the Bible uses terms like "spiritual/" or "cosmic/" to convey different realms all still very related to an earthly existence. I will argue throughout this book we should return to a worldview that sees an intersection between the earthly and cosmic working together rather than differentiating them into isolated and disconnected categories.

Jesus. The supernatural and cosmic dimensions are woven throughout that message.

And they are not limited to this short summary of the gospel. These supernatural elements appear throughout the Bible—Old and New Testaments. Imagine what would happen if we took a fresh look at these supernatural and cosmic parts and treated them as more than nice stories from long ago. Think about Lazarus's resurrection, the feeding of the five thousand, walking on water, blind people regaining sight, lame people walking, water turning into wine, demonic exorcisms—the list goes on and on. My point is simply that we must take the supernatural realm seriously and then consider the real implications it has for our human earthly existence.

This is exactly what the apostle Paul did when he wrote his letter to the church in Ephesus.[3] Paul employs the terminology of a *household* (*oikos*; οἶκός) to describe the family of God. As we will explore in greater detail throughout this book, the concept of the household or family of God is foundational to the storyline of Scripture. The Bible is all about God's relentless desire to have his family back together—and the lengths he will go to accomplish that goal. We could even summarize the big story of Scripture something like this.

---

3. This author holds to Pauline authorship of Ephesians, following Barth, Abbot, Asting, Harnack, Sander, Schlier, Westcott, and others. For an overview of various positions concerning Ephesians' authorship and defense for Pauline authorship, see Markus Barth, *Ephesians: Introduction, Translation, and Commentary on Chapters 1–3*, Anchor Bible 34 (New Haven, CT: Yale University Press, 2008), 36. See also Thomas Kingsmill Abbott, *A Critical and Exegetical Commentary on the Epistles to the Ephesians and to the Colossians*, International Critical Commentary (New York: Scribner's, 1909), ix–xxvii.

God is a good Father who created good things. The jewel of his creation was humanity created in his likeness and image, who were enticed by a supernatural being (the serpent/*nachash*), rebelled, and shattered the family of God. But God wouldn't sit by with his family in ruins. God was determined to have his family back, reunited, and restored—all those who turned to him in repentance. The means of this restoration is Jesus, the unique and eternal Son of God.

Paul draws on the household (*oikos*) terminology, writing from a worldview that accepted there was ongoing war in the cosmos and, even more recently for Paul, the victory of Christ over rebellious supernatural beings (referred to as "powers, principalities, and authorities" in Pauline language). This cosmic victory was now leading to the regathering of the rejected nations back into the household of God (Eph 1:10–14; 20–21; 3:10; 4:8–12).[4] To put it differently, Paul's reliance on the household (*oikos*) as his framework assumes an ancient worldview that incorporates both a spiritual and physical dimension.[5] The household of God has been broken, and this presents a conflict. A battle is now being waged for

---

4. Michael S. Heiser, *The Unseen Realm: Recovering the Supernatural Worldview of the Bible*, 1st ed. (Bellingham, WA: Lexham, 2015), 279n5. Heiser identifies this family as "circumcision neutral" and is not tied to Abraham's physical descent; instead, it is Abraham's spiritual family.
5. In the same way ethnicity is not obliterated or denied upon entry into the family of God at conversion, ethnicity is not rejected or lost "spiritually" in the eschaton. Rather, it will be retained and celebrated in the new heavens and new earth. Thus, the ethnic aspect of redeemed humanity will be present in the eschaton as the nations gather around King Jesus (Rev 7:9) along with the heavenly host, God's first family-household. More on God's cosmic family in chapter 2.

INTRODUCTION

the people within the household. You and I find ourselves amid this unseen battle. On the one hand, the battle is spiritual and is therefore unseen. We are largely unaware of it happening around us. On the other hand, the skirmishes in this ongoing battle can be felt and seen in the physical realm.

This ancient, cosmic worldview stems from texts such as Genesis 11, Deuteronomy 32:8–9, and Daniel 10. Deuteronomy 32:8–9 frames the conflict between Israel and the nations as a byproduct of God's judgment of humanity at Babel, where the nations were allotted to lesser gods (*elohim*; אֱלֹהִים), who are members of the heavenly host (cf. Deut 4:19–20; 17:1–3; 29:23–26; 32:17). Daniel's notion of cosmic powers behind geopolitical empires presumes this worldview (Dan 10). Paul's description of cosmic powers of darkness in geopolitical dominion terms (e.g., principalities, powers) also presumes this worldview. As we will see, Deuteronomy 32:8–9 is a key passage for unlocking this understanding, as it sets two households against each other in earthly and cosmic terms: the household of Yahweh versus all other households on earth—the nations, their people, and their gods.[6]

In the New Testament Paul picks up where the story of the Old Testament leaves off in describing this unseen battle. He believes the gods of the nations were real, fallen supernatural beings who went into rebellion against God and are now determined to lead humanity into rebellion with them. This pattern of rebellion is present three times

---

6. Greco-Roman culture shared this worldview, where city-states, empires, etc. worshiped certain gods because those gods had been allotted to them at the behest of the highest gods (e.g., Plato, *Critias* 109).

xvii

in the first twelve chapters of Genesis, though many of us miss the cosmic dimension behind these narratives. These stories—found in Genesis 3; 6; and 11—are three rebellions that frame why we have this ongoing earthly and heavenly battle waging around us. The Great Commission of Jesus to bring good news to the nations is not a new or novel idea. God's plan is to have his family back together, recapturing the wayward children (the gentile nations) from captivity to the gods of those nations. This is the unseen battle, a battle against the gods of the nations. This is spiritual warfare, a war against the principalities and cosmic powers. And there is really good news in all of this: Jesus is victorious.

But let's back up and start from the beginning. Where did this war begin? How did it all get started?

It begins in a garden, the garden home of Yahweh where his human and supernatural family once lived together—a place called Eden.

ONE

THE GARDEN HOUSE OF GOD

ome is a sacred place. We go there to rest. It's the place where we can relax and enjoy peace and escape from the pressures of the world. It's where we live in relationship with our family. Home is a special place shared freely with those we love, a place we invite our friends for meals and fellowship, and it is a place that deserves to be protected from any who might want to destroy it.

In the opening pages of Genesis, we meet God as he plants a royal garden called Eden. Within this garden he creates humanity, beings made in his likeness to cultivate, steward, and guard his garden from outside enemies. God also wants his family to remain distinct from those outside the garden. He wants this to be a special place—a holy place. God's vision in creating this garden is to have his newly created human beings expand the goodness of his creation from within Eden out to the ends of the earth. There is a key point here that can easily be overlooked: Eden was a parcel of Mesopotamian land on earth, but all of earth was not Eden.[1]

---

1. I first heard this statement from Michael Heiser.

When God creates earth and then humanity in his likeness and image (Gen 1:26), he places Adam and Eve in the
garden of Eden.[2] It is in Eden that we see God dwelling
with humanity, and Eden is also the meeting place for God's
heavenly (cosmic) and earthly (human) family. In Eden we
see God's human and heavenly family united. Where do we
see this? The evidence lies in the cultural context for how
we understand this garden as a type of temple, located on
a mountain, as well as the description of Adam and Eve as
they are placed in Eden. Let's take a closer look at each of
these aspects.

God's placement of Adam and Eve in Eden is of primary
importance, as Eden serves as the first temple sanctuary
where God dwells. As a temple sanctuary, Eden is God's
"home" and the household dwelling for God's blended
family (both human and cosmic): "Eden was the original
home of God on earth, where he visited with Adam and
Eve and where the Tree of Life was located (Gen 3:22)."[3]
Old Testament scholar Gordon Wenham notes that Eden

---

2. Nahum Sarna makes an important observation that will be addressed in
   the subsequent sections relating the "let us" language of Gen 1:26 to the
   expulsion of Adam and Eve in Gen 3:22 and once again in connection to Babel
   in Gen 11:7. See Nahum M. Sarna, *Genesis*, The JPS Torah Commentary
   (Philadelphia: Jewish Publication Society, 1989), 12.
3. Ted Noel and Ken Noel, "A Scientific Paradigm for the Genesis Flood,"
   Journal of the Adventist Theological Society 12 (2001): 113. Wenham notes
   that Gerhard von Rad would disagree here. He holds that Eden was not a
   home of God but merely a gracious gift given to humanity by God. This is
   in response to von Rad's belief that other scholars have read "non-biblical
   mythical ideas about the blessedness of man's original state." See Gordon
   Wenham, "Original Sin in Genesis 1–11," *The Churchman* 104 (1990): 310.
   For von Rad's original work, see *Genesis: A Commentary*, 2nd ed. (London:
   SCM Press, 1972), 75. The language of "dwelling" is essential as it recollects
   Eph 2:22, where God dwells within the believer through the Spirit.

is not just a piece of farmland in the Mesopotamian region but an "archetypal sanctuary, that is, a place where God dwells and where man should worship him."[4] Eden is the place where God enjoyed the presence of both his human and supernatural family, all dwelling together.

Eden has ties to the broader ancient Near Eastern (ANE) context where sacred space was associated with natural locations (for example, a hill, one or more trees, a stone, or a cave).[5] As a garden planted by God, Eden can be understood parallel to an ANE context that associated the deity's or king's dwelling with a natural formation such as a garden. Eden was not merely a garden located on the plains, but it existed on a mountain that was home to the headwaters of several large rivers. This presents a vital connection to other ANE myths in which the gods established their homes on mountains as a residence and "meeting place" that connected the earth and heavens.[6]

---

4. Gordon J. Wenham, "Sanctuary Symbolism in the Garden of Eden Story," *Proceedings of the World Congress of Jewish Studies* 9 (1986): 19.

5. Daniel T. Lioy, "The Garden of Eden as a Primordial Temple or Sacred Space for Humankind," *Conspectus Volume* 10 (2010): 30.

6. G. K. Beale, *The Temple and the Church's Mission: A Biblical Theology of the Dwelling Place of God*, New Studies in Biblical Theology 17 (Downers Grove, IL: IVP Academic, 2004), 76. Beale makes further connections with gardens, temples, rivers, and mountains in connection to the ANE religions. Ramses III created a garden in the deity's house and "made to grow the pure grove of thy [the deity's] temple . . . with gardeners to cultivate it." See James Henry Breasted, *Ancient Records of Egypt: Historical Documents from the Earliest Times to the Persian Conquest*, vol. 4, *The Twentieth to the Twenty-Sixth Dynasties* (Chicago: University of Chicago Press, 1906), 4:148, §272. Genesis 2:10 presents a river flowing from Eden and is similar to Ezek 47:1–12, where a river flows from the temple and brings life to the Dead Sea. This points to Eden being elevated, where the river from Eden flows out and into the world. Further, Ezekiel depicts Eden as located on a mountain (Ezek 28:14, 16). For more on Edenic themes in Ezekiel, see Moshe Greenberg, *Ezekiel 21–37: A*

Eden's location on a mountain creates a connection to Israel's temple, which was also located on a mountain, Mount Zion (Exod 15:17).[7] In fact, careful study of the Old Testament shows that Eden and the temple are closely connected. God as king establishes an earthly family and gives them his image and likeness as evidence of their sonship. This concept was not uncommon in the world of the ancient Near East.[8] The king's establishment of a son or royal court also had a purpose. The king's children were given responsibilities and duties related to the management of the household and the kingdom. This is equally true of Adam and Eve, who are given specific assignments

---

New Translation with Introduction and Commentary, Anchor Yale Bible 22A (New Haven, CT: Yale University Press, 2008), 591.

7. For more on land as an inheritance in connection to Eden/temple, see Oren R. Martin, *Bound for the Promised Land: The Land Promise in God's Redemptive Plan*, New Studies in Biblical Theology 34 (Downers Grove, IL: IVP Academic, 2015), 31–115.

8. In ancient Egyptian mythology, Amon Re says to Amenophis III, "Thou art my beloved son, come forth from my limbs, my very own image, which I have put upon the earth. I have permitted thee to rule over the earth in peace." This quotation makes a connection between deity, kingship, and household/family. Cited in Claus Westermann, *Genesis 1–11*, Continental Commentary (Minneapolis: Fortress, 1994), 153–55. The idea of sonship based on the king was also present in the ANE. Gentry notes, "The ancient Near Eastern and Canaanite cultural context is significant. In Egypt, from at least 1650 B.C. onwards, people perceived the king as the image of god because he was the son of god. What is stressed is that the behavior of the king reflects the behavior of the god. The king as the image of god reflects the characteristics and essential notions of the god." Peter J. Gentry, "Rethinking the 'Sure Mercies of David' in Isaiah 55:3," *Westminster Theological Journal* 69 (2007): 284. Additional claims of sonship can be attributed to Adam's function as a prophet/priest in Eden, the garden-temple. Michael Morales argues that sonship is related to priesthood and kingship. See David Schrock, "Old Testament. Review of God's Mediators: A Biblical Theology of Priesthood by Andrew S. Malone," *Themelios* 43 (2018): 102. The concept of priesthood attached to sonship works itself out in the New Testament as well, where Christians receive their status as sons and daughters as an inheritance (household function and language) and are welcomed into the family and household of God (Gal 3:16, 26–29; Eph 1:11; 2:19–22).

following their placement in Eden, which served as God's two-family household dwelling.[9] Adam and Eve are given tasks as members of God's household, evidence that Adam and Eve are trusted stewards in the house of God and have a responsibility to both the house and the head of the house.[10] Lioy says it well: "The Creator did not bring Eden into existence 'strictly for the habitation of humans'; instead, they were stewards whom He 'invited to enjoy and cultivate' His garden."[11]

Something that may be surprising to us is that humanity was not alone in the garden of Eden. Your first thought may be of the animals that were with humans in the garden. But there were other family members of God's household also present, even while creation was coming into existence. But more on this in the next chapter.

---

9. Adam is told to "cultivate," and "guard/keep" Eden in Gen 2:15. In a sense, these commandments can be viewed as household requirements and expectations. Beale, *The Temple and the Church's Mission*, 68, observes, "The notion of divine 'commanding' (*ṣāwâ*) or giving of 'commandments' (*miṣwôt*) not untypically follows the word 'guard/keep' (*šāmar*) elsewhere, and in 1 Kings 9:6, when both 'serving' and 'keeping' occur together, the idea of 'commandments to be kept' is in view." The 1 Kings passage is important as God commands Solomon not to "serve other gods," a continued thread of household requirements. The failure of such results in the act of rebellion with a consequence of disinheritance.
10. Trevor J. Burke, *Adopted into God's Family: Exploring a Pauline Metaphor*, New Studies in Biblical Theology 22 (Downers Grove, IL: IVP Academic, 2006), 186n16. Burke quotes Adams, saying, "The formulation reflects an Adamic soteriology. The 'glory' to which reference is made is the pristine glory meant for Adam, eschatologically restored to redeemed humanity. When that glory is revealed, Paul implies, creation will be restored to its intended place, and God's children will be re-established in their status as stewards of the created order and enabled to exercise stewardship properly." See Edwards Adams, "Paul's Story of God and Creation: The Story of How God Fulfils His Purposes in Creation," in *Narrative Dynamics in Paul: A Critical Assessment*, ed. B. Longenecker (Louisville: Westminster John Knox, 2002), 19–43.
11. Lioy, "The Garden of Eden," 28.

HUMAN AND SPIRITUAL FAMILIES IN ONE HOUSEHOLD

The worldview of the ANE understood that gods had both a human and a divine family, and these families were interrelated. This was especially true of both the Egyptians and the Mesopotamians.[12] A closer look at Egyptian and Mesopotamian culture and context can aid us in seeing Israel's unique perspective in contrast to the cultures around them.

Let's start with the Egyptians. The title of their ruler, *Pharaoh*, is made up of two words that mean "great household."[13] As the head of the household or the "king," Pharaoh would appoint trusted individuals within the household into positions of power with responsibility. These individuals make up his council. One of the most coveted positions within the Egyptian royal court was the *T'ate*, or the chief of the whole administration. This chief administrator would be considered second only to Pharaoh and responsible for keeping order and administration within the household.[14] It is likely that Joseph of the Bible held this role as he rose to second in command to Pharaoh.

The Pharaoh himself is often divinized and understood to be one among the gods responsible for creation. An example of

---

12. Goetzmann, "House, Build, Manage, Steward," 247. For a sketch of household terms in the OT and NT, see above.
13. Heiser, *The Unseen Realm*, 25.
14. John Skinner, *A Critical and Exegetical Commentary on Genesis*, International Critical Commentary (New York: Scribner, 1910), 469. Additionally, in Sumerian and Akkadian the word for "palace" includes the Sumerian sign for "house" and combined with the adjective for "great/large" equates to "the Great house." Therefore, the household/kingship/divinity relationships go all the way back to the Sumerians. See I. J. Winter, "'Seat of Kingship' / 'A Wonder to Behold': The Palace as Construct in the Ancient Near East," *Ars Orientalis* 23 (1993): 27–55.

this in the Bible is found in a rhetorical conversation between Yahweh and Ezekiel the prophet in Ezekiel 29:3. Yahweh says, "Behold, I am against you, Pharaoh king of Egypt, the great dragon that lies in the midst of his streams, that says, 'My Nile is my own; I made it for myself'" (ESV). In this text the Pharaoh is understood to see himself as a great sea creature that owns the Nile. Further, it is possible that the Hebrew of Ezekiel 29:3 can be translated as "I have made myself."[15] This understanding mirrors the Egyptian god Atum, who claimed self-creation. It also highlights how the Egyptians saw the divine and human households interacting with each other.[16]

Another example of this can be seen with Amenhotep IV, who replaced the traditional sun god (Amun-Re) with an "iconographically distinct form," the Aten. He also changed his name to Akhenaten, meaning "he who acts effectively on behalf of the Aten." Akhenaten established a new city, Akhetaten, "the place where the Aten manifests itself (in the form of the king)."[17] Bill Arnold comments on the father-son relationship, saying, "With the sole god Aten as his father, Akhenaten was the direct manifestation of the sun and the world's only mediator of the divine presence."[18] For the

---

15. Daniel Isaac Block, *The Book of Ezekiel, Chapters 25–48*, The New International Commentary on the Old Testament (Grand Rapids: Eerdmans, 1997), 137.
16. On the deity of the kings of Egypt, see Henri Frankfort, *Kingship and the Gods* (Chicago: University of Chicago Press, 1978), 24–47.
17. Joel M. LeMon, "Egypt and the Egyptians," in *The World Around the Old Testament: The People and Places of the Ancient Near East*, ed. Bill T. Arnold and Brent A. Strawn (Grand Rapids: Baker Academic, 2016), 176–77.
18. LeMon, "Egypt and the Egyptians," 177. An additional example of the gods in relationship to humanity can be found with Osiris, the son of Sibou (earth god) and Nouit (heaven goddess), who was a personification of man. See G. Maspero, "Egyptian Souls and Their Worlds," *The New Princeton Review* 6 (1888): 23–35.

Egyptians, the household of the king was the connection point, the place where both earthly and spiritual beings resided. There were roles and responsibilities on display in the form of a royal council. The same concept holds true for the Mesopotamians.

In the Mesopotamian context there are at least three terms for *father*, with *ab-ba* meaning the "head of the family." This is the term applied in two epithets of the Mesopotamian deity En-lil, who is called "father of all gods" and thus relates to "the *Pater familias* of the world of the gods."[19] Another central element of the household was the relationship of the household to the gods. Mesopotamian and Egyptian mythology held that the gods' origins were found within the context of family relationships.[20] These examples point to the perception of the Egyptians and Mesopotamians believing they had a real familial connection between themselves and the gods that they served and believed they originated from.[21] They believed the human household emulated the deity's divine household structure. These ANE deities are

19. Helmer Ringgren, "אָב," in *Theological Dictionary of the Old Testament*, ed. G. Johannes Botterweck and Helmer Ringgren, trans. John T. Willis, 17 vols. (Grand Rapids: Eerdmans, 1977), 1:3. Dille makes the important observation that the Hebrew authors named the foreign gods "fathers" of their people (Num 21:29; Mal 2:11). See Sarah J. Dille, *Mixing Metaphors: God as Mother and Father in Deutero-Isaiah* (New York: T&T Clark, 2004), 35. See also David Tasker, *Ancient Near Eastern Literature and the Hebrew Scriptures About the Fatherhood of God* (New York: Peter Lang, 2004). Additionally, "Lord Anshar" is referred to as the "father of the gods" and calls Marduk his son. See James Bennett Pritchard, ed., *The Ancient Near Eastern Texts Relating to the Old Testament*, 3rd ed. (Princeton, NJ: Princeton University Press, 1969), 64.
20. John H. Walton, *Ancient Near Eastern Thought and the Old Testament: Introducing the Conceptual World of the Hebrew Bible* (Grand Rapids: Baker Academic, 2006), 48.
21. Tyson L. Putthoff, *Gods and Humans in the Ancient Near East* (New York: Cambridge University Press, 2020), 51.

described in familial terms that connect them to the creation myths of human beings. For example, in the Enuma Elish, Marduk takes the blood of the deity Kingu and uses it to fashion humans. Tablet 6 says, "They imposed on him his guilt and severed his blood (vessels). Out of his blood they fashioned mankind."[22] This connection between divine blood and humanity creates an ontological link of kinship. As Puttoff states, "Blood is the metaphysical link between humans and the gods. Here human blood is nothing short of the blood of Kingu."[23] Another example of the familial link between the deity and humanity includes the story of Marduk, who is addressed as "father and mother."[24] Marduk has a relationship with the human kings in which he hands down his decrees to them to be followed, similar to a father-son relationship found in the Egyptian context. Gudea, a Babylonian prince, says to a goddess who stands by him, "I have no mother, thou art my mother; I have no father, thou art my father; in a secret place hast thou borne me."[25]

Do We Become Angels?

When we talk about God's two-family household, we mean they are distinct. Angels are part of God's

---

22. Pritchard, *The Ancient Near Eastern Texts Relating to the Old Testament*, 68.
23. Putthoff, *Gods and Humans in the Ancient Near East*, 51.
24. The Ancient Mesopotamian gods Bel/Marduk and Nebo are found in father-son pagan cults. See Kathleen E. McVey, "Edessa," in *The Anchor Yale Bible Dictionary*, ed. David Noel Freedman, 6 vols. (New York: Doubleday, 1992), 2:285.
25. Louis H. Gray, "Ages of the World," in *Encyclopædia of Religion and Ethics*, ed. James Hastings, John A. Selbie, and Louis H. Gray, 12 vols. (Edinburgh: T&T Clark, 1908–26), 1:186.

cosmic family, and humans are part of the earthly family. A popular sentiment is that humans become angels, but the Bible doesn't say that. The Bible is very clear that we are being conformed or made into something much better. We are being conformed to the image of Christ Jesus! We regain our true humanity as it was always intended in Eden (Rom 8:29). Passages like Hebrews 12 and the statement Jesus makes to the thief on the cross in Luke 23:43 ("today you will be with me in paradise") suggest that when we die, our spirit goes to be with the Lord in his divine council. This is the proper place of residence for both God's human and cosmic (angelic) family.

These examples present multiple scenarios where the gods of the nations were understood to be active in both divine and human relationships. These relationships are framed around family and speak to an understanding in the ancient Near East where the gods were understood to have two-family households. Their divine family and human family regularly interacted with each other, and this was normative in the ANE context. In other words, the deities of the nations reflected the same household structure: one of hierarchy, responsibility, rebellion, and even division in the cosmic ranks.[26]

---

26. Walton, *Ancient Near Eastern Thought and the Old Testament*, 106. It was common for families to have household gods. These gods were typically lesser deities who were relied upon by the family to make their appeal to the higher gods. The household gods will take on a more significant role in chapter 3 when we trace the implications of Abraham leaving his "fathers' household"

One is left wondering, however, how this family connection between gods and humans came to be. Where did this framework of a royal divine council that includes the gods of the nations and the humans who worshiped them develop? How is it possible that civilizations separated in time and space had similar conceptions of the relationship between the earthly and spiritual realms? If we are willing to entertain—as many people, including most Christians prior to the modern age have—the idea that these are not just myths and religious fables, but clues pointing us to a deeper spiritual reality, the simplest answer is a common origin story. These spiritual beings long to create counterfeit versions because of a deep jealousy rooted in extreme pride. My argument in this book is that the Bible gives us the true story behind the counterfeits, and that at some point, the gods of the nations participated in this household structure, this divine council in which they served the God of the Bible, but eventually went on to create their own counterfeit versions. God had his own two-family household as he resided in Eden, the holy mountain-garden home of God. For most Christians, there is no debate about whether God has a human family. Yet most who are new to this topic are surprised to learn that God also has a cosmic family, one made up of his heavenly host. So before we go any further, let's take a closer look at the evidence for this in the Bible.

---

and how this would imply that Abraham not only leaves the protection of his father but also of his father's gods.

TWO

GOD'S SUPERNATURAL FAMILY

I s there evidence in the Bible for Yahweh's "heavenly family?" Yes, there is, though it's not written into every verse. Careful study shows evidence of this understanding as the background context for a biblical worldview. We find this context in places such as Genesis 1; Genesis 6; Job 1; 38; and Psalm 82.

The language of the Old Testament also helps us make some important connections. In the Old Testament the Hebrew word *ben* is used "extensively to express family and hereditary relationships . . . [and] when an intimate relationship between two persons or some connection between two things continually exists, this is frequently described in terms of the father-son formula."[1] We first get a hint of the heavenly host in Genesis 1:26, where God says, "let us" make man. Who are the "us" referred to in this statement? A once-popular view was that the plurality

---

1. Jan Bergman, Helmer Ringgren, and H. Haag, "בֵּן," in *Theological Dictionary of the Old Testament*, ed. G. Johannes Botterweck and Helmer Ringgren, trans. John T. Willis, 17 vols. (Grand Rapids: Eerdmans, 1977), 2:149.

of God's speech indicates the Trinity.[2] However, this is incoherent based on the Hebrew grammar and virtually universally rejected among modern scholars.[3] Instead, a more coherent and contextually appropriate view is that the "us" refers to God speaking to his first family, the cosmic household mentioned in Job 38 as the sons of God present at creation.[4] Wenham says the phrase "let us" "should be regarded as a divine announcement to the heavenly court, drawing the angelic host's attention to the master stroke of creation, man."[5] Some have raised concerns about this view,

---

2. Merrill, quoting Nicholas de Lyra, says, "The Hebrews say that this is the word of God to the angels. But this seems false, because the angels are not co-creators with God of the (human) soul, in which the image of God himself endures. Therefore, it must be said that (Scripture) says: 'We will make,' in the plural, to denote the plurality of persons in God." See Eugene H. Merrill, "Rashi, Nicholas de Lyra, and Christian Exegesis," *Westminster Theological Journal* 38 (1975): 66–79. However, Wenham affirms that this interpretation presents a "fuller interpretation," it "is not the word's primary meaning." See Gordon J. Wenham, "Genesis," in *New Bible Commentary: 21st Century Edition*, ed. D. A. Carson et al., 4th ed. (Leicester: Inter-Varsity Press, 1994), 61.

3. For a discussion on the challenges of the "us" language, see D. J. A. Clines, "The Image of God in Man," *Tyndale Bulletin* 19 (1968): 53–103. Clines, following Barth, does not find a heavenly council scenario convincing. His primary concern is the implication that humanity is made in the likeness of the heavenly host and/or that the heavenly host participated in the creation of mankind, which seems to be contrary to the view that God alone created humanity. These issues can be answered if there were closer consideration of the situational rhetoric of the context.

4. For more on the heavenly court view, see David VanDrunen, *Divine Covenants and Moral Order: A Biblical Theology of Natural Law*, Emory University Studies in Law and Religion (Grand Rapids: Eerdmans, 2014), 538–40. Wenham says that the text "should therefore be regarded as a divine announcement to the heavenly court, drawing the angelic host's attention to the master stroke of creation." See Gordon J. Wenham, *Genesis 1–15*, Word Biblical Commentary 1 (Dallas: Word, 1987), 28.

5. Wenham, *Genesis 1–15*, 28. This was also the position of Philo, and modern commentators include Skinner, von Rad, Zimmerli, Kline, Mettinger, and Gispen. See also Skinner, *A Critical and Exegetical Commentary on Genesis*, 31.

fearing the implication that God *and* angelic beings both participated in the creation of humanity. However, if we read the text closely, Genesis 1:27 clearly rules out the idea of cocreation with angels with a singular actor (Yahweh) doing the work of creating.

Though the host is not directly involved in the act of creation, Yahweh addresses the heavenly host in acknowledgment of their presence as witnesses of the event. An example of this in our context would be a husband walking into the labor and delivery room with his wife as she is preparing to have a baby. As he walks in his wife looks at him and says, "Okay, let's do this!" Clearly, the wife is the one in labor and giving birth, but she acknowledges the husband's presence.

This divine-council scenario is repeated elsewhere in Scripture (1 Kgs 22:19–22; Isa 6:8; Pss 29:1–2; 82; 89:6–7; Job 1:6; 2:1), most notably at the Babel event (Gen 11:7). As we have hinted already in our references to Job, these heavenly host/divine council members are also referred to as "sons of God," language we find in Psalms 29:1 and 89:7.[6] Most commonly they are referred to as *elohim*, a word we commonly translate as God or gods that can also

---

6. Additionally, the Septuagint has either *huios tou Theou* ("sons of God," Gen 6:4) or *angeloi tou Theou* ("angels of God," Job 1:6), showing that the translators saw both a familial and cosmic context between the "sons of God" and Yahweh. Gesenius further understands *bene* to "denote membership of a guild or society (or of a tribe, or any definite class)." This follows the concept of a tribe or pantheon of beings that are related intimately. The classification of family should not be stretched too far. These cosmic beings are created with purpose to serve Yahweh. See Friedrich Wilhelm Gesenius, *Gesenius' Hebrew Grammar*, ed. E. Kautzsch and Sir Arthur Ernest Cowley, 2nd English ed. (Oxford: Clarendon, 1910), 418. For further discussion of the Septuagint translation of *huioi Theou*, see Gareth Lee Cockerill, "Hebrews 1:6: Source and Significance," *Bulletin for Biblical Research*, 9 (1999): 58–59.

be translated as "divine or spiritual being." This council resembles the ANE councils of Mesopotamia and Ugarit, *though it is distinct from those in that this council is led solely by Yahweh.* In other words, there is a clear difference between what the Bible teaches about God and his divine or heavenly sons and the way other nations understood their gods to relate to one another. As Mike Heiser has helpfully summarized: "Yahweh was an אֱלֹהִים [elohim], but no other אֱלֹהִים [elohim] was Yahweh—and never was nor could be."[7] What Yahweh is, in comparison to other spiritual beings, is "species unique."[8] However, the other *elohim* do relate to Yahweh as his heavenly host. These "sons of God" (*bene elohim*; בְּנֵי אֱלֹהִים) belonged to Yahweh, and the nature of that belonging is not impersonal but personal and portrays a familial context.[9]

God reveals to us that these sons of God were present while he was laying the very foundations of the earth (Job 38:4–7), thereby informing us of their presence during creation *before human existence.* Throughout the book of Job it is clear that the sons of God are cosmic beings.[10] In Job 38:7 the "morning stars" depict an ANE belief in which the stars

7. Michael S. Heiser, "Monotheism, Polytheism, Monolatry, or Henotheism? Toward an Assessment of Divine Plurality in the Hebrew Bible," *Bulletin for Biblical Research* 18 (2008): 29.
8. This author first came across this term from Michael Heiser.
9. Paul Joüon and T. Muraoka, *A Grammar of Biblical Hebrew* (Roma: Pontificio Istituto Biblico, 2006), 440. Beckwith suggests the use of the phrase *sons of God* may be in reference to their being made in the image of God based on the same phrase used of Adam in Luke 3:38. See Roger Beckwith, "The Creation and Fall of the Angels," *The Churchman* 124 (2010): 39. This may be possible and speaks to the language of a creator in terms of father-son relationship that *bene* can also refer to.
10. Marvin H. Pope, *Job: Introduction, Translation, and Notes*, Anchor Yale Bible 15 (New Haven, CT: Yale University Press, 2008), 9.

represent the gods, who play a special role in the royal court or pantheon.[11] Therefore, the "morning stars" can be seen in parallel with the "sons of God" who are celestial beings.[12]

This same phrase, *sons of God*, is also used in Genesis 6:2–4. However, their identity is debated in Genesis, and most notably in this passage:

> The sons of God saw that the daughters of humans were beautiful, and they married any of them they chose. Then the LORD said, "My Spirit will not contend with humans forever, for they are mortal; their days will be a hundred and twenty years."
>
> The Nephilim were on the earth in those days—and also afterward—when the sons of God went to the daughters of humans and had children by them. They were the heroes of old, men of renown. (NIV)

The various interpretive options for these verses include the Sethite view, the divine kingship view, and the angelic view.[13] The first two options see the sons of God as human beings versus the final option, which takes a more supernatural perspective. The Sethite view argues that the sons of God

---

11. John E. Hartley, *The Book of Job*, The New International Commentary on the Old Testament (Grand Rapids: Eerdmans, 1988). Hartley says the "morning stars" are a synonymous parallel with the "sons of God," who serve a role in the divine council of Yahweh.
12. John F. Hobbins, "Critical Biblical Theology in a New Key a Review Article," *Journal for the Evangelical Study of the Old Testament* 1 (2011–12): 89.
13. George C. Gianoulis, "Is Sonship in Romans 8:14–17 a Link with Romans 9?," *Bibliotheca Sacra* 166 (2009): 75. Gianoulis interprets "sons of God" in Deut 32:8 to reference Israel in a summary paragraph on page 76. However, he does not refer to the Dead Sea Scrolls or the incongruity of this translation and any attempts at providing a solution to the challenges of "sons of God" as a reference to Israel in Deut 32:8–9.

in Genesis are descendants of Seth who married daughters of worldly men.[14] These daughters were from the ungodly line of Cain. The supporters of this view, such as Keil and Delitzsch, argue that *elohim* refers to godly and righteous individuals (Ps 73:15; Hos 1:10; Ps 80:17).[15] This view is unconvincing because it fails to account for the fact that the phrase *sons of God* does not appear as a "collective term for the Sethites" elsewhere in Scripture.[16] Additionally, scholar Meredith Kline questions the logic that "Nephilim-Gibborim" (Gen 6:4), what are elsewhere considered giants or mighty men, would be the result of someone marrying an unbeliever.[17] For this and many reasons, the Sethite view is largely unconvincing.

The second option, the divine kingship view, holds that the sons of God are sons of nobility who marry nonroyal daughters. Kline, in defending this view, says, "From the titulary of this pagan ideology of divine kingship the term *benê-hā'elōhîm* was appropriated in Genesis 6:1–4 as a designation for the antediluvian kings."[18] The defense of this

---

14. For a survey of the Sethite and human rulers views, see Willem A. Vangemeren, "The Sons of God in Genesis 6:1–4: An Example of Evangelical Demythologization?," *Westminster Theological Journal* 43 (1980): 333–39.

15. Carl Friedrich Keil and Franz Delitzsch, *Commentary on the Old Testament*, 10 vols. (Peabody, MA: Hendrickson, 1996), 1:81. Supporters of this view throughout church history include Sextus Julius Africanus, Augustine, Thomas Aquinas, Martin Luther, and John Calvin. See Frank Jabini, "Sons of God Marrying Daughters of Man: An Exercise in Integrated Theology," *Conspectus* 14 (2012): 86.

16. See David J. A. Clines, "The Significance of the 'Sons of God' Episode (Genesis 6:1–4) in the Context of the 'Primal History' (Genesis 1–11)," *Journal for the Study of the Old Testament* 13 (1979): 33.

17. See Meredith G. Kline, "Divine Kingship and Genesis 6:1–4," *Westminster Theological Journal* 24 (1961): 190. The Septuagint has *huioi tou Theou* ("sons of God") in Gen 6:4.

18. Kline, "Divine Kingship and Genesis 6:1–4," 191–92.

position is based on reading *elohim* as "judges" (Exod 21:6; 22:68). Yet these judges are never called *elohim* in these passages, and without that connection, we should not come to that definition.[19] Ultimately, this option is not possible when *adam* is used in reference to a "lower class" and is contrasted with *ben* (Ps 49:2), not *elohim*.[20] In addition, the Nephilim are said have been on the earth at the time of Genesis 6:1–2, which means they could not exclusively refer to the result of marriages between kings and nonroyal daughters, as this happened at other times in history.

The third possibility, and what I believe is the best interpretive option, is that the sons of God are the very same sons of God from Job 1:6; 2:1; and 38:7.[21] They are the cosmic beings created by Yahweh who served in his divine council. This view is also affirmed by the New Testament (Jude 5–7; 2 Pet 2:1–10), which refers to the sons of God as angels.[22] Why does this matter? Well, our interpretive decision in Genesis 6 and Job has a direct impact on how we read Psalm 82. Psalm

19. See Michael S. Heiser, "Should אלהים with Plural Predication Be Translated 'Gods'?," *The Bible Translator* 61 (2010): 123–36.
20. James Crichton, "Sons of God (OT)," in *The International Standard Bible Encyclopedia*, ed. James Orr et al., 4 vols. (Chicago: Howard-Severance, 1915), 2835.
21. See also 1 Kgs 22:19; Pss 29:1; 89:5–7; and Hos 2:1.
22. Jabini, "Sons of God Marrying Daughters of Man," 108. New Testament scholars affirm the correlation between these New Testament texts and the events at the time of Noah and the flood when the "angels sinned." See Peter H. Davids, *The Letters of 2 Peter and Jude*, Pillar New Testament Commentary (Grand Rapids: Eerdmans, 2006), 3; Michael Green, *2 Peter and Jude: An Introduction and Commentary*, Tyndale New Testament Commentaries 18 (Downers Grove, IL: InterVarsity Press, 1987), 68; Jerome H. Neyrey, *2 Peter, Jude: A New Translation with Introduction and Commentary*, Anchor Yale Bible 37C (New Haven, CT: Yale University Press, 2008), 120–22. Additionally, while Gen 6:1–4 does not give the punishment, Peter has these sons of God held in bondage in Tartarus until judgment day. This is reflected in 1 Enoch, which may have informed Peter and Jude.

82 relates to Genesis 6 because it correlates to the *sons of God* language and affirms their cosmic identity. In Psalm 82 we also see a continuance of the narrative begun in Genesis—the "judgment" for the sons of God in response to their rebellion.[23]

Psalm 82 introduces readers to a scenario in which God (*elohim*) takes his place in the divine council among the gods (*elohim*), where he holds judgment. Similar to Genesis 6, interpreters have concluded that the sons of God are either humans (Jewish rulers or kings) or cosmic beings.[24] Thus, how we interpret the identity of the sons of God in Psalm 82 correlates directly to Genesis 6. Some interpreters have attempted to take a human reading for Psalm 82, which they read back into Genesis 6, determining that the sons of God there are humans as well.[25] However, a human reading for Psalm 82 is highly improbable, and here's why.

In Psalm 82, we know that the initial *elohim* in this passage is referring to a singular entity (God). However, we know that the second *elohim* is plural because of the preposition *beqereb*.[26] Essentially, because God (singular) is

---

23. The judgment aspect of Ps 82 will be discussed in greater detail later in this chapter. However, the *sons of God* terminology must be discussed first to establish the identity of the sons of God and thus their relationship to Yahweh and humanity. In a sense, Ps 82 serves as a fact check for the interpretive decision of Job and Gen 6. If the identity of the sons of God is different in each text, there must be a plausible explanation for such discrepancy. Otherwise, it seems interpretive continuity in these passages is the best scenario.

24. It may be that the desire to read humanity into the *sons of God* language comes more from the goal of theological preservation or an attempt at philosophical theology rather than exegesis. See Vangemeren, "The Sons of God in Genesis 6:1–4," 320.

25. Michael S. Heiser, "Divine Council," in *Dictionary of the Old Testament: Wisdom, Poetry, and Writings*, ed. Tremper Longman III and Peter Enns (Downers Grove, IL: IVP Academic, 2008), 112–16.

26. The presence of plural *elohim* in passages like Pss 82 and 89 have led some scholars to believe that the early ancient Israelite religion was first polytheistic and then evolved into monotheism. This issue is compounded when considering

unable to stand in the midst of himself or another singular entity, the second *elohim* must be plural. Yet this leads us once again to the key question: the identity of these plural *elohim*. Some Christian and Jewish scholars have attempted to interpret the *sons of God* as meaning "humans" based on Moses being referred to as *elohim* (Exod 4:16; 7:1) or Israel being called "Yahweh's son" (Exod 4:23; Hos 11:1).[27] However, when we consider the phrase *sons of God* in both its ANE context and its natural placement within Psalm 82 exegetically, a better interpretation would be the cosmic beings that are part of the household of God.[28] The plural *elohim* of Psalm 82:1 is referenced once again as *elohim* a

---

passages in Deuteronomy that suggest there are other gods. However, the presence of the plural elōhîm and the accounts in Deuteronomy need not require a polytheistic background to make room for the presence of a divine council. A more acceptable and accurate term related to monotheism is monolatry, which may present a system that more closely reflects the Israelite religion. Monolatry was "coined to express not belief in the sole existence of one god, but restriction of worship to one object of trust and loyalty, although other races might admittedly have other cosmic helpers. However, what Yahweh is, in comparison to other spiritual beings, is 'species unique.' Therefore, a more helpful term may be mono-Yahwism." Michael S. Heiser, "Does Divine Plurality in the Hebrew Bible Demonstrate an Evolution from Polytheism to Monotheism in Israelite Religion?," *Journal for the Evangelical Study of the Old Testament* 1 (2011–12): 2; see also Peter Hayman, "Monotheism—A Misused Word in Jewish Studies?," *Journal of Jewish Studies* 42 (1991): 1–15 (esp. 1–2, 15); Robert Mackintosh, "Monolatry and Henotheism," in *Encyclopædia of Religion and Ethics*, ed. James Hastings, John A. Selbie, and Louis H. Gray, 12 vols. (Edinburgh: T&T Clark, 1908–26), 8:810. Additionally, one may consider henotheism, in which "there are many gods but one all-powerful god who reigns over them is henotheistic religion." See K. L. Noll, *Canaan and Israel in Antiquity: An Introduction*, The Biblical Seminar 83 (New York: Sheffield Academic Press, 2001), 131.

27. Heiser, "Monotheism, Polytheism, Monolatry, or Henotheism?," 19.
28. This also applies to Gen 6:1–4. For further treatment of the "sons of God" interpretive conversation on Gen 6:1–4, see John H. Walton, "Sons of God, Daughters of Man," in *Dictionary of the Old Testament: Pentateuch*, ed. T. Desmond Alexander and David W. Baker (Downers Grove, IL: IVP Academic, 2003), 793–798.

few verses later in Psalm 82:6, where it is further defined as "sons of the Most High." As Michael Heiser notes, "It is well known that the phrases בְּנֵי אֱלֹהִים [bene elohim], בְּנֵי הָאֱלֹהִים [ben ha elohim], and בְּנֵי אֵלִים [bene elim] have certifiable linguistic counterparts in Ugaritic texts to a council of gods under El, and that the meaning of these phrases in the Hebrew Bible points to divine beings."[29] Heiser thus concludes that the *elohim* of Psalm 82:1 are the very same *elohim* of Psalm of 82:6, who are further described as *sons of the Most High*, a term that is linguistically related to *sons of God*.

In addition to the linguistic parallels just cited, the very logic of seeing the sons of God as human beings in Psalm 82 is incoherent on several levels. First, the judgment God renders on the sons of God is that they will die like men. But what does this mean if these are already human rulers? Dying is a natural and expected consequence for all human rulers, so how is this a threat?[30] Second, these elders have responsibility over the nations of the world, but if this is referring to the elders of the Jewish community, they did not have jurisdiction over the nations. Third, the cosmic consequences outlined here seem grossly disproportionate for human rulers. Fourth, the timeline is inconsistent, as the sons of God were allotted to the nations *before* Israel was ever a nation (Deut 32:8–9 and Gen 11:1–9, which we will explore in more detail later). Fifth and finally, the history of interpretation supports a cosmic view. The sons of God being understood as cosmic beings is well represented in apocalyptic literature, "as well

---

29. Heiser, "Monotheism, Polytheism, Monolatry, or Henotheism?," 19.
30. Heiser, "Divine Council," 114.

as the belief held by early Church fathers such Justin (2 *Apol.* v. 3), Irenaeus (iv. 36. 4;), Tertullian (*De idol.* ix. 1; *De cult. fem.* i. 2;), and Clement (Alex., *Paed.* iii. 2. 14; *Strom.* iii. 7. 59)."[31] In favor of angelic beings, Philo says, "Those beings, whom other philosophers call demons, Moses usually calls angels; and they are souls hovering in the air."[32] Additionally, Josephus and the book of Jubilees both point to angelic beings.[33] Thus, the weight of evidence, both exegetically and historically, points to an understanding that the sons of God of Psalm 82 should be understood as cosmic beings within the cosmic household of God.

Now that we've established that God has a two-family household, let's turn to story itself. What happens when you have conflict in your family—a conflict that extends to both dimensions, the earthly and the heavenly? The result is rebellion and warfare, a lengthy battle that continues to this day. At the core of this unseen battle is a conflict over the prize possession of Yahweh, his human children distinctly made in his likeness and image and given rule over the earth.

---

31. J. N. D. Kelly, *The Epistles of Peter and of Jude*, Black's New Testament Commentary (London: Continuum, 1969), 256. One must take 1 Pet 3:19 and Jude 6, 7 into consideration for appropriate interpretation of the sons of God of Gen 6:1–4. Additionally, Athenagoras, "A Plea for the Christians," 141, says, "God, and concerning these gods were not of opinion, some that they are demons, others that they are matter, and others that they once were men,"

32. Philo, *The Works of Philo: Complete and Unabridged*, ed. Charles Duke Young (Peabody, MA: Hendrickson, 1995), 152. In Philo we see fallen angels and sons of God equated to demons. In reference to Gen 6, Philo says, "When the angels of God saw the daughters of men that they were beautiful, they took unto themselves wives of all of them whom they chose."

33. See Flavius Josephus, *The Works of Josephus: Complete and Unabridged*, ed. William Whiston (Peabody, MA: Hendrickson, 1987), 32. See also Charlesworth, *The Old Testament Pseudepigrapha*, 2:61–62.

For this reason I kneel before the Father from whom every family in heaven and on earth is named
(Eph 3:14-15 CSB)

The Godhead (Father/Son/Spirit)
Yahweh - the uncreated creator

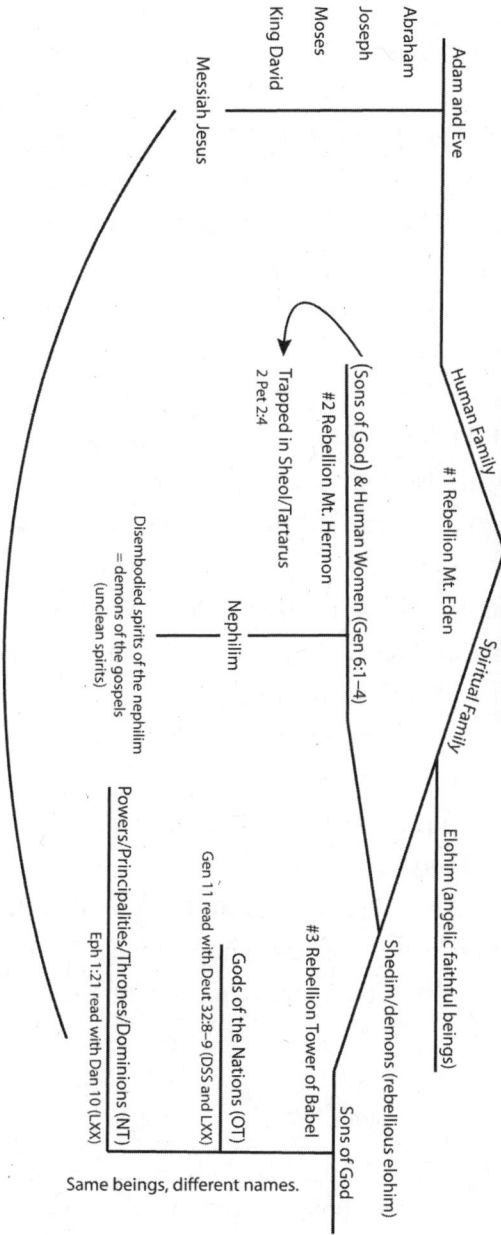

Human Family

- Adam and Eve
- Abraham
- Joseph
- Moses
- King David
- Messiah Jesus

#1 Rebellion Mt. Eden

Spiritual Family

- Elohim (angelic faithful beings)
- Shedim/demons (rebellious elohim)
- Sons of God

#3 Rebellion Tower of Babel

Gods of the Nations (OT)
Gen 11 read with Deut 32:8-9 (DSS and LXX)

Powers/Principalities/Thrones/Dominions (NT)
Eph 1:21 read with Dan 10 (LXX)

Same beings, different names.

(Sons of God) & Human Women (Gen 6:1-4)

#2 Rebellion Mt. Hermon

Trapped in Sheol/Tartarus
2 Pet 2:4

Nephilim

Disembodied spirits of the nephilim
= demons of the gospels
(unclean spirits)

Justice for rebellion (both human and spiritual family members) takes place at the cross. The possibility for redemption is offered to God's human family, for those that repent and return to the household through the Messiah, Jesus. There is no redemption for the rebellious supernatural family of God as their indictment for sin is established in Ps 82.

As we work through Scripture, and more specifically through the first twelve chapters of the Old Testament, we find a pattern developing—and patterns always have a purpose in the biblical text. We find rebellion in both spheres of God's family, the earthly and heavenly/supernatural. We learn that Adam and Eve were not the faithful vice-regents God intended them to be.[34] They failed to follow the one prohibition God gave them—not to eat of the tree of the knowledge of good and evil—after being enticed by the serpent/*nachash* (Gen 2:17). Their failure, which was an act of household rebellion, required a consequence, and they were cast out of the house of God, his garden-mountain of Eden. Yet there was also a consequence for the spiritual being who plays a pivotal role in all of this, and the serpent/*nachash* received judgment for his part in the rebellion.

But this isn't the only place we find this pattern of earthly and supernatural rebellion coinciding in one narrative framework. In fact, the first twelve chapters of Genesis have three rebellions, three foundational instances where God's human and supernatural family participate in rebellion against Yahweh, setting in motion the unseen battle we are in the midst of still today.

All battles have a prize in mind, something the two sides are fighting over. In the next chapter we'll see that this battle's prize is humanity, the crown jewel of Yahweh's creation.

---

34. For the development of Adam and Eve as vice-regents and an ANE background, see Lioy, "The Garden of Eden," 33.

THREE

THE REBELLIONS OF GENESIS 3 AND 6

W hy is there so much evil in the world? Most Christians today probably go straight to Genesis 3 and the fall. We know this story well. You may not even need to look up the reference. In fact, you probably don't have to be a Christian to be at least somewhat familiar with the story. The first human beings God created, Adam and Eve, fell into temptation and followed the deception of the serpent in eating of the tree of good and evil and going into full-blown rebellion against God. Simple and straightforward, right? Well, not quite. If you asked this same question to those living in the context of Second Temple Judaism, they would have agreed that we see evil in the world because of Genesis 3 and the fall—but they wouldn't have stopped there. "Don't forget Genesis 6 and the problem of the Nephilim, spreading rampant evil in the world, and the resulting flood," they would say. And the cherry on top of it all for them would be Genesis 11 and the tower of Babel, a story they would read in light of Deuteronomy 32:8–9 when Yahweh disinherited the nations and placed them under the rule of the gods of the nations, members of his divine council. In other words, it's not such a simple story. There is more than Genesis 3 and the fall. The unseen battle we are smack in the middle of today is the result of not one rebellion, but three rebellions, that occurred in *both* the earthly and spiritual realms.

THE FIRST REBELLION IN EDEN

The first time we encounter spiritual warfare is in the garden home of God, Eden. As we've established, Mount Eden was the place where God's earthly and supernatural family dwelt together and where they were led by the head of the household, Yahweh. But in Genesis 3, we suddenly meet a figure identified as the "serpent." What is this being? Where does it come from? And most importantly, as it begins to dialogue with Eve, why doesn't she freak out? Why does the story seem to suggest that talking with the serpent was perfectly normal for her, nothing out of the ordinary?

Let's start by taking a closer look at the Hebrew word *nachash*, the word we translate as serpent in English. The Hebrew *nachash* can mean a serpent, but it can also mean a divine throne guardian, or something that more generally speaking has a fiery and bronze-like appearance. In Genesis 3, it's likely that all three of these are in play when we read *nachash* in the text. The idea of a *nachash* as a throne guardian may explain why there is a sense of familiarity between the *nachash* and Eve. These throne guardians are angelic beings, and they are referenced elsewhere in Scripture as well. For example, in Isaiah 6 we have a picture of seraphim guarding the throne of God. Interestingly, the Hebrew *saraph* can also refer to a kind of serpent (Isa 14:29; 30:6) or a "fiery serpent shape" (Num 21:8). This is even more interesting when we consider the description of Lucifer/Satan/*nachash* in Ezekiel 28:12–17 and Isaiah 14:12–14, where Lucifer is represented as a "shining/bright star." These passages all bring to mind the serpent of Genesis 3 and the three ways we can understand the term *nachash*.

However, the key to understanding the conflict that arises in Genesis 3 isn't necessarily related to the appearance of the *nachash* but rather the substance of what the *nachash* says. This is the essence of spiritual warfare and how it utilizes *deception*. In this case, it may have been their familiarity with the *nachash* as an angelic throne guardian that was the conduit to humanity's ultimate failure and disobedience. Notice as well that the serpent at the tree with Eve and Adam doesn't create a new narrative for them. The *nachash* doesn't recreate the wheel, so to speak. Instead, he starts dismantling the spokes of the wheel so that it no longer works the way it was intended. He distorts the already existing true story given by God and introduces doubt about its truth.

Take note: *This is how spiritual warfare is fought.* The unseen battle is ultimately a conflict between what is true and what is false. The most deceptive and powerful tactics of spiritual warfare present half-truths as the full truth when they are nothing but a full lie. The serpent reframes what is real by distorting reality to present what he wanted Adam and Eve to believe was true. From the very beginning, spiritual warfare is a reframing and distortion of truth. It is an effort to induce compromise through "coercion by deception." It's dangerous to the human beings listening because there are enough vestiges (original pieces or fragments) of the truth still in place that it seems trustworthy and true. But those fragments are there to distract them from the subtle lies that have been inserted to manipulate them into believing, talking, and acting in ways contrary to God's desires for his children.

Every rebellion requires a response. God is a good Father who won't sit back and let his household stay in shambles. In response to the rebellion of both humanity and the *nachash*, God hands out punishment that is balanced with promise. The punishment for Adam and Eve was their expulsion from the garden-home of God. Adam would now experience toil and trouble in his working of the soil. Eve would now experience the pangs of childbirth. The *nachash* is also punished, made to crawl on his belly and eat the dust of the ground. This is a fascinating turn of events when you consider that humanity was originally created from the dust of the ground. The Hebrew word for man/humanity is *adam* and is closely related to the Hebrew word *adamah*, which refers to the ground or soil. The related Akkadian term *adamātu* means "dark, red soil," showing how these words were conceptually linked in the ANE world.[1] Thus, in an ironic reversal, the *nachash* who attempted to bring humanity down ends up crawling on the ground himself, forced to eat the very dust used to create humanity (Gen 3:14). This also hints at

---

1. J. G. Plöger, "אֲדָמָה," *Theological Dictionary of the Old Testament*, ed. G. Johannes Botterweck and Helmer Ringgren, trans. John T. Willis, 17 vols. (Grand Rapids: Eerdmans, 1977), 1:88.

some kind of ongoing link between the *nachash* and the two humans as their ongoing toil and productivity will be where the serpent naturally feeds.

This isn't the end of the story, however—far from it! We know this because there is a hint of good news embedded in the punishment of the human pair, a promise present in God's judgment on their rebellion. In Genesis 3:15, which is sometimes referred to as the "protoevangelium," or the first glimmer of the gospel, God makes Adam and Eve a promise of future restoration. To the serpent, God promises nothing but future judgment and total defeat. Genesis 3:15 prophesies that the offspring of Eve (her singular seed) would one day prevail and destroy the offspring of the serpent.[2] But who are the offspring of the serpent? In context, this would include all those who are opposed to Yahweh from *both sides* of his household. This would include the supernatural sons of God who have already or will in the future turn against him in rebellion. Yet it also includes those in the human family of God, the descendants of Adam and Eve, who have been deceived into following the ways of the *nachash* and have now joined his household and call him their father (John 8:44).

At this point the Hebrew Bible establishes a pattern in relation to the *zera* or seed of humanity, and especially in future references to the patriarchs of the Old Testament. The

---

2. Douglas Mangum, *The Lexham Glossary of Theology* (Bellingham, WA: Lexham, 2014). There is a larger scholarly discussion on the nature of Hebrew *zera*/seed and whether or not it should be rendered singular or plural. This author holds to the singular translation based on the Septuagint's rendering of this text. For more on this discussion see Jared M. August, "The Messianic Hope of Genesis: The Protoevangelium and Patriarchal Promises." *Themelios* 42, no. 1 (2017): 46–62. See also Jack Collins, "A Syntactical Note (Genesis 3:15): Is The Woman's Seed Singular Or Plural?," *Tyndale Bulletin* 48, no. 1 (1997): 139–47.

Genesis 3:15 promise of Yahweh is seen again and again as a recurring pattern among the descendants of Adam and Eve. We will examine this in more detail later, but for now it's enough to note one key instance of this in Gensis 22 when God promises Abraham a *zera*/seed who will bless all the nations (Gen 22:17–18). God then reiterates this promise to Abraham's son Isaac through his *zera*/seed that all the nations of the earth shall be blessed (Gen 26:4). And God again tells Isaac's son Jacob that his *zera*/seed would be the conduit of blessing of the nations (Gen 28:14).[3]

Sadly, we also see how the *zera*/seed of Adam and Eve would be split in terms of their faithfulness and faithlessness. This understanding helps us to better identify what is happening in the notoriously difficult chapter of Genesis 6. There is a tendency to skip the first four verses of this chapter and jump right into the narrative of Noah and the flood. But doing so misses something extremely important: the second rebellion and the reason why God brings judgment a second time on the human beings he has created. As before, several of those in God's rebellious, earthly household sin. But there is also an act of rebellion among his heavenly household as well. And that's when things get a little wild.

THE SECOND REBELLION IN GENESIS 6

In Genesis 6 we encounter a world permeated by rampant evil and sin. But how did we get here? How does evil spread

---

3. Jared M. August, "The Messianic Hope of Genesis: The Protoevangelium and Patriarchal Promises," *Themelios* 42, no. 1 (2017): 58.

to fill the earth such that "every inclination of the thoughts of the human heart was only evil all the time" (NIV)? How do things get so bad that it necessitates a flood to cleanse the world of this evil?

The prelude to all of this is a *second rebellion* prompted by fallen angelic beings engaged in an unholy union with humanity. In the first rebellion of Genesis 3, we find humanity seeking to become like God, rising to the level of Yahweh in determining what they think is good and evil. Adam and Eve attempt to secure something for themselves they were not given. Now, in this second rebellion, we find dynamic movement in the other direction—divine beings lowering themselves to the level of humanity. We see other members of God's household trying to secure for themselves something they were never given.[4] The result of this second rebellion is the rampant *spread* of evil.

Admittedly, when it comes to unpacking the nuances of these first verses of Genesis 6, the "problems are legion," as one commentator has noted.[5] The first interpretive question is the identity of the sons of God, the *bene elohim*, which we briefly examined in the previous chapter. There I outlined why it is incoherent to have a nonsupernatural view of the sons of God when the immediate context and numerous other instances in the Scriptures point to the reality that these are divine beings, what we today would call angels. Additionally, the earliest witnesses attest to this supernatural reading, so it is not something new being read into the text.

---

4. Nahum M. Sarna, *Genesis*, JPS Torah Commentary (Philadelphia: Jewish Publication Society, 1989), 45.
5. I read this from E. A Speiser, *Genesis: Introduction, Translation, and Notes*, vol. 1, Anchor Yale Bible (New Haven, CT: Yale University Press, 2008), 45.

The angelic view is the oldest view and the one assumed in the earliest of Jewish writings (1 En 6:2; Jub 5:1; Gen 6:1–4 LXX; Philo, *De Gigant* 2:358; Josephus, *Ant* 1.31; the DSS 1QapGen 2:1; CD 2:17–19).

Even the earliest Christian writers and interpreters of Scripture affirmed this view. For example, while commenting on Genesis 6, Justin Martyr says: "God, when He had made the whole world, and subjected things earthly to man, . . . committed the care of men and of all things under heaven to angels whom He appointed over them. But the angels transgressed this appointment, and were captivated by love of women, and begat children who are those that are called demons."[6] Justin goes on to talk about how the human race was ultimately subdued and deceived when these rebellious angelic beings enticed humanity into false worship and introduced them to things like magic that Yahweh forbade. Justin seems to be drawing on other literature for this interpretation, as several of these details aren't explicitly mentioned in Genesis 6. We will get to that in a bit. The point here is to note that Justin isn't the only early Christian writer to hold this view. In addition to Justin we find it in Irenaeus, Clement of Alexandria, Tertullian, and Origen, among several others.[7]

All of this raises the question as to why modern readers and critical scholars dismiss or seek to refute a supernatural reading of Genesis 6. As I mentioned in the introduction, the demythologizing of the Scriptures may be a way to make the

---

6. Justin, *Apology* 2.5
7. Gordon J. Wenham, *Genesis 1–15*, vol. 1, Word Biblical Commentary (Dallas: Word, 1987), 139.

text appealing to the modern mind. But even this motive is incongruent with the heart of the Christian faith and tradition because our gospel is inherently supernatural. Gordon Wenham concludes, "If the modern reader finds this story incredible, that reflects a materialism that tends to doubt the existence of spirits, good or ill. But those who believe that the creator could unite himself to human nature in the Virgin's womb will not find this story intrinsically beyond belief."[8] Such staunch demythologizing may inevitably lead to a deconstruction of Christianity that is self-destructive.

These four verses only appear troublesome when we strip them from their historic interpretive tradition, namely one that allows for a supernatural interpretation. When we reinsert them into a supernatural or cosmic framework, we find a more cohesive understanding that fits a larger ANE and biblical worldview. While modern readers might see these four verses as being disconnected from the rest of the narrative, that is a surface-level reading of the text. Every text has a context, and for the first readers and hearers of the Bible, these four verses hinted at well-known stories that filled in many of the gaps we have as modern readers.

What do I mean by gaps? Well, let's consider an example. If I asked you today who the G.O.A.T. was, MJ or LeBron, what would you say? If you said Michael Jordan, you are right of course! But wait, let's back up a bit. What did I mean by G.O.A.T.? And how did you know I was talking about basketball in the first place? What clued you into the fact that I was talking about Michael Jordan and not Michael Jackson? The answer to all these questions is the context.

---

8. Wenham, *Genesis 1–15*, 140.

In this case, as someone reading this today in a twenty-first century Western context, you are more likely privy to knowledge that *fills in the gaps*. You know that G.O.A.T. is an acronym for the "greatest of all time." You can deduce that MJ must be Michael Jordan because the comparison is with LeBron James, arguably the second greatest basketball player to play the game.

The first four verses of Genesis 6 function in much the same way. The sparse details indicate this must have been a story that was quite familiar to the people of that time.[9] And we know there were several stories in the ANE world at that time depicting battles between supernatural beings and the presence of demigods who were the product of the union between divine beings and humans. A well-known Greek myth (see Hesiod, Pseudo-Apollodorus) depicts the battle between Uranus, who fights his children only to be defeated by his son Cronus. Cronus experiences that same fate as he is defeated by his son Zeus. Zeus then has to fight the "giants" (*gigantas*), who are also known as Titans. This series of mythic stories are also connected to a Phoenician tradition told by Philo of Byblos referencing an ancient author, Sanchuniathon. However, with the discovery of the Hittite texts containing the translations of Hurrian myths, we have moved even closer to a level of certainty in drawing connections between these stories. As one scholar notes, "These myths parallel the Uranid cycle in such striking detail as to preclude any possibility of coincidence."[10] In these texts

9. Sarna, *Genesis*, 45.
10. E. A. Speiser, *Genesis: Introduction, Translation, and Notes*, Anchor Yale Bible 1 (New Haven, CT: Yale University Press, 2008), 46.

the sky god Anu fights and emasculates his son Kumarbi. However, Kumarbi is defeated by Teshub, the storm deity. All of this is a striking parallel to the Greek narratives of Cronus, Uranus, and Zeus. One important detail in all of this is that the battle between Kumarbi and Teshub takes place near Mount Hazzi, which also happens to be the scene of Typhon's battle with Zeus.[11] This Hurrian text dates back to the second millennium, suggesting that it is the likely source of the later Phoenician and Greek stories.

So how does what we read here in Genesis 6:1–4 relate to these ANE stories? The first four verses of Genesis 6 serve as a polemic or refutation of these ANE myths. Michael Heiser describes it as "a literary and theological effort to undermine the credibility of Mesopotamian gods and other aspects of that culture's worldview."[12] For example, one of the more significant Mesopotamian stories also involves a catastrophic flood and a boat that saves humans and animals. Sound familiar? In this story there is a group of wise, nonhuman beings referred to as the *apkallus*. Many of them were considered evil, and after the flood the offspring of the *apkallus* were called human, but they were also two-thirds *apkallu*. The *apkallu* and human women produced offspring, and an example of their offspring is the character Gilgamesh, who was also a giant.[13] Now, let's compare this

---

11. See H. G. Güterbock, "Oriental Forerunners of Hesiod," *American Journal of Archaeology* 52 (1948): 123; cf. also Güterbock, "The Song of Ullikummi: Revised Text of the Hittite Version of a Hurrian Myth," *Journal of Cuneiform Studies* 4 (1951): 145

12. Michael S. Heiser, *The Unseen Realm: Recovering the Supernatural Worldview of the Bible* (Bellingham, WA: Lexham, 2015), 102.

13. See Andrew George, *The Babylonian Gilgamesh Epic: Introduction, Critical Edition and Cuneiform Texts* (Oxford: Oxford University Press, 2003); George, "The Gilgamesh Epic at Ugarit," *Aula Orientalis* 25 (2007): 237–54.

to Genesis 6. Here we have divine, nonhuman beings called the sons of God who saw the beauty of the daughters of men and took them for themselves producing offspring called the *Nephilim*, also considered to be giants. There are striking similarities, but also some important differences.

Should We Read Ancient Sources and Mythology to Better Understand the Bible?

Let me ask you a hypothetical question. If you are a die-hard Chicago Bulls fan visiting the United Center, and someone said they had the ability to give you a tour of the lockers, a close-up of the championship rings and trophies, and perhaps hidden, unseen tapes of basketball practices with Jordan, Pippen, and Dennis Rodman and the entire Bulls team, would you say yes or no? Of course, if you are a true Bulls fan, the answer is an emphatic yes. The more you walk the United Center, the more context you will have to understand the historic journey of the Chicago Bulls under Jordan. Watching those unseen tapes would give you additional insight into the team dynamics. Who wouldn't want or benefit from this additional context?

So why would we want to reject having additional social, historical, and cultural context as we interpret and seek to understand the Bible? Ancient sources, writings, and even mythologies that are contemporaneous to the biblical texts give us insight into the mind of the ancient reader. By reading this, we broaden and expand our ability to understand the unique perspective of people living at that time and in cultures far closer to the biblical writer than our own, as we are distanced by thousands of years. The key issue for many people, however, is what authority or level of influence we give these writings and if we are reading them in their appropriate context. In this, we need to be careful that we don't read too much into them, but neither should we neglect them. Should we read and utilize ancient writings to better understand the Bible? Of course we should. Are these texts as authoritative as Scripture? Not at all.

So why don't we get more details behind the story of Genesis 6:1–4? Are we limited to drawing parallels with similar ANE stories from other cultures? No. We also have evidence in several Jewish texts from the intertestamental period commenting and elaborating on the events of Genesis 6. It is difficult for us to determine which text came first, either the Septuagint (an early Greek translation of the Hebrew Bible) translation of Genesis 6:1–4 or 1 Enoch, but both of these are considered early witnesses. The Septuagint translation of Genesis 6:1–4 has the Hebrew phrase *bene elohim* rendered in Greek as either *uios tou theou* (sons of God) or *angeloi tou theou* (angels of God). The phrase *angels of God* is supported by Codex Alexandrinus, as well as Philo and Josephus, who both wrote in the first century AD.[14]

---

14. It is important to note *huioi* is the majority reading in extant manuscripts.

It is, however, also possible that 1 Enoch is older than the Septuagint. Sections of 1 Enoch provide interesting background to Genesis 6 that gives us clues to how Genesis was interpreted and understood. The book of 1 Enoch 6:1–2 says: "In those days, when the children of man had multiplied, it happened that there were born unto them handsome and beautiful daughters. And the angels, the children of heaven, saw them and desired them; and they said to one another, 'Come, let us choose wives for ourselves from among the daughters of man and beget us children.'"[15] In 1 Enoch, these rebellious angels are given the title of "watchers." Some may be surprised to find this same term is also used in Daniel 4 to describe supernatural beings. The book of 1 Enoch tells us that the watchers rebel against Yahweh by taking human women as wives and producing offspring that were giants (1 En 7). However, the watchers not only take wives for themselves but also begin to teach humanity various arts, including "magical medicine, incantations, the cutting of roots, and taught them (about) plants."[16] Plants on earth are natural and can be used for good. However, they can also be abused and utilized to create an altered state of mind through hallucinative experiences. This was a common practice among those known as witches and mediums, who used these plants as a means of opening human beings to the spirit realm—in a way God did not intend. Yahweh strictly and explicitly forbade this practice (Lev 19:31; 20:6–8).

---

15. James H. Charlesworth, *The Old Testament Pseudepigrapha*, vol. 1 (New Haven, CT: Yale University Press, 1983), 15.

16. Charlesworth, *The Old Testament Pseudepigrapha*, 1:16.

It doesn't end there; 1 Enoch tells us that one of the watches named Azazel taught the people how to make swords, knives, and shields. Another named Amasras taught incantations and cutting roots. Tam'el taught the seeing of the stars, a reference to the practice of astrology. Again Yahweh warned his people against partaking in such practices (Deut 4:19). Another verse in 1 Enoch seems to directly reference what we read in Genesis 6 in a fascinating way. In the middle of narrating how the watchers were teaching humanity and corrupting them through forbidden knowledge, we read: "There were many wicked ones and they committed adultery and erred, and all their conduct became corrupt."[17] Compare this to Genesis 6:5, where we read: "When the LORD saw that human wickedness was widespread on the earth and that every inclination of the human mind was nothing but evil all the time."

How did evil spread throughout the earth? Reading Genesis 6 in connection with the additional background provided by 1 Enoch leads to the conclusion that the rebellion of the sons of God and their unholy union with human women was the spark that perpetuated the rampant spread of evil throughout the earth. Lest we assume human beings were innocent bystanders or victims in all of this, we should carefully note the hints in the text suggesting they are active participants.

Let's begin by looking at the pattern of rebellion and how it is always linked to both the spiritual and earthly realms. The action of the sons of God in Genesis 6 follows a pattern we first saw with Eve in the garden of Eden. Eve

---

17. Charlesworth, *The Old Testament Pseudepigrapha*, 1:16.

saw the fruit of the tree was good. She desired it. Then she took it. The pattern is "see, desire, and take." Of importance in noting patterns are the words *saw* (*ra'ah*) and *took* (*laqah*). We'll want to pay attention to the context whenever we find these words paired together throughout the rest of Scripture.[18] And one of the first places we see this is in Genesis 6. Coincidence? I don't think so.

> The woman *saw* [*ra'ah*] that the tree was good for food and delightful to look at, and that it was desirable for obtaining wisdom. So she *took* [*laqah*] some of its fruit and ate it. (Gen 3:6)

> The sons of God *saw* [*ra'ah*] that the daughters of mankind were beautiful, and they *took* [*laqah*] any they chose as wives for themselves. (Gen 6:2)

And we see it in later passages in Genesis as well:

> When Abram entered Egypt, the Egyptians *saw* [*ra'ah*] that the woman was very beautiful. [15]Pharaoh's officials saw her and praised her to Pharaoh, so the woman was *taken* [*laqah*] to Pharaoh's household. (Gen 12:14–15)

> When Shechem—son of Hamor the Hivite, who was the region's chieftain—*saw* [*ra'ah*] her, he *took* [*laqah*] her and raped her. (Gen 34:2)

---

18. I first was introduced to this pattern by Matthew J. Lynch in his book *Flood and Fury: Old Testament Violence and the Shalom of God* (Downers Grove, IL: InterVarsity Press, 2023). Emphasis added to the CSB text that follows.

This pattern suggests that the sons of God in Genesis 6 "seeing and taking" human women is likely connected to violence against them. Some scholars have suggested that the issue at hand is rape, but the language used to describe the union doesn't support this. What we can say is that evil is being done to these women. Within the cultural context of the ANE it is highly likely that the fathers of these women were involved. Possibly, these men gave their daughters over (by selling or trading them) to the sons of God in marriage.[19] In more modern terms, we would say that what we find in Genesis 6, when read within the context of 1 Enoch, points to the origin of evils like sex trafficking. The likelihood of this possibility increases when we take into account how the Enochic texts also show an exchange of goods as part of the transaction. The sons of God receive human women in marriage to produce their own seed, while humankind, likely the fathers of these women, receives forbidden knowledge— knowledge that furthers the spread of evil and ultimately ends in their own destruction.

These rebellious angelic beings saw the beauty of the daughters of men and desired them. Seeing, desiring, and taking are actions of the rebellious, not the righteous. In Eden, Eve saw the fruit and it created an internal desire. That internal desire prompted her and Adam to take of the fruit and enter into rebellion against Yahweh. In a similar pattern, the sons of God (*bene elohim*) saw the beauty of the daughters of men, desired them, and took them in sexual union. In both instances, the act of seeing and taking leads to direct rebellion against Yahweh.

---

19. Wenham, *Genesis 1–15*, 141.

◇◇

Are There Really Angels Trapped Under the Earth?

After reading the title of this sidebar, you might be thinking, "I've never wondered about that before—where does that question come from?" It originates in Jude 6, but it only becomes odd if you don't connect it to its Old Testament background. Jude 6 hyperlinks us back to the Genesis 6 event, giving us a clue that he is referring to sinning angels. The text of Jude 6 says: "And the angels who did not keep their own position but abandoned their proper dwelling, he has kept in eternal chains in deep darkness for the judgment on the great day." In Genesis 6 the sons of God participate in rebellion against Yahweh and his household. The Sons of God see human women and leave their designated place to pursue an unholy alliance. In Jude, we learn that these specific angels are given a punishment. Charles says, "The angels' fate is commensurate with their privilege. Having been exposed to light and glory, they are eternally consigned to darkness and judgment."[20]

Jude seems to be getting his source material from Genesis 6 as well as the broader Enochic tradition. There are certain verbal parallels to note between Jude 6 and Enoch.

---

20. Daryl J. Charles, "The Angels under Reserve in 2 Peter and Jude," *Bulletin for Biblical Research, Vol. 15* (2005): 46.

- Binding and darkness (1 En 10:4)
- The great day (1 En 10:6)
- Abandoning high heaven (1 En 12:4)
- Kept in eternal chains (1 En 54:5)

At the very least we can know the Enochic literature was within Jude's literary framework.

The passage indicates these angels are bound or tied up in eternal chains as they await the judgment of Christ. So where do we get the idea that they are "trapped under the earth"? This usually stems from the phrase *deep darkness* (*hypo zophon*), which can be a reference to Hades or Sheol as attested to in other Greek literature. For example, Aeschylus, Euripides, and even Homer use this same phrase to refer to the underworld.[21] This understanding fits well with the Hebrew conception of Sheol and matches what we find in the Enochic text, specifically in 1 Enoch 10:12: "When they and all their children have battled with each other, and when they have seen the destruction of their beloved ones, bind them for seventy generations underneath the rocks of the ground until the day of their judgment and of their consummation, until the eternal judgment is concluded."[22] Combining Jude 6 with the background in Enoch and the connotations with Greek literature seems to indicate that there are impris-

---

21. For the same form in Greek refer to Homer, *Odyssey* 11.57; *Iliad* 21.56; *Persians*, 839); *Hippolytus*, 1416.
22. James H. Charlesworth, *The Old Testament Pseudepigrapha*, vol. 1 (New York; London: Yale University Press, 1983), 18.

oned rebellious angels who are under judgment in a location that could very well be Sheol (the underworld) where they are awaiting the final day of judgment.

So what can we say about the fruit of this union, the mysterious Nephilim? The Nephilim were the result of an unholy union between divine beings and human women. Ambrose bishop of Milan, a patristic father, says, "The author of the divine Scripture does not mean that those giants must be considered, according to the tradition of poets, as sons of the earth but asserts that those whom he defines with such a name because of the extraordinary size of their body were generated by angels and women."[23] As we noted earlier, the Greek and Roman myths of the demigods such as Hercules, Theseus, Achilles, and others must have had an origin story. Genesis 6:1–4 gives us that origin story. As we've also noted, God doesn't sit back and allow rebellion to go unpunished. There is always a punishment and a promise rooted in each rebellion. In this second rebellion the punishment for the sons of God is being cast into the depth of Hades, or Tartarus, as 2 Peter 2:4 notes: "God didn't spare the angels who sinned but cast them into hell· and delivered them in chains [*seipais*] of utter darkness to be kept for judgment."[24] The word chains (*seipais*) fits the description of the watchers who are punished in 1 Enoch and Jubilees, an indication

23. Andrew Louth and Marco Conti, eds., *Genesis 1–11*, Ancient Christian Commentary on Scripture (Downers Grove, IL: InterVarsity Press, 2001), 126.
24. *Christian Standard Bible* (Nashville, TN: Holman Bible Publishers, 2020), 2 Pe 2:4.

that the writer of 2 Peter was likely aware of those texts. Additionally, Jude 6 refers to the angels who are in chains, and verses 14–15 contain "a quotation that appears almost word-for-word in *1 Enoch* 1:9, so it is difficult to argue that Jude knew nothing of *1 Enoch* 6."[25] We also learn that humanity was punished as well, suggesting that they were not victims but were complicit in taking what they learned from these divine beings and using that knowledge for evil. The flood was God's answer to the moral decay and sinful rebellion of humanity. However, as we noted, embedded in that punishment was a promise of rescue. One family, the family of Noah, was saved not *from* the flood but *through* the flood, along with pairs of animals as a means of restarting the creation so it would one day reflect the ideal of Eden.

But humanity's new start would be short-lived. Even with a fresh beginning, they chose to continue in the path of rebellion. Instead of going out into the world to spread God's glory and goodness, they traveled to the plains of Shinar in an attempt to force God to come down to them as they built the tower of Babel. This takes us to the third rebellion.

---

25. Robert C. Newman, "The Ancient Exegesis of Genesis 6:2, 4," *Grace Theological Journal* 5, no. 1 (1984): 29.

FOUR

THE THIRD REBELLION AT BABEL

In Genesis 3, rebellion created division between God and humanity. In Genesis 6, the rebellion of the sons of God resulted in separation between the angelic beings and God and also instigated evil in the world, further separating humanity from God. Now, in Genesis 11, we have a third rebellion. Here we find further human rebellion leading to division between peoples and nations, once again instigated by supernatural beings. Where do we see this? Again, we need to let the Scriptures interpret the Scriptures by reading Deuteronomy 32:8–9 as the backdrop to the Genesis 11 Babel event.

Even though humanity was cast out from God's household due to rebellion, the divine decree to multiply and be fruitful remained intact. This is evident in God's repeated command not only to Adam and Eve (Gen 1:22, 28) but also to Noah, Adam's descendant (Gen 8:17; 9:1, 7).[1] In

---

1. The phrase *peru urevu* is not limited to these occurrences. It is repeated in Gen 35:11, where God changes Jacob's name to Israel and promises not only a nation but an "assembly of nations" would come from him. This is an

Genesis 9:9 Yahweh establishes his covenant with the sons of Noah: "Behold, I establish my covenant with you and your offspring after you" (ESV). In context, the offspring are the descendants of Shem, Ham, and Japhet. In other words, the covenant has in mind everyone known to the biblical writer. Therefore, Noah's descendants play an important role in the events of Genesis 10 and 11.

Since this universal scope is presented in Genesis 9:9, Genesis 10 and 11 may present a conceptual challenge to the interpreter.[2] We must first determine the universality or the locality of the event of Babel. This determination will play an important role in subsequent chapters, where we look at Acts 2 and the reversal of Babel through the unification of the nations via a common understanding of God in the gospel. Even if the Babel event was a local phenomenon, this does not negate the conclusion that the covenant had in mind everyone known to the biblical writer—and was thus intended to be taken universally.[3]

One consideration is the translation of the Hebrew word *erets* and whether it is intended to mean the "whole earth" or a geographic "land." Paul Penley surveys the usage of

---

important note as it indicates national growth and expansion and household expansion and growth. See also Jer 3:16; 23:3; Ezek 36:11.

2. One option that may be plausible is that Gen 11 happens chronologically before Gen 10. See Andrew E. Steinmann, *Genesis: An Introduction and Commentary*, Tyndale Commentary Series 1 (London: Inter-Varsity Press, 2019), 131.

3. The same argument can be made concerning the Great Commission. We do not limit the mandate of the Great Commission to the Mediterranean and the Middle East. What was the "known world" to the author should encompass what we now know to be true of the known world. In the same way, even if the event at Babel was an isolated local event, the language of the biblical writer makes clear that it had in mind "all people" known to the writer at that time and thus encompasses a universal perspective.

erets before Genesis 11 and finds that the majority of these instances require a translation of "land" or a limited geographical location (Gen 10:5, 10, 11, 20, 31). Additionally, the seventeen instances after Genesis 11:1–9 seem to refer to a limited geographic region (Gen 11:28, 31; 12:1, 5, 6, 7, 10; 13:6, 7, 9, 10, 12, 15).[4] While this argument is compelling, it does not speak to the question of the "one language" (*saphah*) that the whole earth spoke. In other words, even if the land is limited geographically, the reference to one language seems to indicate that all of the earth (including the isolated land of Shinar) spoke one language.

Gordon Wenham notes that "one language" literally means "one lip" and has a "Sumerian parallel to the idea that at one time all mankind spoke the same language."[5] Additionally, the "one language" is combined with "one kind of speech," which is not simply a repetition, as these two phrases cannot be used interchangeably.[6] If Genesis 11 takes place after Genesis 10, we must account for the multiple languages in Genesis 10 and the one language of Genesis 11,

---

4. Paul T. Penley, "A Historical Reading of Genesis 11:1–9: The Sumerian Demise and Dispersion Under the Ur III Dynasty," *Journal of the Evangelical Theological Society* 50 (2007): 697–98. Kidner observes that if the translation of "land" is excepted, the RSV translation of "few words" is possible and lends to the possibility of a limited geographical location based on a group of settlers in a localized area. See Derek Kidner, *Genesis: An Introduction and Commentary*, Tyndale Old Testament Commentaries 1 (Downers Grove, IL: InterVarsity Press, 1967), 119. For a defense of a localized view of language in Gen 11 and a historical Babel event, see Dale S. DeWitt, "The Historical Background of Genesis 11:1–9: Babel or Ur?," *Journal of the Evangelical Theological Society* 22 (1979): 13–20.
5. Wenham, *Genesis 1–15*, 238.
6. Victor P. Hamilton, *The Book of Genesis, Chapters 1–17*, The New International Commentary on the Old Testament (Grand Rapids: Eerdmans, 1990), 351.

as it seems that there were both multiple languages and one language spoken on the earth.[7] Victor Hamilton provides the best possible solution that retains the integrity of the language, culture, and ideological roots of ethnic development and diversity due to Genesis 11.[8] Hamilton suggests Genesis 11 presents the phenomena of lingua franca, "a medium of communication among representatives of different speech groups."[9] Therefore, in addition to the "local languages" of Genesis 10, Genesis 11 presents a "world language" that made communication across ethnic boundaries possible.[10] This is familiar to us today. I am Indian and my family speaks Telugu, a major dialect of India. However, there are a variety of languages that Indians

---

7. Gen 10 is connected to Gen 11 and Gen 5 and the genealogy present there. However, Gen 10 is distinct as the focus is on the development of "nationality" and "ethnicity." Smith says, "Genesis 10 is really a table of nations instead of a classical genealogy. The plural forms and names of cities make it clear that the author was more concerned with humankind's expansion." See Gary V. Smith, "Structure and Purpose in Genesis 1–11," *Journal of the Evangelical Theological Society* 20 (1977): 311–13. Additionally, it is not necessary, and arguably unlikely, that a chronology is intended by the author, who may instead be concerned with connection. Wenham, *Genesis 1–15*, 209, notes the two chapters are linked by key words and phrases—scatter, spread out, country of Shinar, and build. Therefore, it would be best to be seen in the context of establishing symmetry, not necessarily chronology.

8. In addition to Hamilton's observations, the ANE belief of a universal human language fits with Gen 11 conceptually. A fragment, "Enmerkar and the Lord of Aratta," says that the speech of mankind was "confounded as a result of strife and jealousy between two gods." See Sarna, *Genesis*, 81.

9. Hamilton, *Genesis, Chapters 1–17*, 350. The same phenomena can be seen today in Africa and India, and some may suggest that English is taking on a similar "world" language.

10. This solution's appeal correlates to Acts 2 and Pentecost and Eph 2:12–22, where the ethnic groups are unified through shared understanding. In this sense, the lingua franca is a divine gift enabled by the Spirit to provide one understanding while preserving each representative's local ethnic languages. Hamilton follows C. H. Gordon, *Before Columbus: Links Between the Old World and Ancient America* (New York: Crown, 1971), 107, 165–66.

speak, such as Tamil, Malyalam, and Urdu. Even the villages have distinct spins on these languages similar to how we would say those who live in the South have a unique flair to their English. However, the national language of India is Hindi. So you have one language that unites all people while still retaining distinct regional languages.

The unity of one language in Genesis 11 enabled the people to communicate and set their desires on common goals. This sparked creativity and ingenuity that was intended to help the people fulfill their commission. Genesis 11 tells us that the people migrated "from the east" and found a plain in the land of Shinar.[11] There are two important observations here. First, they migrate from the east, a reversal of direction following the Edenic expulsion. The repetition of *east* suggests that humanity is initiating this act of reversal (see Gen 3:24; 4:16) by seeking to reverse the exile of Eden and attempting to return. Their motivation may be a desire to "be like God," which is indicated through building a "tower with its top in the heavens" and working to "make a name" for themselves (Gen 11:2–4). This calls to mind the dangers of misguided desire in previous rebellions, as we reflect on the desire of Eve and Adam in Genesis 3 and the sons of God in Genesis 6.

A second observation is that the people settle in a plain. A plain has no mountains, and as we noted earlier, mountains were where heaven and earth met. Without mountains, how could humanity meet with deity? The question underlying

---

11. There are at least three possible approaches to the historicity of Gen 11:1–9: ahistorical primeval event, agnostic historical event, and known historical event. For a summary of these three approaches, see Penley, "A Historical Reading of Genesis 11:1–9," 691–95.

the narrative is whether humanity will take things into their own hands by rebelliously usurping authority, or will they follow the command and decree of the head of the human-divine household and work toward a future regathering only after members of the household have fulfilled their duty? At Babel, we see the former, an act of rebellion and insurrection.

If the people's desire is to be reunited with deity, then constructing a tower in the middle of a flat plain makes perfect sense. Seen another way, the tower's construction may express a desire to return to the mountain of God, Eden, the original home where God met with humanity. As we saw in prior acts of rebellion, the pattern of seeing, desiring, and taking rears its ugly head yet again. The people *see* they are not in Eden. They *desire* to return to their Edenic status. So they decide to *take* what they want by constructing a tower to get it. The text suggests the desires behind the people's efforts were not pure or good. The inclusion of the phrase "make a name for ourselves," alongside the desire to build a tower with its "head in the heavens," suggests both pride and an act of rebellion.[12]

The desire to make a name for themselves directly recalls Adam and Eve's original sin with their desire to "be like God," which is ironic since they alone among creation were

---

12. Hiebert disagrees with any notion of pride and arrogance associated with the tower of Babel account. For Hiebert, the sole and exclusive reading of Gen 11:1–9 is "exclusively about the origins of cultural differences and not about pride and punishment at all." Hiebert's ambition to "retrieve" the cultural origins found within Gen 11 is admirable. This author agrees that the "pride and rebellion" motif should not relegate the cultural diversity to a background element. However, Hiebert goes too far in arguing for an exclusivity of cultural difference as the point of Gen 11:1–9. See Theodore Hiebert, "The Tower of Babel and the Origin of the World's Cultures," *Journal of Biblical Literature* 126 (2007): 29–58, https://doi.org/10.2307/27638419.

made in the image and likeness of God. In attempting to be like God, Adam and Eve forfeited their nearness to God, and those at Babel follow the same pattern. Desiring to be near to God, they build a tower that focuses the glory on themselves.

The Great Ziggurat of Ur
Photo credit: frog/stock.adobe.com

The Hebrew word for tower (*migdal*) indicates an elevated structure typically used for protection. The tower (*migdal*) of Babel was almost certainly a ziggurat, which is derived from an Akkadian word translated as "temple-tower." The people are building a temple, a reality that should lead us to pause as we recall that the temple was the abode or home of deity.[13] Following this line of thought, the tower of Babel was

---

13. Walton notes, "We cannot say that the building project described in Genesis 11 was exclusively a temple complex, but a temple complex certainly was included and is the focus of the story." Thus, it is likely that the people are in the beginning stages of building a large city working from the inside out. Thus, the ziggurat (step-pyramid) would have been located adjacent to the temple and near other city buildings. See John H. Walton, "The Mesopotamian Background of the Tower of Babel Account and Its Implications," *Bible and Spade* 9 (1996): 78–89.

given the name *Etemenanki*, meaning "The House of the Foundation of Heaven and Earth."[14] The people attempted to build a temple-tower that would serve as the house of the deity. To put it simply, they are trying to create a counterfeit Eden. The people at Shinar act on their sinful desires and in defiance of the decree of Yahweh to re-create a new Eden where heaven and earth meet.[15] They are trying to twist the Lord's arm to reconvene his human household, evidence of their inflated view of self, their pride, and their rebellion.

Are There Aliens in This World?

One of the questions that comes up often is the origin story of the ancient pyramids. The ziggurat temple tower closely resembles pyramids, and they served similar functions. They were temples/houses that were connected to the gods of the nations. They were constructed in locations that didn't have mountains because mountains were viewed as the meeting place of god and humans. The prevailing thought (of some) is that ancient humans did not have the technology to build these structures. So clearly alien beings are the alternative option. I actually think Christians are in a good place to

---

14. Kerr D. Macmillan, "Exegetical Theology. Review of Light on the Old Testament from Babel by Albert T. Clay," *The Princeton Theological Review* 6 (1908): 663–64.

15. Babel's construction language reflects the building language associated with *oikos* terminology. However, there is a certain sense of irony as Paul in Ephesians identifies a fulfillment in the process that is left unfinished at Babel. More on this elsewhere in the chapter.

answer this question. In addition to the question of pyramids, the past few years have seen more news coverage, viral clips, and questions about the presence of extraterrestrial life forms in our universe. I believe that what the world calls "aliens," the Bible refers to as "spiritual beings" who reside in the "unseen realm." At times, the unseen realm breaks through into the physical realm, and in those instances we may see glimpses of spiritual beings. What the mind can't comprehend, we've labeled as aliens. But in reality, this type of encounter is commonplace in the Bible. Think about the story of Elisha in 2 Kings 6.

> Elisha said, "Don't be afraid, for those who are with us outnumber those who are with them."
> Then Elisha prayed, "LORD, please open his eyes and let him see." So the LORD opened the servant's eyes, and he saw that the mountain was covered with horses and chariots of fire all around Elisha. (2 Kings 6:16–17)

Elisha prays, and the Lord opens the servants' eyes to see into the unseen realm. Imagine what someone in the twenty-first century would say about this situation. How would they try to describe it? They might call this an "alien encounter" when in reality they had a peek into the spiritual realm described in the Bible and experienced an encounter with spiritual beings.

Additionally, the question about advanced technology can be answered by Genesis 6 and the issue of the watchers with the background context of the Enochic literature. The sons of God could have easily given advanced instruction for technology and knowledge to create structures, and of course they would do it precisely to construct their own temples/houses as a counterfeit to Yahweh's family. However, all of this is quite different from what some have labeled the "ancient alien" view that is popular today. In that view, the assumptions are that these beings are extraterrestrials from another planet and that the Bible is simply one among many sources providing evidence that we have been visited from other planets. I firmly reject this view.

In response to this activity, Yahweh does not simply sit back and watch. We find both punishment and promise in this third rebellion as well. In Genesis 11:7 the Lord says "let us go" (NIV). Again we find a reference to plurality, recalling Genesis 1:26 where God first declares "let us." The biblical author essentially copies and pastes "let us" (*na'aseh*) from Genesis 1:26 into the Genesis 11 account. The "let us" language is also used of humanity in expressing their desire to build a tower (Gen 11: 3). But when this same language is repeated a few verses later by Yahweh, he is speaking to his first family, the heavenly host, indicating he is once again engaging in household business (Gen 11:7).

However, this time God is not calling attention to what

he has done; he is calling attention to the rebellious activity of his human family and his response. Humanity's rebellion requires a response, and as punishment God diversifies the tongues of man, accomplishing his original divine decree despite human rebellion. In Genesis 10, we see the pattern that guides our understanding. All the families of the earth have their own lands and clans and languages. This is *before* Babel. Then, in Genesis 11, the opening sentence tells us they also had one language. This means humanity originally had *distinction through diversity within unity.*

But things go tragically wrong.

1. God's *gift* of ingenuity and unity to the people was used for rebellion, *not* loyalty to their Creator.
2. God's *commission* was to go out into the world, *not* up into the heavens.
3. God's *aim* for the people was the expansion of his name and glory, *not* the people's fame and name throughout the earth.

The consequence of rebellion was the loss of the one language that provided unity, understanding, and common ground. This forced the spread of people outward into the world as God intended, but with the tragic loss of their unity, a unity that was supposed to mark them as a common family.

As we shall see, a seed planted here will be redemptively grown in the New Testament in Acts 2 at Pentecost. At Pentecost God sets right all that went wrong at Babel. This was more than a reversal of what was lost; it was a redemptive reinstitution of God's plans and purposes for his family.

THE THIRD REBELLION AT BABEL

1. God's *gift* to the nations of the world that are represented at Pentecost (the list of nations in Acts 2:9–10 reflects the table of nations of Genesis 10) is the promised and long-awaited Holy Spirit.
2. God equips the nations of the world to accomplish his original *commission* by giving them a unified understanding (one language) to knit them together as one family.
3. God's *aim* for the people of God is redeemed and reinstituted through the Holy Spirit as the fame and glory of God is spread throughout the nations of the world.

At Pentecost the people don't have to climb up because God in the person of the Holy Spirit comes down. The church at Pentecost doesn't need to build a new temple to meet with God because they have become the temple where God is present. The people's ambitions and aims are no longer self-centered but God-ordered as they fulfill his plans for their lives unto his glory. And the most redemptive aspect of Babel is God's refusal to let their ethnic distinctions be lost or obliterated.

Let's not lose Genesis 10 in the story of Babel. Prior to Babel there was both ethnic diversity and unity. In Genesis 12, the Abrahamic covenant gave us a clue to God's plans with his promise to reunite the families of the earth. In Acts 2:8, we see the redemption of Babel in the answer to the question, "How is it that we hear, each of us in his own native language?" (ESV). God through the Holy Spirit could have given humanity common understanding yet again through one of the national languages of the time (perhaps Greek or Aramaic). Instead, God does something wonderful. For the first time, the people of the nations can hear the good news of the gospel in the intimate context of their unique family language. Pentecost is, in fact, spiritual warfare because it is a return to the ideal of Genesis 10. It is a right ordering of human ambition and a godly fulfillment of the rebellious aim of Genesis 11. And it is the fulfillment of the promise made to Abraham in Genesis 12.

Why does any of this matter? Because it helps us to more clearly see what the unseen battle is over, the prize behind spiritual warfare. From ancient times, the unseen battle has been about people: Who will claim the human household? Each of these rebellions has humanity at its center. The first rebellion questioned God's good and loving fatherly intentions for his children. The second rebellion was an attempt to further corrupt the human family with improper relations and forbidden knowledge. Now this third rebellion, an attempt to reverse God's decree, leads to a rejection of a portion of the human family as an act of familial discipline. But again, we cannot forget that a promise is embedded in the punishment.

The Three Rebellions and the Three Temptations of Christ?

The gospel writers seem to be connecting the three rebellions of the Old Testament and the three temptations of

Jesus in the New Testament.[16] In his incarnation, Jesus is retelling the story of Israel. However, where Israel failed, in all the ways that Israel was faithless, Jesus was faithful. This is specifically highlighted in the wilderness temptations. In the wilderness, Jesus is tempted in three ways that directly hyperlink back to the wilderness wandering and the Israelites' sinfulness. However, Jesus remains faithful, and he quotes three passages in Deuteronomy (Deut 8:3; 6:16; 6:13). But I don't think this is the only connection being made. I believe there is an additional conceptual tie in back to the three rebellions of Genesis 3, 6, and 11.

Temptation 1: The Temptation of Selfish Satisfaction

The devil asks Jesus to turn the stone to bread. The devil seems to be replaying the first temptation in Eden when he convinced Eve and Adam to take something that was never theirs so their selfish desires could be fulfilled (to be like God). In this scenario, the devil attempts to convince Jesus to take the divine the power that was within his rights to use, but to use it for selfish purposes. Jesus is not tricked. He quotes Deuteronomy 8:3 and stops just

---

16. As I was finishing this manuscript, I sent it out to an early reader group who gave me crucial insights and feedback. I'm indebted to them for their diligence in reading a far from finished manuscript and pouring into it as if it was their own words. One of the readers in particular drew my attention to a concept that I had overlooked. Once again, a friendly reminder that theology should always be done in the context of community.

short of the rest of the verse, which says, "...but on every word that comes from the mouth of the LORD." In the first rebellion, Eve and Adam did not hang on the words that came from the mouth of the Lord and instead clung to the deceptive words that flowed from the father of lies, the serpent and the devil. Jesus does what Eve and Adam should have done in Eden. He returns to the truth spoken by the Father when presented with the lies of the enemy.

Temptation 2: The Temptation of Worldly Possessions

The devil offers Jesus the world. Which is an irony, considering the world already belonged to Jesus (as the world's creator) and was waiting to be reclaimed by Christ as God's anointed king. Jesus responds by saying, "Worship the Lord your God, and serve him only" (NIV), a quote from Deuteronomy 6:13. But note the very next verse, Deuteronomy 6:14, which explicitly commands us not to follow other gods. What was the nature of the third rebellion following Babel, as detailed in Psalm 82? The sons of God sought to elicit worship from the nations they were commissioned to steward and instead led them into deeper rebellion against God. The nations worship what should not have been worshiped and fall into grave sin. Here, Satan attempts to elicit the worship of Jesus, but unlike the Israelites and the wayward nations, Jesus remains steadfast in his devotion to the Father. Through his obedience to the Father, Jesus will ultimately inherit even more than what Satan promised—rule over the nations of the world as well as rule over every principality and power in the cosmos.

Temptation 3: The Temptation for Power

In the final temptation, Satan again attempts to manipulate Jesus into exercising his divine power for selfish gain. At the core of this temptation was the freedom to do whatever, whenever just because he could. Jesus responds by saying, "Do not test the Lord your God" (Matt 4:7, quoting Deut 6:16). However, just a few verses later, Deuteronomy 6:18 says, "Do what is right and good in the Lord's sight." In the second rebellion in Genesis 6, all of humanity did what was evil in the sight of God. They gave their daughters to the sons of God in exchange for forbidden knowledge that would give them power, and the resulting fruit of that union, the Nephilim. For their part, the sons of God saw what they desired (human women) and took of it because of their own selfish desires. Here, Jesus rejects the temptation to power by returning to a posture of faithful obedience. Though he has divine power, he refrains from exercising it, choosing to remain within the limits and boundaries of his incarnation as a human being, the path of the obedient Son of his heavenly Father.

In all three temptations we see the tactics of spiritual warfare. There is always the visible battle over the temptations being offered, but there is also the unseen battle waging within our hearts. Each temptation asks about the ultimate object of our affection. Will we revere, honor, and love God? Or will we give into self-obsession? Jesus shows us the way to fight these spiritual battles through the Word, by the power of the Spirit, and for the glory of the Father.

I'm a big fan of Marvel movies, and one of the iconic features of a Marvel movie is the postcredits scene. I believe Deuteronomy 32:8–9 gives us the postcredits scene for Genesis 11. Deuteronomy 32:8–9 serves as a conclusion to the rebellion of God's human family and brings another element into the narrative—God's heavenly family. Here we learn that the punishment of humanity is not limited to their dispersion throughout the earth but is far more significant. Babel results in the disinheritance of the nations, an act that will ultimately lead to division within the divine council and the sons of God.

THE DEUTERONOMY 32 WORLDVIEW

God rules and makes decisions through a council of divine beings who are part of his household, often referred to as a divine council. Sometimes people question why God would do this. We can get at the answer by asking another question: Why did God create humanity? The answer to this is kind of simple: He did so because he wanted to. Kings get to do what they want to do! That's how I tend to think about the divine council. Why does God work this way? God chooses to work through a divine council because it is his divine prerogative.

The idea that God utilizes a divine council to delegate rule over the nations of the world is sometimes referred to as the "Deuteronomy 32 worldview." The Deuteronomy 32 worldview is an ancient biblical worldview well understood by Old Testament scholars and specialists in Second Temple Judaism. This is particularly true since the discovery of the Qumran scroll reading of Deuteronomy 32:8 ("sons of God"), which provided Hebrew support for the Septuagint rendering of this passage. Deuteronomy 32:8–9 also holds an important interpretive clue to the aftermath of the Babel event.

Genesis 11 teaches us that God disperses the people among the earth. But Deuteronomy 32:8–9 suggests there was something else going on during this dispersal, something happening in the unseen realm as well. As we shall see, the consequence of humanity's household disobedience and rebellion resulted not only in geographical separation but in familial separation. Deuteronomy 32:8–9 reads as follows: "When the Most High gave to the *nations* their *inheritance*, when he divided mankind, he fixed the borders of the peoples *according to the number of the sons of God. But the* LORD's *portion is his people, Jacob his allotted heritage*" (ESV).[17] Deuteronomy 32:8–9 tells us that at the Babel event

---

17. Emphasis mine. The translation follows the Septuagint (or LXX) and the Dead Sea Scrolls with "sons of God." Many Old Testament scholars today follow the Dead Sea Scrolls' reading of "sons of God." The Septuagint also follows this reading. Among one of the first New Testament scholars to see an indication of "sons of God" was G. B. Caird, who saw the presence of

Yahweh disinherited the nations and gave them over to the "sons of God," establishing the boundaries of the nations. Deuteronomy 4:19 reinforces this understanding. Here we learn that Yahweh "allotted" the "host of heaven / sons of God" to "all the peoples under the whole heaven." The "allotment" (*chalaq*; Deut 4:19; see also 4:19–20; 29:23–26) and "inheritance" (*hanchel*) language of Deuteronomy 32:8–9 depicts Yahweh as the head of a household giving stewardship of the nations to the trusted members of his divine council, the sons of God. This section points us to Babel as the originating event for the formation of the subsequent Jew-gentile division. From this point forward in the text, the gentile nations are now disinherited and allotted to the sons of God. They are no longer Yahweh's portion

<hr/>

a "heavenly host" in the Septuagint of Deut 32:8–9, where he amended the "sons of Israel" in the Masoretic Text to "sons of God" based on his reading of the Septuagint. Caird comments that his translation decision was initially "a conjectural emendation, based on the LXX" but has been confirmed since discovering the Qumran texts and a fragment of the Song of Moses. See G. B. Caird, *Principalities and Powers: A Study in Pauline Theology: The Chancellor's Lectures for 1954 at Queen's University, Kingston Ontario* (Eugene, OR: Wipf & Stock, 2003), 17. See also Patrick W. Skehan, "A Fragment of the 'Song of Moses' (Deut. 32) from Qumran," *Bulletin of the American Schools of Oriental Research* 136 (1954): 12–15. Skehan proposes that the Septuagint reflects the original text. Soon after Skehan published an important article on this passage in 1951, a Qumran fragment of the text of Deut 32:8 was found that reads "sons of God." This discovery is the first example of a Hebrew manuscript that favors the reading of the Septuagint. It is thus suggested by many that the fragments of 4QDeut preserve the original reading. For more on the Septuagint and Old Latin manuscripts that favor the reading of "sons of God," see David E. Stevens, "Does Deuteronomy 32:8 Refer to 'Sons of God' or 'Sons of Israel'?," *Bibliotheca Sacra* 154 (1997): 133–34. Stevens ultimately prefers the Masoretic Text reading over the Septuagint and Dead Sea Scrolls. His primary reasons for this conclusion are based on the excellent preservation of the Hebrew text of Deuteronomy and the historical context of the Septuagint that may have favored a focus on "angelology." While this is true, Stevens is unconvincing based on previously noted issues of the "sons of Israel" reading.

among humanity. Yahweh's portion will now exclusively be the Jews (Israel/Jacob) through the line of his chosen person, Abraham. Only through the promise to Abraham will the disinherited nations, now given over to lesser divine beings, have any hope of rejoining the household of God.

Deuteronomy 32 begins with an extended introduction (a poem) and then turns to the table of nations, another textual connection between this passage and Genesis 10 and 11. As John Sailhamer comments: "It was there [Babel] that God apportioned each of the nations its own inheritance of land; and it was there that he also gave Israel, 'his people,' the inheritance of their land (Deut 32:8–9)."[18] The language of *inheritance* is significant in considering the household context as background for what is occurring. The Hebrew verb *nachal* means that a "joint heir has received his portion by succession."[19] Further, it has connotations of an individual who receives a portion of a patriarchal estate.[20] Here

---

18. John Sailhamer, "Creation, Genesis 1–11, and the Canon," *Bulletin for Biblical Research* 10 (2000): 102. For more on the form and structure of Deut 32, see Matthew Thiessen, "The Form and Function of the Song of Moses (Deuteronomy 32:1–43)," *Journal of Biblical Literature* 123 (2004): 401. For "covenant lawsuit," see G. Ernest Wright, "The Lawsuit of God: A Form-Critical Study of Deuteronomy 32," in *Israel's Prophetic Heritage: Essays in Honor of James Muilenburg*, ed. Bernhard W. Anderson and Walter Harrelson (New York: Harper, 1962), 26–67. For wisdom literature, see James R. Boston, "The Wisdom Influence upon the Song of Moses," *Journal of Biblical Literature* 87 (1968): 198–202. Deuteronomy 32 has been argued to be a covenant lawsuit, wisdom literature, or a hymn. Thiessen argues for the hymnic perspective; however, it may not be necessary to discount the wisdom and covenant lawsuit perspectives. This author sees all of the aforementioned elements in Deut 32 that lend to household language. The household can be understood in a covenant, wisdom, and even hymnic aspects.
19. E. Lipiński, "נחל," in *Theological Dictionary of the Old Testament*, ed. G. Johannes Botterweck, Helmer Ringgren, and Heinz-Josef Fabry, trans. David E. Green, 17 vols. (Grand Rapids: Eerdmans, 1998), 9:320.
20. This is specifically applied to the noun *nachalah*.

we see a combination of household and covenant language, which should not be surprising, as the head of household in both the Old Testament and Greco-Roman worlds regularly administered inheritance rights and responsibilities to household members. Additionally, this inheritance language intersects with the concept of fatherhood. The fatherhood of God is not unique to the New Testament and has its roots in the Old Testament. As Dan Lioy notes, "Deuteronomy 32:6 serves as an important reminder that the 'fatherhood of God' did not originate with the New Testament; instead, the concept has 'deep roots in the relationship between God and Israel' (cf. Exod 4:22; Isa 63:16; 64:8; Jer 3:19; 31:9; Hos 11:1; Mal 2:10)."[21]

Yet the question remains: By whom are the nations "inherited"? Following the Septuagint's and the Dead Sea Scrolls' reading of the "sons of God," the inheritance equates to the nations and thus suggests each divine being is paired with a nation. This is where we get the "gods of the nations" concept of the Old Testament.[22] The appointment of divine beings to

---

21. Dan Lioy, "A Comparative Analysis of the Song of Moses and Paul's Speech to the Athenians," *Conspectus* 16 (2014): 13. As DeRouchie says, "Yahweh alone is Israel's 'father' (32:6), their redeemer (4:20; 4:34; etc.), covenant maker (29:1), warrior (1:30; 3:22), protector (33:26–29), guide (1:33; 8:2; 32:12), instructor (1:3; 4:2; 6:1–2), prayer answerer (4:7; 9:19; 10:10), provider (2:7; 8:16–18), disciplinarian (8:3, 5; 11:2), tester (13:3), judge (1:17; 5:9; 7:10), restorer (4:40–41; 30:1–10; 32:34), and savior (4:31; 33:29)." See Jason S. DeRouchie, "From Condemnation to Righteousness: A Christian Reading of Deuteronomy," *The Southern Baptist Journal of Theology* 18 (2014): 107.

22. Tigay notes "that the number of nations equals the number of 'sons of the divine,' suggests that each of these beings is paired with a nation. Jewish sources of the Hellenistic and Talmudic periods elaborate on this picture, indicating that God appointed divine beings to govern the nations on His behalf. See Jeffrey H. Tigay, *Deuteronomy*, The JPS Torah Commentary (Philadelphia: Jewish Publication Society, 1996), 514. Regarding the variant readings, three different manuscripts help determine the correct reading of

the nations by God, as father and head of the household, is a direct result of the Babel rebellion in Genesis 11.

The events of Babel, when read alongside Deuteronomy 32:8–9, present us with a picture of God handing over the rebellious, disinherited nations to the sons of God. In Deuteronomy 4:19–22, we find the same event but in reverse: God "allotting" the gods to the nations.[23] The implications of Deuteronomy 32:8–9 should be seen in correlation with Deuteronomy 4:19–20, where we find clearer inheritance and allotment language. Michael Heiser refers to this as the "other side of the punitive coin."[24] The head of the household is functioning administratively with both his human and cosmic/divine family. The allotment (*chalaq*) speaks to land, inheritance, division, and placement of property.[25] Yahweh

---

Deut 32:8b. The Masoretic Text, the Samaritan Pentateuch, and the Qumran scrolls. The Masoretic Text and Samaritan Pentateuch agree on "sons of Israel,"' and the Septuagint and the Dead Sea Scrolls agree on "sons of God." This concept will be pickup up further in the next section discussing Dan 10 and the biblical theology of the Deut 32 worldview put on display in connection to the "sons of God" as "princes" with geopolitical influence. Sirach 17:17 says, "Over every nation he places a ruler, but the Lord's own portion is Israel." Skehan and Di Lella make the following translation note: "Before this verse, GII inserts "For in the dividing up of the nations of all the world," an allusion to Deut 32:8–9, on which Ben Sira's v 17 depends." See Patrick W. Skehan and Alexander A. Di Lella, *The Wisdom of Ben Sira: A New Translation with Notes, Introduction and Commentary*, Anchor Yale Bible 39 (New Haven, CT: Yale University Press, 2008), 277. See also 1 En 89:59–67, which includes household language. The seventy shepherds equate to angels, while the sheep represent seventy nations.

23. Daniel L. Block surveys the "Deity-Territory Tie" and comes to the conclusion that, "To date, no ancient Semitic text provid(es) a detailed account of how specific gods came to be associated with specific lands." Block goes on to state that the earliest evidence for an association between deity and people comes from the Hebrew Bible, specifically Deuteronomy 32:8–9. See Block, Daniel I. *The Gods of the Nations: Studies in Ancient Near Eastern National Theology.* Second Edition. Eugene, OR: Wipf & Stock, 1988, 21–35.

24. Heiser, *The Unseen Realm*, 114.

25. When allotment (*chalaq*) is in the *qal* (as it is in Deut 4:19), it is, "used generally for inheritance within a family (Prov. 17:2; Neh. 13:13; not far

acts decisively by subjecting the nations under the rule and authority of the sons of God (Deut 4:19–20) while at the same time rejecting his own direct rulership of rebellious humanity.[26]

God gives the sons of God the responsibility to care for and steward (or guard) the nations according to his decrees and laws. They are responsible to enact justice and righteousness among those they rule over. However, rather than executing the divine task assigned to the sons of God, they instead pervert justice and accept human worship. As Heiser says, "We aren't told how the *elōhîm* Yahweh assigned to the nations became corrupt, only that they were."[27] While we may not be told explicitly how the *elohim* became corrupt, the biblical record throughout the Old Testament is clear that the nations worshiped these gods and tempted Israel to worship along with them, an

---

removed is 2 S. 19:30[29])." M. Tsevat, "חָלַק," in *Theological Dictionary of the Old Testament*, ed. G. Johannes Botterweck and Helmer Ringgren, trans. David E. Green, 17 vols. (Grand Rapids: Eerdmans, 1980), 4:449. There is a possible background connection to the events of Gen 11 and Deut 32:8–9 in Deut 21:18–21 that indicates the seriousness of the offense of humanity's rebellion (and, as we will see, the rebellion of the sons of God). There are familial issues at play and legal issues with the household children, who are also considered heirs. Burnside says, "This arises from the legal (as opposed to the filial) relationship that existed between parents and children in the ANE. The parties are related not only biologically as parents and children but also legally as testators and heirs. This may add a further dimension to seriousness of offence. Deut. 21:18–21 may not simply be a case of being a bad son (filial disobedience) but also a bad heir." See Jonathan P. Burnside, *The Signs of Sin: Seriousness of Offence in Biblical Law*, Journal for the Study of the Old Testament Supplement Series 364 (Sheffield: Sheffield Academic Press, 2003), 71.

26. Heiser, "Monotheism, Polytheism, Monolatry, or Henotheism?," 26.
27. Heiser, *The Unseen Realm*, 116. See the earlier discussion of the sons of God and their acceptance of human worship as indication of their familial rebellion.

illegitimate abuse of their authority and an act of idolatry (Deut 4:19–20; 17:3; 29:25; 32:17).[28]

At some point, the sons of God assigned to the nations entered into an act of cosmic rebellion, bringing further division within the household of God. In Deuteronomy 4:19–20, the text stops just short of saying the nations *worship* the "heavenly bodies, but this might be implied (cf. Jer. 10:1–16; 2 Kgs. 17:16; Zeph. 1:5)."[29] Not only do the nations allotted to the "sons of God" eventually fall into idolatry, but Israel, God's possession and inheritance, is also guilty of the worship that the sons of God accept. Heiser says it this way:

> Attention need only be drawn to Deut 32:17, a text that, alluding to the failures of Israel in disobeying the warnings of Deut 4:19–20, quite clearly has Moses referring to the other אֱלֹהִים [*elohim*] as evil spiritual entities (שֵׁדִים): "They [Israel] sacrificed to demons (לַשֵּׁדִים) who are not God (אֱלֹהַּ), to gods (אֱלֹהִים) they did not know; new ones that had come along recently, whom your fathers had not reverenced." While these lesser אֱלֹהִים [*elohim*] are linked to the statues that represented them in the mind of their worshipers (Deut 4:28; 7:25; 28:64), these beings must

---

28. Further evidence for the rebellion of the *elohim* can be found in the Septuagint translation of Ps 95:5, where the psalmist declares all the gods of the people are "idols/*daimonia*," thus indicating reverence of the gods is a form of idolatry. This follows with Second Temple literature, where the sons of God are given the nations as an inheritance to bring oversight under the authority of Yahweh. Thus, any action outside of the direction of Yahweh is a form of idolatry. In the "Animal Apocalypse" of 1 En 85–90, we find the shepherds kill more sheep than are allotted and find themselves under household discipline. See Charlesworth, *The Old Testament Pseudepigrapha*, 1:68.

29. Edward J. Woods, *Deuteronomy: An Introduction and Commentary*, Tyndale Old Testament Commentaries 5 (Nottingham: Inter-Varsity Press, 2011), 110.

be considered real spiritual entities. Indeed, it cannot be presumed that ancient people considered a humanly fabricated statue or fetish object to be identical with the god in whose likeness it was fashioned.[30]

Thus, the consequence of rebellion—both human (Gen 3; 11) and cosmic (Gen 3; 6; 11 cf. Deut 32:8–9)—is the formation of competing households in an antithetical relationship with Yahweh and his household.[31] The sons of God are now fallen, leading the nations that were allotted to them into rebellion against God and working against the divine decree of Yahweh.[32] This is the origin story for the gods of the nations that permeate the Old Testament narrative.

Once again, however, we see evidence of the pattern found in other rebellions: punishment and promise. The punishment has been clear—the nations are disinherited by Yahweh—but there is also hope, for God makes a promise of reunion with the nations, a future where they will be welcomed back into the inheritance of Yahweh. This is found in Genesis 12 with Abram and his family, who are called out of the epicenter of the Babel rebellion to be a blessing to the nations of the world. In context, the simple but significant

30. Heiser, "Monotheism, Polytheism, Monolatry, or Henotheism?," 8.
31. See Michael S. Heiser, "Does Deuteronomy 32.17 Assume or Deny the Reality of other Gods?," *The Bible Translator* 59, no. 3 (2008): 137–45.
32. In Deut 4:7 there is a discussion concerning the plurality of the first *elohim*. Bricker argues for the first instance of *elohim* to be translated as plural, which would, in turn, more accurately describe the polytheism of the ancient Near Eastern nations. Thus, a careful look at Deut 4:7 reveals a contrast between Yahweh as the intimate and near God of Israel versus the deities (fallen sons of God) of the surrounding nations. See Daniel P. Bricker, "'God So Near': An Examination of the Ancient Near Eastern Setting for Deuteronomy 4:7 and קרבים," *Bulletin for Biblical Research* 22 (2012): 345–46.

act of Yahweh calling Abram is a declaration of war against the dark forces of the world, the gods of the nations. It is also a clear statement that God has not abandoned his human family. In fact, he will one day reclaim what is rightfully his.

FIVE

ABRAHAM AND THE
BLESSING OF THE NATIONS

A t this point in the story, in the aftermath of Babel, the
future of humanity seems bleak and hopeless. Will the
household of God remain divided? Has God truly abandoned
his human family in putting them under the rule of lesser
diving beings? As we will learn in the ongoing narrative, the
answer is no. God instead reaches into one of these disinherited nations and claims a single man, Abram, later renamed
to Abraham, as his own, declaring his intention to make a
new nation from this one individual.

In Genesis 11 the people desire to "make a name" for
themselves. In response God indicates that he will be the
one to "make a name," and he will do it through Abraham
(Gen 12:1–3).[1] Not only would Yahweh make Abram's name

---

1. L. Michael Morales, *Who Shall Ascend the Mountain of the Lord?: A Biblical
Theology of the Book of Leviticus*, New Studies in Biblical Theology 37
(Downers Grove, IL: IVP Academic, 2015), 67–68. This concept is first
introduced directly after the Babel event in Gen 11:10, which begins with
the genealogy of Shem. Morales says, "Indeed, the verse directly following

great, but he promises to institute the future reconstitution of God's human family through Abraham. Abraham will be a "blessing" to *all* the nations, and the nations would be "blessed" by Abraham.[2] This is the seed of Yahweh's plan to put his household back together, and in the story that unfolds, as we witness God's people forging their way among the hostile nations of the world, an unseen battle is being waged in the cosmic and supernatural realm. Yahweh has made it clear that he will reinherit the nations and bring them back within his family, and he has chosen Abraham and his descendants for this purpose.

ABRAHAM'S POLYTHEISTIC BACKGROUND

In Genesis 11:31–32, we meet Abram in Haran with his father, Terah, and brother, Nahor. At first it might seem that God called Abraham out of Haran, where Abraham had settled for a time with his father's family. However, Stephen in Acts 7:2–4 informs us that God's call of Abram did not begin at Haran, but in Ur. Luke may be drawing from Genesis 15:7 (ESV): "He said to him, 'I am the LORD who brought you out from Ur of the Chaldeans to give you this land to possess.'"[3] In agreement with Genesis 15:7 and

the tower story (Gen. 11:10) begins with the genealogy of Shem, the son of Noah whose name means 'name,' and whose lineage leads to Abram, to whom YHWH promises, 'I will bless you and make your name [*šēm*] great' (12:2)."
2. Gen 12:3 will be discussed in further detail throughout this chapter. For further discussion see Joel S. Baden, "The Morpho-Syntax of Genesis 12:1–3: Translation and Interpretation," *Catholic Biblical Quarterly* 72 (2010): 223–37.
3. Nancy Calvert-Koyzis, "Abraham," in *Dictionary of the Later New Testament and Its Developments*, ed. Ralph P. Martin and Peter H. Davids

Nehemiah 9:7, Philo suggests that the call to Abram occurs in both places (Philo, *Abr.* 62, 85). These details help us locate the residence of Abraham first in Ur, placing him and his relatives near Babel. Further, we are told that Abraham's father, Terah, worshiped other gods, which brings to mind the fallen sons of God allotted to the nations as they are scattered around the world. In the context of the Babel event, Yahweh's actions with Abraham are not arbitrary or random but intentional. The clear message is that Yahweh is beginning a plan to reclaim his inheritance from among the very nations that have been disinherited and given over to lesser beings on his divine council.

There are several reasons why it is significant that Abraham and his family resided in Ur. In Genesis 15:7 Yahweh says to Abraham that he brought him out of "Ur of the Chaldeans." This designation clearly presents the city as Babylonian. This geographic reference places the family origins with Babel and the Babel event, the location of "the archetype of rebellion against God."[4] After the events of Babel, the disinherited nations allotted to the sons of God worshiped these cosmic beings, and as an act of cosmic rebellion, the sons of God accepted their worship and established themselves as the patron deities of various nations.[5] This is the context and situation we find from historical study of Ur as well. The people there worshiped Nanna, the moon goddess, and within the center of the city was a fortress

---

(Downers Grove, IL: IVP Academic, 1997), 2. Both Gen 15:7 and Neh 9:7 explicitly affirm that Yahweh first called Abram from Ur.

4. George Van Pelt Campbell, "Refusing God's Blessing: An Exposition of Genesis 11:27–32," *Bibliotheca Sacra* 165 (2008): 278–79.

5. See chapter 4.

housing the temple of the moon goddess. The ziggurat at Ur was world famous.[6] As previously noted, ziggurats were temple structures or staircases that served as entry points and a type of dwelling place for the deity. Ur's city center housed a deity, a picture of a rival household to Yahweh, one in rebellion against him.

The residents of this city (including Terah, Abraham, and Nahor) were either active participants in this rebellion through idolatry (as we know of Terah and Nahor) or were influenced in some way (as could be said of Abraham) by this idolatrous city.[7] Second Temple literature, such as the *Apocalypse of Abraham*, presents a picture of Abraham serving the gods of his father. New Testament scholar Nijay Gupta, commenting on the opening section of this work says, "The opening scene of the apocalypse borders on satirical."[8] Abraham is sent to sell cult statues, and on the way his donkey gets scared and tosses the "gods," crushing the statues. Abraham then reflects on the fragility of the statues and his own religion. Regardless of the historicity of this account, which is dubious at best, the literature presents a historical and cultural context showing Terah, Abraham, and Nahor

---

6. Irvin Himmel, "Abraham's Decision: To Walk by Faith (Genesis 12:1)," *Christianity Magazine* (1990): 12. Himmel presents Ur as a city that was designed like a medieval castle.
7. In later sections we will explore the situation of Abraham in Ur and Haran. The Old Testament presents Abraham as the passive recipient of Yahweh's call. In other words, he does not do anything to earn the opportunity. This is God's gracious call and an extension of mercy and opportunity. However, Second Temple literature attempts to present Abraham as a righteous individual who rejects the gods of his father. Thus, as a reward for righteous action, Yahweh extends the promise of inheritance to Abraham.
8. Nijay K. Gupta, "'They Are Not Gods!' Jewish and Christian Idol Polemic and Greco-Roman Use of Cult Statues," *Catholic Biblical Quarterly* 76 (2014): 716.

living in a world where the gods were an active part of the culture. For humanity to serve and give worship to these gods was an act of idolatry, and ultimately an act of rebellion against Yahweh.

Signs of the spreading post-Babel rebellion are evident through the influence of the moon god's presence in both Ur and Haran. As noted previously, Ur and Haran both had worship centers dedicated to Nanna, the moon god,[9] and this presents important background for Terah's desire (some may say willingness) to migrate from Ur with his son, Abraham.[10] It is possible that Abraham's call from Yahweh influenced Terah to begin a journey, yet it is highly unlikely that Terah and his other family members were able to shake their inner attraction to their gods. They appear to be unable to abandon their gods when faced with that decision.[11] As Genesis 11:31 notes, while Terah may have had an initial desire to go to Canaan with Abraham, when he arrived at Haran and saw the temple of his god, he relented and settled there, a land that provided him protection. In the ancient world, leaving the geographic area of your gods was extremely dangerous. People understood that the protection of the gods was connected to those gods' geographical boundaries. This will resurface again later when we look at the story of Rachel and the *teraphim*. At this point in the narrative, we can sur-

---

9. Daniel Goepfrich, "The Nature of the Coming Messianic Kingdom as Found in Its Covenants," *Journal of Dispensational Theology* 18 (2014): 213.

10. It is possible that Terah was influenced to move from Ur by his son Abraham. Because Terah was a polytheist, he could have seen Abraham's call from another deity as a significant opportunity. But when he arrives at Haran and faces the familiarity of household gods and the security they promise, he may have decided to relent and stay in Haran.

11. Campbell, "Refusing God's Blessing," 280.

mise that Terah may have panicked when he realized that following Abraham meant leaving the domain of his gods. By leaving Ur and Haran, the family would be abandoning their gods, leaving them unprotected and alone.

We know that Abraham's father, Terah, was a polytheist, and it should not be surprising that he still lived in fear of enemy gods, spirits, and evil forces that could attack him and his household. Terah most likely observed the practice of his culture and social setting in the ANE. He believed his "house would have been protected and his property secured by figurines such as Rachel later stole from Laban (Gen 31:19)."[12] In Haran, the religion of Terah and his household is settled, yet Abraham and his household choose to continue onward after Terah's death, following Yahweh's call toward the promised land. Understanding Terah's polytheistic background and beliefs help us to see that Abraham was once included in a household that belonged to other gods. In leaving Ur and Haran, Abraham leaves behind his family and abandons the household of other gods, following Yahweh alone into the wilderness.

There is a lesson for us here as well. The call of Abraham was more than just a call to go to a strange, unknown land. This call had spiritual implications, perhaps akin to a declaration of war. Spiritual warfare is fundamentally about obedience. Will we follow the call of God and leave behind the safety and security of our "other gods," whatever they may be? This is the question Abraham faced. Will he remain in the household of the familiar gods he knows, or will he

---

12. Lael Caesar, "Hermeneutics, Culture, and the Father of the Faithful," *Journal of the Adventist Theological Society* 13 (2002): 91–114.

follow this new God who calls him to a new land? Abraham's entrance into the promised land of Canaan is a continuation of the unseen battle between warring households. The promised land is directly connected to the promise God makes to Abraham, to be a blessing to the nations of the world.

ABRAHAM CALLED TO BE A BLESSING TO THE NATIONS

One of the most important aspects of Abraham's call is God's initiative. In Joshua 24:3 the Hebrew "took" suggests an intervention with purpose.[13] This is a repeated theme elsewhere with David (2 Sam 7:8), Amos (Amos 7:15), and especially Israel (Deut 4:20; Jer 3:14). The language of *taking* recalls the inheritance and possession language we saw earlier, as Yahweh claims what was already his. Yet it contrasts with the pattern of *see, desire, and take.* In this sense, God is creating a brand-new beginning for Abraham by taking him out of the land of his father—one marked by idolatry—and leading him to a new land and establishing a new household belonging to Yahweh.[14] Abraham was pulled out, or *taken,* from the domain of the gods of nations to reestablish the household of God.[15] It may be best to think of this act as the

---

13. E. John Hamlin, *Inheriting the Land: A Commentary on the Book of Joshua,* International Theological Commentary (Grand Rapids: Eerdmans, 1983), 193. There is another interesting play on words involving the language of *took/take* in Gen 11:31, where Terah takes his family and again in Gen 12:5 where Abram takes Sarah and Lot. Here we are reminded that human action is still subject to God's intention.
14. Marten H. Woudstra, *The Book of Joshua,* The New International Commentary on the Old Testament (Grand Rapids: Eerdmans, 1981), 345.
15. Richard D. Nelson, *Joshua: A Commentary,* The Old Testament Library

first step in reclaiming what is already his. As Reed observes, foreign nations "may be ruled by demons, but they are not forces of independent evil; all nations belong to God, who rules directly over his chosen Israel (Jub 15:31)."[16] God's act of *taking* Abraham is an act of reclaiming what was already his, the next salvo in the battle, and God's response to the rebellion of his divine council.

The taking of Abraham had consequences. By leaving the land, Abraham left his nation. His obedience means Abraham is rejecting his ancestral deities. Leaving his father's household left him unprotected physically and spiritually. However, Abraham is not left alone, and blessing accompanied him as he walked out obedience to Yahweh's calling. These blessings include Yahweh's covenant promise to Abraham: the promise of becoming a great nation and the father of many nations. First, Yahweh enters a covenant with Abraham and establishes Abraham and his descendants as his own.[17] Second, Yahweh makes a promise to

---

(Louisville: Westminster John Knox, 1997), 269. The Hebrew verb *took* in Josh 24:3 is the same as in Deut 4:20 that depicts God *taking* the Israelites out of the iron furnace of Egypt to be his possession and inheritance.

16. Reed, *Demons, Angels, and Writing in Ancient Judaism,* 304. Reed's reference is to Jubilees, where she argues that demonization is "dramatically expanded." Demons are the rulers of Gentiles (Jub 1:11; 11:4), and they are the "rulers of the nations (Jub 15:31; 48)." Further, there is a correlation between the destruction of the enemies of Israel and the defeat and destruction of demons (Jub 23:29; 40:9; 46:2; 50:5)

17. David Andrew Dean, "Covenant, Conditionality, and Consequence: New Terminology and a Case Study in the Abrahamic Covenant," *Journal of the Evangelical Theological Society* 57 (2014): 307. Dean outlines the flow of covenantal relationship with Abraham through a unilateral covenant. Dean distinguishes between *covenant obligations,* which include each party obligating themselves to the covenant, and *covenant regulations,* in which the suzerain imposes a regulation on the vassal to regulate behavior based on the covenant. This discussion ventures outside of the scope of this dissertation, but the technicalities on covenant are related and thus require discussion. See

turn Abraham into a great nation (Gen 12:2). In doing so, "God will continually direct the grand drama of redemptive history through covenantal promises."[18] That Abraham is called to be a blessing to the *nations* is important because this term is distinct from *people*. *Nations* have in mind the connections people have through various cultural ties. The term *people* has in mind the connections people have by blood, those with genetic ties. God wants to create a family that moves beyond blood and genetics and is in fact multinational and multiethnic.[19] Therefore, Yahweh's intention with Abraham reaches beyond genetic blood ties and has in mind multinational ties with many people groups through their common bond of faith in Yahweh.

In Genesis 17:5 Yahweh refers to Abraham as the "father of a multitude of nations," continuing and expanding the original covenant promise of Genesis 12. This promise to Abraham is fulfilled by "the nation of Israel, the descendants of Ishmael (Gen 25:12–18), the descendants of Abraham's concubine Keturah (Gen. 25:1–5), and the descendants of Esau (Gen 36:1–19, 31–43)."[20] Here we see how the language of *father* expands beyond blood and genetic terms

Dean, "Covenant, Conditionality, and Consequence," 286–92, for Dean's delineation of covenant language and terms.

18. Jeong Koo Jeon, "The Abrahamic Covenant and the Kingdom of God," *The Confessional Presbyterian* 7 (2011): 124. Jeong argues the Abrahamic covenant, viewed within its ancient Near Eastern context, reflects a covenant of royal grant established between a suzerain and faithful vassal. This understanding of the covenant between God and Abraham is cohesive with the two-family household argument from chapter 2.

19. Cleon L. Rogers Jr., "The Covenant with Abraham and Its Historical Setting," *Bibliotheca Sacra* 127 (1970): 253–54.

20. Chee-Chiew Lee, "גים in Genesis 35:11 and the Abrahamic Promise of Blessings for the Nations," *Journal of the Evangelical Theological Society* 52 (2009): 473.

into a metaphorical understanding or a spiritual sense (Gal 3). This "metaphorical usage of ab/ אב 'father' suggests that Abraham's fatherhood goes beyond genealogical linkage and implies that Abraham shall be a spiritual benefactor of many nations, 'the mediator of God's blessing to them.'"[21] This promise is not limited to Abraham but is restated in Genesis 35:11 to Abraham's grandson, where God tells Jacob that "a nation and a company of nations shall come from you." The phrase *company of nations* (*qehal goyim*) is related to Genesis 17:4–5 and is thus a restatement of the Abrahamic promise of a multiethnic family.[22] Paul in the New Testament affirms this understanding in Romans 4:18 when he refers to Abraham as the "father of many nations." We should also read Romans 4:18 in light of Romans 4:13, where Paul says that Abraham and his offspring with be "heir[s] of the world" (ESV). Paul's understanding of Abraham as the "father of many nations" helps us see that the application of Genesis 17:5 is much larger than a collection of random nations and has the whole world in mind.[23]

The redemptive reversal of Babel begins here with Abraham. God has promised to make Abraham's name great, in contrast to the name-seeking rebels at Babel. He will do this as a gift and promise, in contrast to those at Babel who sought to achieve it through their own might

---

21. Lee, "גים in Genesis 35:11," 473.
22. The intentional usage of *nation* versus *people* speaks to the connection of a multinational and multiethnic group. In Gen 28:3 and 48:4 the phrase *qahal 'ammim* ("a company of peoples") is used in reference to a people group knit together by kinship or blood relations. For more on the distinction between the terms and the relationship between Gen 35:11 and Gen 17:4–5 see Lee, "גים in Genesis 35:11," 468–69.
23. Michael Heiser pointed out this connection to me from Rom 4:18 and 4:13.

and purpose. The connection to Babel can be further seen through Yahweh's promise to bless all the "families" or "clans" (*mishpakhah*) of the earth through Abraham. This reference to *mishpakhah* connects to the table of nations (Gen 10:5, 18, 20, 31, 32), making it clear that the call of Abraham has in mind the reunion of the families of the earth.

The covenant promise to Abraham not only is central to the formation of the patriarchal narratives but also frames Yahweh's prerogative to rescue and reclaim all the families of the earth through Abraham.[24] In the storyline of the unseen battle we participate in today, this is done through gospel proclamation to those in the disinherited (gentile) nations who have not yet been brought back into the family of God. Yahweh tells us he will provide "blessing" through Abraham to the nations. The verb *bless* could be taken as descriptive or prescriptive, a result of a command.[25] Regardless of the

---

24. Lee, "גים in Genesis 35:11," 471.
25. For a discussion of the grammar, see Rogers, "The Covenant with Abraham and Its Historical Setting," 255. Rogers deems the best translation option of the *niphal* verb as a passive, and the preposition *in* as a sphere with the referent being the seed of Abraham, Christ. Lee notes, "The verb ברך 'to bless' is in the *niphal* stem in Gen 12:3b and in its reiterations in Gen 18:18; 28:14, but it is in the *hithpael* stem in the reiterations in Gen 22:18 and 26:4." Additionally, Lee gives three convincing arguments for a passive reading. Two are particularly relevant. First, the variation is intentional and present a particular nuance. In Gen 10 *mishpakhah* appears with *goy* four times showing the development of a clan into a nation. Second, the narratives of the patriarch's present how people are either cursed or blessed based on their relationship with Abraham and his posterity (Abimelech, Laban, Potiphar, Pharaoh, Egypt). See Lee, "גים in Genesis 35:11," 471–72. Much discussion surrounds the proper translation of *bless*, which occurs in the *niphal* stem in Genesis 12:3; 18:18; 28:14 and in the *hithpael* stem in Gen 22:18; 16:4. We can summarize the debates about these nuances by saying the *niphal* deals with the "state of being blessed" while the *hithpael* relates to the "process" that takes place in order to achieve the blessing. Benjamin J. Noonan, "Abraham, Blessing, and the Nations: A Reexamination of the *Niphal* and *Hitpael* of ברך in the Patriarchal Narratives," *Hebrew Studies* 51 (2010):

interpretive option we choose, we are left with a covenant promise and the expectation that Abraham and his descendants (physical and spiritual) will be the ones to transmit the blessing of Yahweh onto others.[26] Thus, there is a continuation of God's initial decree to humanity to flourish and multiply. However, now a key part of that flourishing and multiplication is through the inclusion of gentiles into the family of God, reuniting the human household into one family with one father. This is why the unseen battle is primarily waged through the proclamation of the gospel to the nations. As the disinherited nations hear the invitation to come home and then return to Yahweh's family, the tide of the battle shifts and the victory of Christ as Lord of lords and King of kings (over all lesser spiritual and human rulers and powers) is affirmed.

GENTILE INCLUSION IN THE OLD TESTAMENT

I realize that some reading this may think of the idea of gentile inclusion into the household of God as something reserved for the New Testament and the preaching of the gospel. But that is incorrect. While it is not widespread in

---

74. Noonan argues for a passive or middle translation in Gen 12:3; 18:18; and 28:14, seeing Abraham as the "means" or "instrument" of blessing to the nations. Noonan turns to ancient translations that reflect this reading (Septuagint, Vulgate, Targums, Peshitta). Modern interpreters that seek to create cohesion between the *hithpael* of Gen 22:18 and 16:4 are flawed for two reasons according to Noonan (85–87). First, there is no basis for giving the *hithpael* preference over the *niphal*. Second, there is no clear analysis in the Hebrew Bible of the *niphal* used as a reflexive or reciprocal.
26. M. Daniel Carroll R., "Blessing the Nations: Toward a Biblical Theology of Mission from Genesis," *Bulletin for Biblical Research* 10 (2000): 22.

the Old Testament, the inclusion of gentiles is anticipated, setting the stage for its fulfillment in the New Testament. At various times throughout the Old Testament, prophets refer to the nations as "the people of God." For example, Zechariah 2:11 says, "Many nations shall join themselves to the LORD in that day, and shall be my people. And I will dwell in your midst, and you shall know that the LORD of hosts has sent me to you" (ESV). Second Temple literature also shows that the language of *joining themselves with Israel* has in mind an intimate and personal relationship. The nations do not simply observe, but they participate in the fulfillment of God's eschatological promise. Additionally, the language of *dwelling* recalls temple and household language. This is reminiscent of Eden, the abode of Yahweh and humanity, and once again we see Yahweh dwelling among all his people.

The inclusion of the gentiles among the people of God is also a prominent theme in Isaiah and is recapitulated in Isaiah 19:18–25 and again in Isaiah 56:7 in anticipation of the day when foreigners, in this case the Egyptians, will worship the Lord. This is a striking concept considering the reality that the Egyptians are a primary enemy of the Israelites. Once again, we find that the intersection of ethnicities (Egyptian) with the people of God (Israelites) is not random. The prophet Isaiah pushes forth God's plan for equal salvation among all people and nations, and as Psalm 72:17 showed us, this plan of salvation would come through the messianic king as a fulfillment of the promise first made to Abraham. As J. Daniel Hays notes, "The prophet paints an eschatological picture of people from all nations blending together with the remnant of Israel as the true people of Yahweh."[27] Isaiah pictures a blended family made up of all the nations of the earth incorporated in the household of God.

Isaiah's eschatological communications involve judgment for a wayward Israel that finds its culmination in a future regathering and restoration with an addition of all nations. Isaiah 2:2–4 puts this on display: "It shall come to pass in the latter days that the mountain of the house of the LORD shall be established as the highest of the mountains, and shall be lifted up above the hills; and all the nations shall flow to it" (v. 2 ESV).[28] The hope of 'a future regathering of the nations derives from "the blessing pronounced on Abraham."[29] The blessing of Israel is not isolated to the Israelites but, according to the covenant made with Abraham, would overflow to the nations that turn from their idolatry and turn toward Yahweh.[30] The events described in Isaiah 2:2–4—based on the promise made to Abraham—culminate in Jerusalem at Pentecost (Acts 2). The church is established as a "great agency for spreading the saving gospel."[31]

Isaiah 11:10–12 correlates well with Psalm 72:17 as it promises that the coming Messiah will gather the remnant from the four corners of the earth:

---

27. J. Daniel Hays, *From Every People and Nation: A Biblical Theology of Race*, ed. D. A. Carson, vol. 14, New Studies in Biblical Theology (Downers Grove, IL; InterVarsity Press, 2003), 106.
28. Mic 4:1–3 provides an additional example of this prophetic vision for a future multiethnic gathering of God's people.
29. Calvin E. Stowe, "Review of Jahn's History of the Hebrew Commonwealth Translated by Calvin E. Stowe," *Biblical Repertory* 5 (1829): 328.
30. Anthony R. Petterson, "The Book of Malachi in Biblical-Theological Context," *The Southern Baptist Journal of Theology* 20 (2016): 16.
31. H. C. Leupold, *Exposition of Isaiah*, 7 vols. (Grand Rapids: Baker, 1971), 5:77.

In that day the LORD will reach out his hand a second time to reclaim the surviving remnant of his people from Assyria, from Lower Egypt, from Upper Egypt, from Cush, from Elam, from Babylonia, from Hamath and from the islands of the Mediterranean.

He will raise a banner for the nations
and gather the exiles of Israel;
he will assemble the scattered people of Judah
from the four quarters of the earth.
(Isa 11:11–12 NIV)

May his name endure forever;
may it continue as long as the sun.
Then all nations will be blessed through him,
and they will call him blessed. (Ps 72:17 NIV)

Assyria represents not only a national superpower but also serves as a geographical marker to represent the far north regions. In similar fashion, Cush represents the far southern region. Isaiah and the psalmist both envision a future when the banner of the Messiah will call all people from all corners of the earth together under the perfect dominion of God in fulfillment of the Abrahamic promise first made in Genesis 12.

The promise God made to Abraham was clearly evident in the minds of the prophets.[32] Isaiah 2:2–4; Amos 9:7; and

---

32. For further references to prophetic witness of the nation's coming under the kingship of the Messiah, see Jer 3:17; Zech 8:20–22; Hag 2:6–9; Isa. 60; 66:22–23.

other Old Testament Scriptures clearly had in mind the Abrahamic promise (Gen 12:2–3; 22:16–18).[33] However, there was a significant barrier to bringing the disinherited nations back into his household. Before Yahweh could claim the people of the nations, he would have to deal with the gods of those nations. And they would not give up their rule and authority without a fight.

---

33. J. Alec Motyer, *Isaiah: An Introduction and Commentary*, Tyndale Old Testament Commentaries 20 (Downers Grove, IL: InterVarsity Press, 1999), 58.

SIX

GODS OF THE NATIONS AND THE WAR OF THE HOUSEHOLDS

To have a battle, there must be an enemy. As we've progressed through the storyline of Scripture, we've met several enemies. We learned that at some point in the distant past, one or more of God's first family, a race of supernatural beings we sometimes refer to simply as angels, rebelled. In so doing they enticed humanity, God's second family, to do the same. The battle between the cosmic family and the human family, between the sons of God ruling over the disinherited nations and Yahweh together with his people Israel, sets the background for much of the Old Testament. This is a cosmic conflict that takes place in both spiritual and earthly realms—and it is deeply embedded throughout the Hebrew Bible.

Let's consider one example. When Joshua says, "Thus says the LORD, the God of Israel, 'Long ago, your fathers lived beyond the Euphrates, Terah, the father of Abraham and of Nahor; and they served other gods" (Josh 24:2

ESV).[1] Who were these other gods? Keil and Delitzsch say, "Nothing definite can be gathered from the expression 'other gods,' with reference to the gods worshipped by Terah and his family; nor is there anything further to be found respecting them throughout the whole of the Old Testament. We simply learn from Gen. 31:19, 34, that Laban had תְּרָפִים [teraphim], i.e., *penates*, or household and oracular gods."[2] However, despite what Keil and Delitzsch say, there may be *much* more we can know about the *teraphim* (תְּרָפִים).[3] When we recall Ur and Haran as locations of worship for the moon god and correlate this to a Deuteronomy 32 worldview, we find a connection between the *teraphim* and the fallen sons of God whom the nations worship.[4]

Genesis 31:53 and 49:25 also indicate there were patriarchal gods, or "gods of the father." In Genesis 31:53, Laban is

---

1. In Joshua 24:2 we have the presence of a plural verb "served" and a plural noun "your fathers." Heiser shows that there is not a clear distinction that separates Abraham from the description of those that worshiped false gods. Thus, the most straight forward reading presents Abraham as one who also worshiped the false gods before his conversion. See Heiser, Michael S. "Should Elōhîm with Plural Prediction Be Translated 'Gods'?," *Bible Translator* 61, no. 3 (2010): 123–36.
2. Carl Friedrich Keil and Franz Delitzsch, *Commentary on the Old Testament*, 10 vols. (Peabody, MA: Hendrickson, 1996), 2:167.
3. It is probable that Terah passed on his idol worship to his family. In Jubilees Abraham is taught to read by Terah, whom Jubilees connects to idolatry (Jub 11:16). However, it is through reading that Jubilees identifies Abraham as rejecting idolatry. Jubilees also says Terah gave Abraham books in Hebrew (a language lost after Babel that Terah could not read). See Annette Yoshiko Reed, *Demons, Angels, and Writing in Ancient Judaism* (New York: Cambridge University Press, 2020), 262–63.
4. This is seen through the plural verb *yishpetu*. The Deuteronomy 32 worldview refers to the disinheritance of the nations (Gen 11) and the allotment of these nations to the sons of God (Deut 32:8–9). Further, it recalls the sons of God and their judgment for leading the nations astray and thus entering into rebellion themselves against the head of the household, Yahweh (Ps 82). For more on this, see chapter 2.

in a conversation with Jacob in which they establish a covenant between them to ensure peace between their households.
Laban refers to two distinct deities: the "God of Abraham"
and the "god of Nahor."[5] That the other nations (Ur and
Haran) served other gods is not surprising.[6] To serve "other
gods" can also be translated to serve "foreign gods" or "the
gods of the people in that land." It may also be expressed as
"gods other than me, the Lord."[7] The indictment of serving
other gods and the consequence of such actions is specifically
placed on Israel, God's chosen inheritance.[8]

---

5. Edward J. Young, "The God of the Fathers," *Westminster Theological
Journal* 3 (1940): 35. The Septuagint removes the phrase *elohe Abraham* and
translates the verb as singular (*ho Theos Abraam kai ho Theos Nachōr krinei
ana meson ēmōn*). But as Young states, this does not solve the tension and is
not the best reading. For a further discussion on the grammar, see Young,
"The God of the Fathers," 32–35. Additionally, the context of these passages
is a covenant pact between two parties. Thus, it seems to be the practice in
the ANE when two parties had different religious backgrounds for each to
swear by their deity as the "guarantor of the covenant" (Young, "The God
of the Fathers," 36). We may also recall that Joshua 24:2 and Genesis 31:53
are related to each other as both verses have a plural predicator with *elohim*
as its subject. Heiser points out three possible interpretive options with the
most likely (based on the phrase "Fear of Isaac") being that each occurrence
of *elohim* should be read as semantically singular. In other words, the supreme
deity of each individual would be called upon as their witness. This would
preserve Abraham's depiction as a YHWH worshiper. See Heiser, "Should
Elōhîm with Plural Prediction Be Translated 'Gods'?," 123–36.
6. See Deut 12:20, 30.
7. Robert G. Bratcher and Barclay Moon Newman, *A Translator's Handbook on
the Book of Joshua*, UBS Handbook Series (New York: United Bible Societies,
1983), 300.
8. Walton and Walton observe this special relationship between Israel and
Yahweh as a treaty, and idolatry for Israel is breach of treaty. However, the
Waltons also conclude that the absence of this relationship/treaty with the
other nations leaves the nations free to worship whomever they may desire.
They state, "Yahweh did not make a treaty—that is, a covenant—with any
nation other than Israel, and so accordingly the nations are never said to
'rebel' against Yahweh by setting up another lord over themselves (i.e., by
serving their own gods)." See John H. Walton and J. Harvey Walton, *Demons
and Spirits in Biblical Theology: Reading the Biblical Text in Its Cultural
and Literary Context* (Eugene, OR: Wipf & Stock, 2019), 154. The Waltons'

The Old Testament uses a variety of terms to describe these other gods as malevolent spirits, but one reference in particular is connected to the fallen sons of God, the Hebrew *shed* ((שד translated as "demons" (Duet 32:17; Ps 106:37). This is made explicit in Deuteronomy 32:17: "They [Israel] sacrificed to demons [*shed*], not God [*'eloah*], to gods [*elohim*] they had not known, new gods that had just arrived, which your ancestors did not fear." The term *elohim* can refer to messengers, the familial god, or Yahweh.[9] As Heiser notes, "Earlier passages in Deuteronomy show that the 'sons of God' allotted to the nations in Deuteronomy 32:8 were considered gods (*elōhîm*)."[10] Therefore, we can connect these *shed* to the *elohim* referenced in Deuteronomy that were allotted to the nations and connected to a territory.

Furthermore, *shed* is also connected to the Akkadian term *shedu*, which refers to a "territorial spirit" that guarded the entry way to temples.[11] The relationship of these "territorial spirits" and the temple is important, as temples served

---

argument is essentially an argument from silence. The absence of an explicit treaty between Yahweh and the nations does not mean these nations are not under the rule (indirectly) of Yahweh. The same argument that Walton makes can be made from the other angle. Silence of a treaty with the nations may mean expectation that nations are under the authority of Yahweh and that their "care" has been deferred to the "sons of God." In fact, this is a more coherent understanding because it fits the theme of the suzerain-vassal relationship in the ANE (see chapter 2 and the household in an ANE context).

9. Reed, *Demons, Angels, and Writing in Ancient Judaism*, 74. Reed also points to 1 Sam 28:13, where the shade of Samuel is referred to as *elohim*.

10. Michael S. Heiser, *Demons: What the Bible Really Says about the Powers of Darkness* (Bellingham, WA: Lexham, 2020), 22.

11. Additionally, the *shed* and the connected Akkadian term *shedu* are more than just territorial entities. They can also be linked to people, families (especially royal families), and the king, his gods, and his land. *Shedu* can be a "spirit or demon representing the individuals vital force." It can also be an "orthostat" that guarded gates, entrances to cities, temples, and palaces. See CAD š 2:256, *šēdu* A.

as the abode (i.e., household) of the deity. The temple was literally the deity's house. For example, the Hittites referred to temples as "divine house" or "ritual house."[12] R. D. Wilson notes: "As to שֵׁד [shed], there is no doubt that it is the same as the Babylonian word shedu, defined by Muss-Arnolt as (a) a destructive god and (b) a protecting deity."[13] Another scholar had noted that if you changed the Masoretic pointing system, there is a very close parallel to Psalm 106:37, which relates to shedu—that is, a protecting spirit.[14]

The connection between the shed and shedu points to the territoriality of these spiritual beings and suggests they were also viewed as "protective spirits." As we've seen, mention of the shed in the Hebrew Bible present them as dangerous due to the "blurring of boundaries between Israel and other nations."[15] Thus, these shed (or fallen sons of God) are likely the nations' patron deities, and they influence not only the nations but also the households that reside within that

12. Tyson L. Putthoff, *Gods and Humans in the Ancient Near East* (New York: Cambridge University Press, 2020), 130.
13. R. D. Wilson, "The Names of God in the Psalms," *The Princeton Theological Review* 25 (1927): 16. Italics removed from Hebrew. For *shedu*, see William Muss-Arnolt, *A Concise Dictionary of the Assyrian Language* (New York: Nabu, 2010), 1014. It seems the *shedu* also protected the body, "May the protecting shedu, the protecting lamassu, Settle upon his body." See Morris Jastrow Jr., *The Religion of Babylonia and Assyria* (Boston: Ginn, 1898), 290. The connection to the personal protection will be expounded in the next section discussing the *teraphim*.
14. Aune references Albright, who "suggests changing the Masoretic pointing of *laśśîḏ* [RSV 'to lime'] in Am. 2:1 to *laśśēḏ*, making the verse a very close parallel to Ps. 106:37, a probable emendation, which is related to the Assyr *šēdu*." See D. E. Aune, "Demonology," in *The International Standard Bible Encyclopedia*, rev. ed., ed. Geoffrey W. Bromiley, 4 vols. (Grand Rapids: Eerdmans, 1979–88), 1:919. See also Victor P. Hamilton, "2330 שֵׁד," in *Theological Wordbook of the Old Testament*, ed. R. Laird Harris, Gleason L. Archer Jr., and Bruce K. Waltke (Chicago: Moody, 1999), 906.
15. Reed, *Demons, Angels, and Writing in Ancient Judaism*, 198.

national territory.[16] We see this most clearly with reference to the *teraphim* in connection to Laban, the descendent of Nahor who follows in serving the other gods of his descendent, Terah.

HOUSEHOLD GODS

Laban's familial connection to Abraham remains an important bond, so much so that Laban's family is the ideal choice for a marriage between the families. In that time and culture, any marriage between households would also include navigating the couple's alliance to their household gods. Therefore, the influence of Laban (and therefore Nahor) in Haran comes into direct conflict with the new family that Abraham has established. Abraham desires a wife for his son Isaac, but he does not want Isaac to marry a Canaanite. Rather, he wants a woman from his own land. Therefore, in Genesis 24:11 the servant of Abraham goes out to Mesopotamia, to the "city of Nahor" (ESV). This city is not necessarily named Nahor. It is more likely simply a reference to the city where Nahor lived. It may refer to Haran, the city in which the shepherds knew Laban, son of Nahor (Gen 29:4–5).[17] This could mean that Abraham's servant, who is seeking a wife for his master's son, Isaac, now finds himself in the land of Haran, where Abraham left his father, Terah, and brother, Nahor, who subsequently

---

16. The understanding of the "sons of God"/*shed* correlating to the household gods will be seen in the next section through the connection of the *teraphim*, *tarpis*, and *shedu*.
17. Richard S. Hess, "Nahor (Place)," in *The Anchor Yale Bible Dictionary*, ed. David Noel Freedman, 6 vols. (New York: Doubleday, 1992), 4:997.

settled there and continued to serve other gods (*shed*).[18] It is
from this family lineage that Laban descends. In Genesis 31:19
we learn that Laban is in possession of "household gods"
(ESV) that Rachel would later steal.[19] But what were these
household gods, what did they represent, and how are they
connected to *shed*?

Before we continue with this conversation, I want
to pause here to acknowledge that some portions of this
book—including this next section—may dive a little deeper
into a topic than many readers might wish to go. Because
this section on the household gods leans more scholarly, I've
moved most of this discussion to an appendix at the end of
the book. However, I want to add a personal note as to why
I'm still very passionate about this specific section. Much
of the content of this book was first developed as my PhD
dissertation, and this section is one of the topics that was of
particular interest for my doctoral advisor, Michael Heiser,
to whom this book is dedicated. When I was first writing
on this topic, Mike was pretty skeptical of the links and
connections I was suggesting. In several different ways he
encouraged me to abandon mission on this line of thinking.
But I persisted, and after sharing the argument I was developing further, he was intrigued. He wrote to me:

---

18. Deut 32:17 reinforces this claim that the *shed* are *elohim*.
19. Walton and Walton, *Demons and Spirits in Biblical Theology*, 158, reject
    the notion of the *teraphim* as "cosmic demonic powers" and refer to them as
    purely "ineffective or impotent." However, this seems to be a rejection based
    on Waltons' stance against "conflict theology." This section will show that
    teraphim should be seen in connection to the "sons of God"/*shed* of Deut
    32:17. Further, this is made more explicit when considering Deut 32:17 with
    1 Cor 10:17 and Paul's reflection on demons and idols. See Michael S. Heiser,
    The Unseen Realm: Recovering the Supernatural Worldview of the Bible
    (Bellingham, WA: Lexham, 2015), 340–41.

This will be interesting. I'm not aware of a connection between the *teraphim* and territorial gods of the nations. Typically, *teraphim* are connected to ancestor remembrance (or worship if the context requires). But the "household" context in your dissertation makes this intriguing.

Then, after reading the section I've included in the appendix, I was blown away when he commented on the connections I was drawing between the *teraphim* and the work of a German Hittite expert:

Nice job! Very good for sure for this (he was a Hittite expert). Nice connections; I did not know this—helpful to me personally.

So while I'm summarizing my research in a paragraph or two to make this book more accessible, my hope is that readers who wish to dig a little deeper will take the time to read the appendix as well. Hopefully, this short pause has increased your appetite for the discussion!

In short, the big challenge with the *teraphim*, or household gods, was the lack of evidence connecting these idols and the spiritual entities behind them to anything of substance beyond ancestor remembrance. But there is a significant connection. These *teraphim* are connected to the Akkadian *shedu* and Hebrew *shed* through an amazing discovery in 1966 by a German Hittitologist H. Otten. Otten was exploring the Hittite *tarpis*, which were territorial protective spirits closely associated linguistically and culturally to the household gods/*teraphim*. Otten discovered a Babylonian column that defined the Hittite *tarpis*, a territorial protective spirit, as the Babylonian *shedu*. This is significant because, if you recall, the Babylonian *shedu* are linguistically connected to the Hebrew *shedim*, which we translate as demons.

This discovery has a vital implication for how we understand the meaning of *teraphim*. If the *teraphim* are, in fact, to be understood as synonymous or similar spirits to the *tarpis*, and the *tarpis* are referred to as *shedu*, then this suggests that the household gods of Terah, Nahor, and Laban that Rachel steals are conceptually related to the *shed*, the two terms we find in Deuteronomy 32:17.

Remember, Hittite temples were considered "houses of the deity," and the *tarpis* protected these houses. These linguistic connections strongly suggest an overlapping of identity and function. In other words, the *teraphim* were a type of territorial spirits that protected the house, and these spirits were none other than demons (*shedu*). Furthermore, these demons are categorically *elohim* and are connected to the fallen sons of god, the gods of nations.

WHY RACHEL STEALS THE HOUSEHOLD GODS

With this background in place, we may have a better clue as to why Rachel steals her family's *teraphim*. Rachel may have stolen the household gods to protect herself from the possible loss of her inheritance, as well as her own fear of leaving the land of her father and thus the protection of the gods of her father. Rachel's actions remind us of her ancestor, Terah, who abandons the journey to Canaan to settle in Haran for the comfort, safety, and security of the gods he knew. Additionally, this may have been Rachel's way of establishing priority for her own son as heir and the next clan chief.[20]

The connections between Babel, the Deuteronomy 32 worldview, and Rachel's narrative in Genesis 31:9 are intriguing.[21] Rachel steals Laban's *teraphim* when leaving Haran, which is connected to Babel and is the place where Terah, Abraham, and Nahor stop on their own journey. While Abraham leaves, Nahor remains, continuing in the idolatrous ways of his father (Terah) and worships "other gods" (*shed*). If seems likely that the household gods of Laban (descendent of Nahor) are connected to and may even be the very same gods of Terah.[22] If so, this connects the household gods of Laban, which Rachel stole, to the tower of Babel and once again reminds us that God has reached into one of the disinherited nations not only to claim a nation but to create a new nation for himself as an inheritance. We

---

20. E. H. Merrill, "Idols, Idolatry, תְּרָפִים, Household Gods," in *Dictionary of the Old Testament: Pentateuch*, ed. T. Desmond Alexander and David W. Baker (Downers Grove, IL: IVP Academic, 2003), 441.

21. The continuity includes references by Eusebius, who quotes Alexander Polyhistor (fragment 1 and 2) in *Praeparatio Evangelica* (9.17.1–9, fragment 1 and 9.18.2, fragment 2). Fragment 1 assumes that the tower of Babel was created by the giants, and after the destruction of Babel the giants were dispersed throughout the earth. Abraham, generations later, is born and is seen as pleasing God because "he eagerly strove to be pious." Stuckenbruck notes that a correlation of 9.17.3–4 and 9.17.8–9 place Enoch and Abraham alongside each other and even implies that "Abraham's learning is being derived from or linked to Enoch" who in turn was taught by the angels. Further, Abraham's birthplace is identified as Babylon, which correlates to Ur and Haran. See Loren T. Stuckenbruck, *The Myth of Rebellious Angels* (Grand Rapids: Eerdmans, 2017), 7–11.

22. Philip Schaff, ed., *A Dictionary of the Bible: Including Biography, Natural History, Geography, Topography, Archæology, and Literature* (Philadelphia: American Sunday-School Union, 1880), 858.

are also reminded that these gods are tied to the geography of the land and the nation. And the people of these nations are intimately connected to their national gods. The gods of the nations want to retain these people as their prize, their most valuable possession. Once again, we are reminded that this unseen battle is over people and where they belong, or rather, to *whom* they belong.

In addition, we again find a pattern of anxiety over leaving one's homeland and the protection and security that comes with inclusion in the household. Rachel, in the same manner as her ancestors Terah and Nahor, attempts to hold on to the "household gods" (*shed*) of her ancestors, perhaps due to lingering doubt and anxiety over following Jacob and Yahweh. Rachel's actions are an attempt to hold onto the inheritance rights of her ancestor's household, even though Yahweh has promised a new inheritance to Abraham that has now been passed on to Jacob (and thus Rachel by marriage). But as Terah, Nahor, and now Rachel have demonstrated, there is a very real struggle in rejecting the protection and security of one household for another, even when the exchange is the promise of a new household. Yahweh calls his new family forward into a new journey, one in which they will participate in the promise and formation of a new household of God.

The old household gods claimed control over the geographic areas they held power over. Yet it is important to remember that these lands and spaces were first given to them by Yahweh for them to steward (Deut 32:8–9). Though now in rebellion against Yahweh, they still have a claim to the land, but they have deceived the people of the land.

Eventually, these household gods became the national gods of the people living in that geographic area.

The gods of the nations played an ongoing role in later wars and conflicts as the nations of the world battled against Israel, who was often at the epicenter of these battles. Perhaps the clearest example of this unseen battle and its connection to visible geopolitical realities is found in Daniel, more specifically in Daniel 10, where we see the sons of God (the gods of the nations) at work.

DANIEL 10 AND THE UNSEEN BATTLE OF THE SONS OF GOD

The book of Daniel further reinforces the Deuteronomy 32 worldview and is helpful in formulating a biblical theology of spiritual warfare. Daniel 10 makes visible the cosmic struggle and the unseen battle between the gods of the nations and Yahweh, the God of Israel. The formation and development of national angelic patrons was associated with empires, kingdoms, and lands.[23] Behind a national "empire" was a cosmic spiritual power (one of the sons of God or, in Paul's language, "powers and principalities") that influenced and directed nations in opposition to Yahweh and his kingdom, perhaps an attempt to revisit the goal of

23. The notion of angels serving as guardians of nations is attested in early Christianity by Clement and Hippolytus. See Darrell D. Hannah, "Guardian Angels and Angelic National Patrons in Second Temple Judaism and Early Christianity," in *Angels: The Concept of Celestial Beings—Origins, Development and Reception*, ed. F. V. Reiterer, T. Nicklas, and K. Schöpflin (Berlin: de Gruyter, 2007), 429.

Babel. Scholar Stephen Noll says, "The spirit of empire is directed not only against God and his people but against the nations as well. In a reprise of the Babel story, the imperial bureaucrats—the satraps, prefects, governors, counselors, treasurers, magistrates and other officials—are employed in summoning all peoples, nations and languages to worship one idolatrous kingship (Dan 3:1–7)."[24] This concept is also present in Isaiah 24:21 and Psalm 82; however, the most distinct and explicit development is found in Daniel 10:13, 20, 21; 11:1; and 12:1.[25]

◇◇

The Gods of the Nations

Gods of the Ancient Near East

Ba'al: Of all the false gods of the nations mentioned by name, Ba'al has prominence. Worshiped as the storm god who would bring down rain, there was also a connection between rain and sexuality, as rain was necessary for the growth of fertile crops. Consequently, worshipers of Ba'al would perform sex acts in the temple, believing this would increase the sexual activity of the god and result in more rain for crops. This particular deity was also known by other

---

24. Stephen F. Noll, *Angels of Light, Powers of Darkness: Thinking Biblically About Angels, Satan, and Principalities* (Eugene, OR: InterVarsity Press, 1998), 149–50.
25. S. R. Driver, *The Book of Daniel with Introduction and Notes*, The Cambridge Bible for Schools and Colleges (Cambridge: Cambridge University Press, 1900), 157.

names in other people groups (e.g., Chemosh among the Moabites; Num 21:29).[26]

Ashtoreth: A female deity considered a mother goddess and worshiped throughout Palestine. Her area of specialty was fertility (e.g., *asherah* poles; Exod 34:13) and warfare. Her husband is believed to be the god Ba'al. In the book of Judges the Israelites turn to "Ba'al and Ashteroths" (Judg 2:13; 10:6). She also is referred to as the "queen of heaven" (Jer 7:18; 44:17).

El: In the Canaanite pantheon, El was believed to be the father of the gods. Along with his wife Asherah, he fathered seventy minor gods. El eventually fades from the scene and is replaced by Ba'al. Here, we hear an echo of the story of Zeus and Cronos, and there is a reason for this repetition, as many of these stories copy one another. The Bible provides a polemic against these stories, portraying these gods as false gods.

Dagon: As the patron god of the Philistines, he is well attested in the Mari texts as one of the principal deities of the Amorites of Old Babylonian Upper Mesopotamia and was the god of vegetation and fertility. In some mythic stories Dagon was understood to be the father of Ba'al. In 1 Samuel, we find an intriguing story about Dagon where the Philistines

---

26. For this sidebar, see Louis H. Gray et al., "Demons and Spirits," in *Encyclopædia of Religion and Ethics*, ed. James Hastings, John A. Selbie, and Louis H. Gray, vols. 1–13 (New York: Scribner's, 1908–26). See also Leland Ryken et al., *Dictionary of Biblical Imagery* (Downers Grove, IL: InterVarsity Press, 2000).

capture the ark of the covenant and bring it to his house, the temple of Dagon (1 Sam 5:3–4). Dagon falls face down in the presence of Yahweh. In another story, Saul is killed by the Philistines, and they hang his head in the temple of Dagon (1 Chr 10:10).

Marduk: The patron god of Babylon and in Mesopotamia was understood as the supreme ruler of their cosmology. You can read all about him in the Enuma Elish epic, which tells the story of how he rises to the head of the Babylonian pantheon. He appears once in the biblical narrative in Jeremiah (Jer 50:2).

Molech: Arguably one, if not the most, detestable of the false gods of the nations, Molech is closely associated with child sacrifice. This Canaanite deity was the cause of much of Israel's rebellion. The name appears around fifteen times in the Bible (Lev 18:21; 20:3–5).

Re: The Egyptian sun God and the king of the Egyptian pantheon. The pharaohs of Egypt believed they were the representatives of Re and thus often took his name as part of their name to convey they were "Son of Re."

Amon: The Egyptian god of the wind and breath. In time, this deity was combined with Re and called Amon-Re, who was both the state god of Thebes (which eventually became the Egyptian capital) and the king of the gods of Egypt.

Osiris: The Egyptian god of the underworld (akin to the Greek god Hades).

Isis: Goddess of healing and magical arts (akin to the Greek goddess Artemis).

Apis: The Egyptian bull god of agriculture and fertility. Apis doesn't show up in the Hebrew Bible but is referenced in the Septuagint of Jeremiah 26:13–15, affirming the concept of the patron gods of the nations. Babylon is able to defeat Egypt because the Lord weakens, "Apis, your chosen calf."[27]

Gods of the New Testament World

Artemis: Her temple in Ephesus was one of the seven wonders of the world. She was the daughter of Zeus, the twin sister of Apollo, and one of the twelve Olympians (here we see hints of counterfeit symbolism in imagery that parallels the twelve tribes of Israel and the twelve disciples). She is seen as the goddess of midwifery, magic, and sorcery. This is the context for the riot in Ephesus documented in Acts 19:35, as well as Paul's language referring to the powers and principalities in his letter to the Ephesians.

Hermes: He was the attendant and spokesperson of Zeus and was believed to be the guide for both the living and the dead. In Acts 14, Paul and Barnabas are in Lystra and heal a crippled man. The crowds see this miracle and cry out, "The gods have come down

---

27. Froelich, Margaret. "Apis," in *The Lexham Bible Dictionary*, ed. John D. Barry et al. (Bellingham, WA: Lexham, 2016).

to us in human form" (Acts 14:11). They believe Paul is Hermes and Barnabas is Zeus.

Zeus: The supreme god of the Olympian pantheon, the god of the storm and sky. Son of the Titan Cronos and Rhea, Zeus rebels against his father, defeating him, and taking rulership of the Olympians. He creates the home of the gods on Mount Olympus.[28]

In Daniel 10 we also find the household theme conceptually present through the language and imagery of kingship, empire, and princes.[29] The Hebrew *sar* (שַׂר) can mean ruler, leader, or high official in reference to both humans (Gen 21:22, 32; 26:26; Num 21:18; Judg 4:2) and angelic beings (Josh 5:14–15; Dan 8:11).[30] Some commentators and scholars have argued for an interpretation of this as "human rulers." However, this is both incoherent and logically improbable, as *sar* in Daniel 10:13 is a clear reference to Michael, the "chief prince," who is an angelic being.[31] The language of

28. Leonhard Schmitz, "Zeus (Ζεύς)," in *Dictionary of Greek and Roman Biography and Mythology*, ed. William Smith, 3 vols. (Boston: Little, Brown, 1870).
29. In chapter 1, we saw the range of household terms in both Greek and Hebrew extending to *kingdom* and the *royal house*.
30. The idea of an earthly (royal) household having a cosmic household behind the human is well evidenced in the ANE. This concept is seen through kingship, as kings were linked to geography and the gods were also linked to geography. See "Family, Household, and Local Religion at Late Bronze Age Ugarit," in *Household and Family Religion in Antiquity*, ed. J. Bodel and S. Olyan (Oxford: Blackwell, 2008), 60–88.
31. J. Paul Tanner, *Daniel*, Evangelical Exegetical Commentary (Bellingham, WA: Lexham, 2020), 634. For a discussion on the princes of Daniel as human rulers, see T. Meadowcroft, "Who are the Princes of Persia and Greece (Daniel 10)? Pointers Towards the Danielic Vision of Earth and Heaven," *Journal for*

prince is also picked up by Paul in Ephesians (2:2) and is used elsewhere in the New Testament (Matt 9:34, 12:24; Mark 3:22; Luke 11:25; John 12:31; 14:30; 16:11; 1 Cor 2:6, 8). However, before we jump ahead to the New Testament, let's first look at how the *prince* language in Daniel affirms the idea of a war between households.

In Daniel 10 we are introduced to competing and warring kingdoms in both God's earthly and cosmic family. Graham Cole, quoting Matthias Henze commenting on Daniel 10:20–11:1, says this is "a celestial conflict between the angelic princes that is currently raging, in which each prince represents a nation: the 'prince of Persia' and the 'prince of Greece' are fighting against Michael, the warrior and defender of Israel (Dan 12:1; 1 En 9:1; Rev 12:7; see also the War Scroll from Qumran)."[32] Ultimately, we know this is a conflict between the kingdoms of Satan and God. Interestingly, Craig Evans suggests the prince of Persia is, in fact, Satan, and that the "Prince of the host" in Daniel 8:11 (ESV) is probably Yahweh.[33] Evans makes a compelling

---

the Study of the Old Testament 29 (2004): 99–113. Meadowcroft, along with Shea's thesis, "Wrestling with the Prince of Persia," hinges on Cambyses being the "prince of Persia." See William H. Shea, "Wrestling with the Prince of Persia: A Study on Daniel 10," *Andrews University Seminary Studies* 21, no. 3 (1983): 225–50. However, for this to be possible, Cambyses would need to be referred to as both prince and king. For a cohesive and compelling rejection of the human ruler, position see David E. Stevens, "Daniel 10 and the Notion of Territorial Spirits," *Bibliotheca Sacra* 157 (2000): 410–31.

32. Graham A. Cole, *Against the Darkness: The Doctrine of Angels, Satan, and Demons*, Foundations of Evangelical Theology (Wheaton, IL: Crossway, 2019), 62.

33. Craig A. Evans, "Inaugurating the Kingdom of God and Defeating the Kingdom of Satan," *Bulletin for Biblical Research* 15 (2005): 54. Michael S. Heiser, The Unseen Realm: Recovering the Supernatural Worldview of the Bible (Bellingham, WA: Lexham, 2015), 121n8, nn127–48, agrees that the Dan 8:11 figure should be seen as "the second embodied Yahweh."

argument, drawing from evidence in the Dead Sea Scrolls about the "prince of the dominion" that recollects the language of Paul, who refers to Satan as the "prince of the power of the air" in Ephesians 2:2 (ESV).[34]

If the "prince of hosts" in Daniel 8:11 is a Yahweh figure like he seems, this is additional evidence of God's household and family coming under attack by competing households, nations, and gods being led by "the ruler of this world" (John 12:31; 14:30; 16:11).[35]

Additionally, Satan is in this instance a commander of "a large contingent of demonic angels who are organized in different ranks to oppose the Lord God (Eph 1:21; 6:12; Rev 9:1–2, 11)."[36] Daniel highlights the ANE understanding of a cosmic, spiritual kingdom that directly impacts the earthly kingdom and furthermore shows these opposing forces struggling for dominion and power through the conquest of land, territory, and political power.[37] This rival kingdom

---

34. Florentino García Martínez and Eibert J. C. Tigchelaar, *The Dead Sea Scrolls Study Edition (Translations)*, (Leiden: Brill, 1997–1998), 141. For more possible indications that Satan = Prince of Persia, see 4Q225 2 i 9; 2 ii 13–14. 11Q5 19:15, says, "Let not Satan rule over me, nor an evil spirit" (11Q6 4 v 16).
35. The Septuagint for Dan 8:11 has *archistratēgos* in place of *sar-hatsava*. Further, *archistratēgos* is used in Josh 5:15 of the commander of the Lord's army. Thus, if the figure of Josh 5:15 is preincarnate Christ, this correlates well to Dan 8:11 and gives further credence to the war-of-households idea.
36. Tanner, *Daniel*, 635.
37. Tanner, *Daniel*, 635, is critical of the use of *territorial spirit* associated with geographical assignment. Tanner says, "The stress is on *sociopolitical structure*, meaning that this demon was targeting the empire and the human authorities behind that empire. This demon's purpose was to manipulate and control decisions coming out of the Persian court that affected the whole empire. This was relevant to Daniel because the Jewish people at this time were under the authority of Persia. If the demon could turn the hearts of the Persian rulers against Judah and/or influence them to pass laws and commands detrimental to the Jews, then this would thwart God's program." Tanner is following D. E. Stevens, but both Tanner's and Stevens's arguments

concept is not isolated to Daniel and is later picked up by New Testament writers. One of the things we can draw from this instance is that Satan's desire goes beyond individual destruction; his goal is the unraveling and destruction of entire systems and structures, including nations and the people groups that reside within them.[38]

The malevolent spirits opposed to the household of God are not unopposed. The *prince* language extends to Michael (Dan 10:13) and Gabriel (Dan 8:16), who are part of the household of God fighting on behalf of God and the human family (Israel) Yahweh held as an inheritance for himself.[39]

---

are lacking on multiple levels. First, creating a sharp distinction between geographic and political is not practical. In other words, geography is associated with political motives. An empire with no land or geographical context to protect or a desire to expand is problematic. Second, Tanner does not seem to connect Deut 32:8–9 to the background of these fallen angels, whom he rightly identifies as demons. This is crucial in seeing the geographical allotment of nations and boundaries (Deut 32:8–9; 4:19–20). Third, the ANE background would understand the deity's territoriality with land (Heiser, *Unseen Realm*, 116–17). The idea of the deity's desire for territorial expansion is in view, not necessarily a deity's exclusive limitation based on its territory and an inability to expand its power in terms of land and political influence.

38. Christopher Byrley, "Persecution and the 'Adversary' of 1 Peter 5:8," *Southern Baptist Journal of Theology* 21 (2017): 80. Much more can be said of the development of Satan and his role in the Old Testament and New Testament. The New Testament develops this Old Testament concept and refers to Satan as the "ruler of this world" and thus as a kind of "father" over fallen humanity and all that is sinful. Paul in Ephesians refers to Satan as the "prince" of the air. For Paul and the Greco-Roman and Second Temple world, the air was the "dwelling place of evil spirits."

39. In Jude 9 we are told Michael is in a higher position of angel, "archangel." First Enoch refers to both Michael and Enoch among seven archangels of God (1 En 20:5). Goldingay says, "In the Qumran *War Scroll* he is listed as one of the four archangels in 1QM 9:15–16, and, most significantly, he is given authority among the אלים in 1QM 17:6–7." See John E. Goldingay, *Daniel*, Word Biblical Commentary 30 (Dallas: Word, 1989), 292. For more on Michael, see Claudio Gianotto, "Michael the Archangel (Iconography)," in *Encyclopedia of Ancient Christianity*, ed. Angelo Di Berardino and James Hoover, trans. Joseph T. Papa, Erik A. Koenke, and Eric E. Hewett (Downers Grove, IL: IVP Academic, 2014), 795.

Thus, the cosmic battle wages and the impact of these cosmic battles is visible through historical events that affect the outcomes of humanity, nations, leaders, kingdoms, and empires. As Hannah notes:

> In the apocalyptic assumption that earthly realities reflect and mirror heavenly ones, the princes of Persia and Greece, that is, their angelic patrons, oppose the archangels who stand up for Israel. And their order, Persia followed by Greece, parallels the events of terrestrial history: The dominion of the Persian Empire was brough to an end by Alexander the Great and his successors (cf. Dan. 9).[40]

In other words, in Daniel we see the invisible activity of the sons of God, who functioned as the patron gods of the nations. These gods, referred to here as "princes," are in direct conflict with Yahweh and his own cosmic family, who are also referred to as "princes." Additionally, the cosmic warfare in Daniel shows us that the battleground— the prize over which they war—is the nations of the earth and their human rulers and peoples, once again affirming that what takes place in the cosmic realm is mirrored in the earthly realm. The two cannot and should not be disconnected. Paul retrieves this Old Testament background when he writes Ephesians 1 and 2, indicating that he too sees a close connection between the two realms. Paul understands that the sons of God (patron gods of the nations) will be judged for their rebellion against Yahweh. But where does Paul get the additional idea that God will judge the powers

---

40. Hannah, "Guardian Angels and Angelic National Patrons," 413–36.

and principalities (the sons of God)? The answer is found in Psalm 82 and Isaiah 24:21–23; 34:1–4, which form the theological framework for Paul's "already" judgment of the principalities and powers in the New Testament.

PSALM 82 AND COSMIC HOUSEHOLD JUDGMENT

Earlier, we looked at Psalm 82 and its use of the term *sons of God*. Now we want to take one step further and consider how the events described in Psalm 82 are related to these sons of God in light of the Deuteronomy 32 worldview and the events following Babel. Psalm 82 describes a judgment of the sons of God due to their injustice and corruption toward the nations to whom they were allotted, along with the subsequent reinheritance of the nations to Yahweh (Ps 82:2–5, 8).

As Noll says, "Psalm 82 is a vivid depiction of God's determination to end the power of injustice."[41] Our earlier discussion has already indicated that these sons of God are cosmic beings (not human rulers) who have participated in rebellion and injustice against God's household and the disinherited nations to whom they were assigned rule.[42] This

---

41. Noll, *Angels of Light, Powers of Darkness*, 126.
42. Some scholars have suggested that the best reading of the *sons of God* is that they are national rulers who are wicked, and the language of deity can be understood as these human agents working on behalf of the divine. For more on this, see Charles A. Briggs and Emilie Grace Briggs, *A Critical and Exegetical Commentary on the Book of Psalms*, International Critical Commentary, 61 vols. (New York: Scribner's, 1906–7), 2:215. Additionally, Neyrey argues for the sons of God to be seen as Israel at mount Sinai in accordance with John 10. See Jerome H. Neyrey, "'I Said: You Are Gods':

involves interpreting Psalm 82 so it is read with coherence alongside Deuteronomy 4:19–20 and 32:8–9. Psalm 82 is yet another household scenario filled with administrative declarations where Yahweh handles "family business" and finds the sons of God guilty of dereliction of duty. We also find inheritance language (Ps 82:8) that connects this psalm to Babel (Gen 11) and Deuteronomy 32:8–9; 4:19–20, as Yahweh speaks of reinheriting the nations.

The household scene of Psalm 82 is a familiar ANE image, and the "assembly of gods" or "divine council" was present in numerous extrabiblical sources within Mesopotamia. For example, Jabini notes, "In Ugarit, the phrase 'assembly of the gods' was also recognized. The sons of El, who were all members of the assembly of the gods, were called *'ilm*, 'gods.'"[43] It seems likely that some type of divine council scenario, similar to the idea shared among Israel and other cultures in the ANE, is in mind throughout Psalm 82.

The psalm opens without an introduction, and the focus is on a specific *elohim* who takes his place in the divine council among the *elohim* (Ps 82:1). Here we find Yahweh presiding over the divine council and casting judgment on the sons of God for their rebellion and dereliction of duty. We see evidence that Yahweh is the head of the council because he "presides" as judge over the council (Ps 82:1 NIV).[44] But why

---

Psalm 82:6 and John 10," *Journal of Biblical Literature* 108 (1989): 649. For the possibility of human rulers based on the Septuagint in correlation with John 10:34–35, see Daniel A. Keating, "'You Are Gods, Sons of the Most High': Deification and Divine Filiation in St. Cyril of Alexandria and the Early Fathers," *Letter and Spirit* 4 (2008): 237–38.

43. Jabini, "Sons of God Marrying Daughters of Man," 92.

44. Tanner notes, "The *assembly of El* is often referred to as the divine council. This would be a familiar mythological theme in the ancient near East. *'El* is a known name for the king god of the Canaanite pantheon, and his myths

is Yahweh presiding over the council? What situation would require or lead to such a meeting? Deuteronomy 4:19–20 and 32:8–9 have already helped us establish that the sons of God were allotted to the nations following the Babel event, and at some point afterward they accepted human worship, falling into rebellion against Yahweh. Now, based on the charges brought against them in Psalm 82, it appears that the sons of God were expected to perform duties that had been modeled to them by Yahweh, duties that likely reflected the job description of the king of Israel outlined in Psalm 72. This further supports the idea that God's household (both his heavenly and earthly family) is intended to share the same ethics.[45] The issue at hand in Psalm 82 is the corruption of God's justice, specifically as it relates to the nations placed under the care of the sons of God.

The psalm presents a scene of familial judgment within the context of household rebellion and dereliction of duty. Here the language of the *sons of God* in relationship to their fallen state should be considered. The ongoing development of the sons of God throughout the Old Testament indicates they are demons (Lev 17:7; Ps 106:37; see also 1 Cor 10:20).[46] As Lioy notes, "These were malevolent spiritual entities,

---

predate the exodus. The God of the Israelites, the LORD, subsumed this title as an epithet, so that El becomes synonymous with YHWH." Thus, the assembly language of Psalm 82 recalls the ANE Canaanite pantheon image. Further, the function of *El* can be seen subsumed and included interchangeably with Yahweh. See Beth Tanner, "Book Three of the Psalter: Psalms 73–89," in *The Book of Psalms*, The New International Commentary on the Old Testament (Grand Rapids: Eerdmans, 2014), 642.

45. Tanner, "Book Three of the Psalter," 643.
46. Heiser, "Monotheism, Polytheism, Monolatry, or Henotheism?," 22. The following chapter will trace *shed* and *daimonion* in relationship to their use in the Old Testament and Septuagint.

whom the Israelites never knew, especially in the way they had experienced the Creator's overflowing and constant provision."[47] The consequence for these rebellious children of God was to become mortal and die like any "prince," like God's human children (Ps 82:7 ESV). The language of *prince* (Ps 82:7) recollects Daniel 10 and correlates to Deuteronomy 32:17. There is a certain irony here, a promise that the cosmic princes behind the national and political efforts of human princes (Dan 10) would now face the very same demise as the human princes they have been manipulating, namely death. The demise of these sons of God due to their rebellion would also create a vacancy by the deposed gods. Parker makes an important observation about the nature of the judgment of the gods: "The god's fate is clear and their demise anticipated, though not yet accomplished."[48] Paul's later understanding of the "powers and principalities" in his letter to the Ephesians recollects the idea of the future judgment of the sons of God, most notably in Ephesians 3:10, where Paul says the church will make known the manifold wisdom of God to this rebellious faction of God's cosmic family as the reinherited multiethnic family of God. Furthermore, Paul's understanding of the "already" judgment of the principalities and powers is not relegated to Psalm 82 but might include Isaiah 11:10; 24:21–23; and 34:1–4, among other passages.

In Isaiah, for instance, the genre shifts to ironic prophetic rhetoric. Isaiah's focus throughout is on the exclusive role of

---

47. Lioy, "A Comparative Analysis of the Song of Moses," 17.
48. Simon B. Parker, "The Beginning of the Reign of God: Psalm 82 as Myth and Liturgy," *Revue Biblique* 102 (1995): 540.

Yahweh governing the world, thus rejecting the reality of other gods. In Isaiah 41:21–24 Yahweh challenges the gods to act and show themselves as powerful and active, yet that challenge goes unanswered.[49] Further, Isaiah 24:21–23 associates the "host of heaven" with astral worship (Isa 40:26; 45:12; Jer 33:22; Neh 9:6). *Host of heaven* is another term for the sons of God (1 Kgs 22:19; 2 Chr 18:18; Luke 2:13) who would be punished by Yahweh.[50] Additionally, Isaiah anticipates a time when a future Messiah would defeat the enemies of Yahweh and bring back the disinherited nations. The Septuagint translation of Isaiah 11:10 references the root of Jesse, the one who "rises up to rule nations; nations will put their hope in him, and his repose will be honor."[51] The Septuagint has *anistamenos* for "rise," and this is reflected in Romans 15:8–12 where Paul quotes Isaiah and refers to the Messiah who "arises" (*anistamenos*) and is both the ruler and the hope of the gentiles. This same concept is also present in Psalm 82:8, where Yahweh "rises" (*anasta* in the Septuagint) to judge the earth and reinherit the nations.[52] As we will see below, this language closely resembles the ascension language of Paul in Ephesians.

---

49. Parker, "The Beginning of The Reign of God," 554.
50. S. H. Widyapranawa, *The Lord Is Savior: Faith in National Crisis: A Commentary on the Book of Isaiah 1–39*, International Theological Commentary (Grand Rapids: Eerdmans, 1990), 146. See also 1 En 6–10; Matt 24:29; Rom 8:38; Eph 3:10; Col 1:13, 16; Rev 12:4, 9.
51. Rick Brannan et al., eds., *The Lexham English Septuagint* (Bellingham, WA: Lexham, 2012), Isa 11:10.
52. For more connections between Isaiah and Ps 82, see Ronald Bergey, "The Song of Moses (Deut 32:1–43) and Isaianic Prophecies: A Case of Intertextuality?," *Journal for the Study of the Old Testament* 28 (2003): 33–54. See also Mark A. Seifrid, "Romans," in *Commentary on the New Testament Use of the Old Testament*, ed. G. K. Beale and D. A. Caron (Grand Rapids: Baker Academic, 2007), 690.

In Psalm 82:8, Yahweh steps in and does what the gods would not do: execute justice, care for the poor and oppressed, and through this, ultimately, "inherit all the nations" (ESV). Psalm 82:8 presents Yahweh taking back the very nations that had been formerly disinherited (Deut 32:8–9). In fact, it may very well be that as Yahweh presides over the divine council and speaks a judgment on the rebellious *elohim*, he also calls on a singular *elohim* to rise and take up his inheritance. If we were to look at Psalm 82 as a theatrical event, we would picture Yahweh speaking from his throne, casting judgment upon the rebellious *elohim* among the assembly. But there would be another figure, another *elohim* standing off screen, perhaps sharing in Yahweh's growing agitation and anger over the rebellion and disobedience present within the divine council. Who is this *elohim* called by Yahweh to inherit the nations and execute justice? In my estimation, this *elohim* is none other than the preincarnate Christ.

The second half of Psalm 82:8 can be read to mean "you shall inherit all the nations," as in the ESV.[53] Even though the nations were disinherited, the judgment of the sons of God and the giving of the nations to this new figure constitutes a reinheritance, not a new inheritance. Yahweh is regaining what belonged to him in the first place, and here he calls upon the preincarnate Christ to accomplish this and receive the promise.

---

53. Or "as a jussive that carries on the imperative sense קוּמָה [*qumah*] and שָׁפְטָה [*shaptah*]." See Daniel McClellan, "The Gods-Complaint: Psalm 82 as a Psalm of Complaint," *Journal of Biblical Literature* 137 (2018): 844.

CONCLUSION

When we read Deuteronomy 32:8–9 as the aftermath of the events of Babel in Genesis 11, we see how the cosmic family of Yahweh is put in a position of responsibility to care for the disinherited nations that have been spread across the earth. Further, when Genesis 11 is read alongside Deuteronomy 32:8–9, we better understand the source and rationale behind the Jew-gentile distinction. The disinherited nations have been allotted to the members of the divine council, while Yahweh calls out a man living near Babel (Abraham) to create his own nation. At some point soon after Babel, we witness the cosmic side of the human rebellion at Babel by the sons of God, who accept human worship and lead the nations assigned to their care into idolatry. This sets up the ongoing framework for the unseen battle: Whatever impacts the heavenly household has ramifications for the earthly household. This framework is the basis of all spiritual warfare.

We saw evidence of this framework in Psalm 82, Isaiah, and throughout Daniel 10 with the heavenly princes, who were a cosmic force behind earthly geopolitical powers. Daniel 10 makes visible the war of households, where two princes (possibly Yahweh and Satan) are in conflict over people and places. Though the future of the human household initially appeared void of hope after Babel, God quickly initiates a recovery plan by reaching into one of the disinherited nations and reclaiming one man, Abraham. What Yahweh begins with Abraham is brought to completion in Christ Jesus. When Jesus steps onto the world scene in his incarnation, he deals the decisive blow to the enemy, a battle fought in the unseen realm at a most unexpected place, a Roman cross where criminals were condemned to die. Yet by his death, resurrection, and ascension, Jesus makes the judgment declared to the rebellious sons of God in Psalm 82 a reality. He defeats the gods of nations through the cross, nullifying their claim to the disinherited nations, and making it possible for the divided families of the world to be reunited within the household of God.

SEVEN

JESUS AND THE JUDGMENT OF THE GODS

The household conflict that developed through the three rebellions of Genesis 3, 6, and 11 and the unfolding unseen battle that underlies the promise of Abraham and the ongoing narrative of the Old Testament culminate at a single point in human history: the death, burial, resurrection, and ascension of Christ. At the ascension of Christ we see the declarative moment of the reign and rule of Christ as he subjugates and disarms the "powers." These powers and principalities were disarmed and dethroned through the work Christ accomplished in his death, burial, and resurrection, and this was formally declared at his ascension (Eph 1:20–22). We find all of this on display in Paul's letter to the Ephesians.

In Ephesians 1:9–10 Paul identifies the "mystery" of God's plan as the Old Testament anticipatory promise made to Abraham in Genesis 12 and now fulfilled through Christ. The promise refers to a right ordering of God's earthly and heavenly families, but this necessarily means judgment for members of the household who are in rebellion. The reunification of the household of God is a return to an Edenic vision of a united earthly and cosmic household. To show this, Paul makes known the "mystery" (*mystērion*) of God's will that was "set forth in Christ as a plan (*oikonomia*) for the fullness of time to unite (*anakephalaiōsasthai*) all things in him, things in heaven and things on earth" (Eph 1:10 ESV). Paul's use of *mystērion*, *oikonomia*, and *anakephalaiōsasthai* are all instructive, as they work together to recall an Old Testament background and understanding of the reunification plan.

The mystery that Paul refers to has direct connections to Daniel in the Old Testament. Paul places the mystery within an earthly and cosmic scene through his language of *the heavenlies*. When Paul refers to the mystery, he doesn't have something new in mind but is instead trying to broadcast the ancient plan of God into the present moment. Later in Ephesians, Paul makes explicit that the mystery entails the unification and restoration of relationship between Jews and gentiles through Christ, the Messiah (Eph 2:14–15; 3:6). What Paul says in Ephesians 3:6 he first telegraphs in Ephesians 1:9–10 by recalling the Old Testament background to the mystery. There is a direct connection between Paul's use of *mystery* in Ephesians and the book of Daniel, where the word is used to refer to the redemptive plan of God. As we saw in the previous chapter, the context of Daniel is a cosmic, geopolitical battle. At one moment in particular, when the unseen battle breaks through into the visible earthly realm, Daniel is given the ability to comprehend the various ways supernatural forces are working through geopolitical means in the world. Similarly to Paul's context, Daniel's context includes both Jews (Daniel and the remnant of Israel) and gentiles. Paul's intentional usage of the word *mystery* ties us back to this cosmic conflict, one in which the peoples and nations are the prize to be won.

This is further developed when we notice the Greek *mystērion* is a translation of the Aramaic *raz* (*razah*) in Daniel and should be understood as a mystery or secret.[1] In the Septuagint translation of Daniel, *mystērion* (Aramaic: *razah*) refers to God's plan and purpose that involves unification within cosmic dimensions.[2] Daniel 2 presents a secret or mystery that Nebuchadnezzar knew and then forgot, as well as something he did not understand when he "knew" it. Similarly, in Daniel 4:9 the mystery is something the king knows but does not understand. Thus, the mystery (Greek: *mystērion*/Hebrew: *raz*) in Daniel seems to indicate something that is known in a factual sense but cannot be understood.[3] This connection to Daniel is important in interpreting Paul's letter to the Ephesians as it recalls the geopolitical and national activity taking place between God's divided, cosmic, family household.[4] The sons of

---

1. Francis Brown, Samuel Rolles Driver, and Charles Augustus Briggs, *Enhanced Brown-Driver-Briggs Hebrew and English Lexicon* (Oxford: Clarendon, 1977), 1112. They suggest this word is a Persian loan word and thus should be understood as a secret.
2. Lincoln, *Ephesians*, 30. We find usage of the word in Daniel 2 (vv. 18, 19, 27, 28, 29, 30, 47[2x]) and once in Dan 4:9. Dan 4:9 is from the second-century Theodotion translation based on Rahlf's *Septuagint*. See Harold W. Mare, "Paul's Mystery in Ephesians 3," *Journal of the Evangelical Theological Society* 8 (1965): 79.
3. Lincoln, *Ephesians*, 30. This is similar to the Old Testament revelation of gentile inclusion that was understood but had a variety of interpretations in Second Temple literature.
4. Refer to chapter 2 and the language of *prince* as it relates to the cosmic figures

God *allotted to* the nations are working out their rebellion *through* the nations by perpetuating and instigating war and division *among* the nations.

This is a good place for us to pause and reflect on the social and political climate of our own world today. When many Christians think about spiritual warfare, they tend to focus on the individual expressions evident in demonic oppression, possession, or some form of torment. Although we find evidence of this in the Scriptures, we need to expand our understanding of spiritual warfare to include the larger social and political structures of our world. Why does war bring ruin to the world? Why do we feel constantly on the verge of a new world war? What if there is a real enemy working behind the scenes, utilizing geopolitical power and authority to encourage selfish ambition and vain conceit? What if the gods of the nations are still wreaking havoc today in creative new ways? Why is peace, specifically the peace that permeates through the spread of the gospel, such a threat to world powers? The answer to these questions falls under the larger context of the unseen battle, a battle that has in mind the final unification of the nations of the world under the banner of Christ Jesus.

As we have seen in Daniel and as we will see in Paul's letter to the Ephesians, this battle has both cosmic and earthly dimensions. However, simply knowing that these dimensions exist does not mean we understand how they fit into the plans and purposes of God. We can start by noting

---

in Daniel (see Dan 10:13, 20, 21; 11:1; 12:1). Specifically, note that these beings recall the sons of God that are allotted to the nations and are thus acting behind and through the nations of the world as an enemy of the God and his people.

the connection to Daniel in Paul's utilization of *mystery* [*mystērion*] in Ephesians. To bring this mystery into fulfillment, Yahweh must still deal with the rebellious sons of God, rulers of the disinherited nations. As we shall see, Paul has these beings in mind as he describes the unseen battle and the necessity of spiritual warfare throughout Ephesians. Paul simply uses different terms to describe them.

THE HEAVENLIES, POWERS AND PRINCIPALITIES, AND SONS OF GOD

Ephesians 1:10 tells us that God's plan, or *oikonomia*, is to unite all things in heaven and on earth. So what are those things in heaven, and how does this unification take place? To rightly understand the powers and principalities Paul speaks about and place them in their appropriate context, we must first consider what he means by the "heavenlies" and how this relates to the plan (*oikonomia*) of God to sum up (*anakephalaiōsasthai*) all things in Christ.

Paul has much to say about the "heavenlies" (Eph 1:3, 10, 20; 2:6; 3:10; 6:12; cf. 3:15; 4:10; 6:9) as well as the "things on earth" (1:10; 3:15; 4:9; 6:3).[5] Notice first the combination of the things that are unseen (heavenlies) and those things that are seen (earthly). Paul links these, suggesting that a proper understanding of the heavenlies will enable us to see the connection between the heavenly and earthly.

---

5. Peter Thomas O'Brien, *The Letter to the Ephesians*, Pillar New Testament Commentary (Grand Rapids: Eerdmans, 1999), 112.

There are at least three possible meanings for the heavenlies. It can either refer to[6]

1. the eternal house of God,
2. the invisible and nonmaterial spiritual realm in a general sense (this is where all spiritual beings including those that are good and evil reside), or
3. the part of the created world that we refer to as the sky.

The meaning of the heavenlies also raises the question of who abides in the heavenlies. If the heavenlies are understood (as Paul suggests in Ephesians) as being inhabited by cosmic beings, it seems best to understand his meaning here as option 2, the invisible spiritual realm in a general sense.[7] I suggest retrieving this understanding of the heavenlies as the nonmaterial spiritual realm as we consider the unseen battle. The invisible nonmaterial spiritual realm is a place inhabited by both angels and demons (as well as God and the devil) and is the usage most consistent with Paul's cosmic focus. This also reinforces our understanding of the unseen battle as one taking place in both realms of existence, the unseen and seen.

In Ephesians 1:10, we learn that the plan of God is unification. Then in Ephesians 1:20 Christ is identified as the one who executes the plan when he is raised and seated

---

6. Ben Witherington III, *The Letters to Philemon, the Colossians, and the Ephesians*: A Socio-Rhetorical Commentary on the Captivity Epistles (Grand Rapids: Eerdmans, 2007), 232.
7. Witherington, *The Letters to Philemon, the Colossians, and the Ephesians*, 232.

in the heavenly places. Ephesians 1:20 also emphasizes the locality in which Christ ascends and now resides.[8] Here we find a juxtaposition between the earthly and heavenly, and we find that Christ's ascension is also located in the heavens. In Ephesians 2:2 we are introduced to the "prince of the power of the air" who is at work in the "sons of disobedience" (ESV). These cosmic beings are associated with the air, perhaps best understood as something complementary to the heavenlies. All of this matters because, as we will see, the ascension of Christ firmly places Christ as the one who rules both the unseen and seen realm. Nothing is outside the sovereign authority of Christ in whom we (believers) reside. And as we find ourselves amid an unseen battle, this truth should provide us with assurance and confidence.

Paul understands the powers and principalities to be in the heavenlies, ruling out the possibility that they could be human rulers, governing authorities, or earthly institutions.[9]

---

8. This is a concept similar to one that is first introduced in Eph 1:10 with the phrase *ta epi tois ouranois*, which is contrasted with *ta epi tēs gēs*. W. Hall Harris III, "'The Heavenlies' Reconsidered: Οὐρανός and Ἐπουράνιος in Ephesians," *Bibliotheca Sacra* 148 (1991): 77. Harris also observes that in some manuscripts read *en tois ouranois* for *en tois epouraniois*, which creates even closer similarity and connection between *ouranos* and *pouranios*.

9. Witherington, *The Letters to Philemon, the Colossians, and the Ephesians*, 233. This does not rule out the possibility of the powers and principalities using human rulers, governing authorities, and earthly structures in their schemes and plans of discord and division. It is true that the terms ἀρχαί and ἐξουσίαι are used of earthly powers in Titus 3:1. However, the context of the terms in Ephesians rules out this possibility. For a human-ruler argument, see Wesley Carr, *Angels and Principalities: The Background, Meaning and Development of the Pauline Phrase Hai Archai Kai Hai Exousiai* (New York: Cambridge University Press, 2005), 91–112. As noted, this is improbable in both the context of 1 Cor 15:24 and Ephesians. Guy Williams says, "Presumably, it was not uncommon at the time to believe that the supernatural did itself intervene directly in the realm of history, without Carr's epistemological dualism." Guy Williams, *The Spirit World in the Letters of Paul the Apostle: A Critical Examination of the Role of Spiritual Beings in*

THE UNSEEN BATTLE

We should also be reminded that Satan was originally part of God's divine council, a meeting that was believed to reside in the air and take session on mountains.[10] This understanding is found in Second Temple literature such as 1 Enoch 61.10: "He will summon all the forces of the heavens, and all the holy ones above, and the forces of the Lord—the cherubim, seraphim, ophanim, all the angels of governance, the Elect One, and the other forces on earth (and) over the water."[11] The language Paul uses here is also reminiscent of Second Temple Jewish literature that references evil and good angels.[12] That Paul is referencing evil and hostile powers is further reinforced by the language of subjugation, as the hostile forces are "put under [Christ's] feet" (Eph 1:22).[13] These beings should be seen as cosmic beings attempting to

the Authentic Pauline Epistles, Forschungen zur Religion und Literatur des Alten und Neuen Testaments 231 (Göttingen: Vandenhoeck & Ruprecht, 2009), 132–34.

10. Ernest Best, A Critical and Exegetical Commentary on Ephesians, International Critical Commentary (Edinburgh: T&T Clark International, 1998), 175.

11. James H. Charlesworth, The Old Testament Pseudepigrapha, 2 vols. (New Haven, CT: Yale University Press, 1983), 1:42.

12. See chapter 4 for Second Temple literature. Michalak notes the military context of these sections. Obedience is the virtue of the good angels, while disobedience is the mark of malevolent angels. An important aspect of this discussion is the fact that human responsibility for war and chaos on earth is partially "transmitted to the fallen angels who are also generally responsible for the spread of evil and impurity on the earth." Therefore, it becomes all the more necessary for Christ's ascension to include the subjugation of these malevolent and rebellious spiritual beings. For further discussion on the military overtones of angels in 1 En, see Aleksander R. Michalak, Angels as Warriors in Late Second Temple Jewish Literature, Wissenschaftliche Untersuchungen Zum Neuen Testament 2/330 (Tübingen: Mohr Siebeck, 2012), 133–47.

13. Some modern scholars may be hesitant to share the view that Paul was referencing fallen angels and therefore attempt to find, as Muddiman says, "some kind of contextual justification for such a peculiar idea." See John Muddiman, The Epistle to the Ephesians, Black's New Testament Commentary (London: Continuum, 2001), 89.

gain control of the world and the people within the world through its systems, structures, and their rulers.[14]

Paul delineates these cosmic beings with the words *archē* (ἀρχή), *exousia* (ἐξουσία), *dynamis* (δύναμις), *kyriotēs* (κυριότης). The first two words Paul groups together are *rule* (*archē*) and *authority* (*exousia*) (Eph 3:10; 6:12; Col 1:16; 2:10, 15).[15] Interestingly, these terms only have one appearance in the Septuagint, where they refer to angelic beings (Dan 7:27). While this word pairing is not often found in non-Jewish literature, it occurs regularly in Jewish literature, such as the first century Testament of Abraham 13:10: "Death said to Abraham, 'I tell you, in all the creation which God created, there is not to be found one like you. For he searched among the angels and archangels, and principalities and powers [*archai kai exousiai*].'"[16] Often *archē* is also translated as "dominion, power, or position of power."[17] When it comes to "dominion or force," *archē* is always paired with *exousia* (Luke 12:11; Titus 3:1).[18] These rulers and authorities seem to not only have an influence in the heavenlies, but from the heavenlies they impact and intervene in earthly affairs.[19]

---

14. Best, *A Critical and Exegetical Commentary on Ephesians*, 176. The term *cosmic* should not be understood to create a division between the natural and cosmic. The ANE and Greco-Roman world understood the natural and cosmic as interwoven.
15. Bock, *Ephesians*, 55.
16. Charlesworth, *The Old Testament Pseudepigrapha*, 1:901.
17. Gerhard Delling, "Ἄρχω, Ἀρχή, Ἀπαρχή, Ἀρχαῖος, Ἀρχηγός, Ἄρχων," in *Theological Dictionary of the New Testament*, ed. Gerhard Kittel, Geoffrey W. Bromiley, and Gerhard Friedrich, 10 vols. (Grand Rapids: Eerdmans, 1964–), 1:481. The meaning also includes "host, division of a host," which recollects the heavenly host and angelic beings.
18. *Theological Dictionary of the New Testament*, 482.
19. Reid says, "This implies that their power is cosmic in extent." Additionally, Reid sees a possible connection with Paul's language of *archontes* and the "malevolent spiritual powers of this age." Reid goes on to suggest these

The third word Paul uses from this list is *power* (*dynamis*), which he uses to refer to angelic beings (1 Cor 15:24; Rom 8:38; cf. 1 Pet 3:22). This word has its roots in the Old Testament,[20] and the connection between the powers and spiritual beings is seen through the Septuagint usage of *power* as a label for the "host of heaven" (2 Kgs 17:16; 21:3, 5; 23:4–5 ESV), which Israel was warned not to worship (Deut 4:19).[21] In addition, the term *dynamis* became a common word used to describe angelic beings in Second Temple literature.[22] The connection between the *dynamis* and the "host of heaven" of Deuteronomy 4:19 is vital as it establishes a connection between the language of Paul and

spiritual beings "may very well stand behind Paul's usage of ἄρχοντες [*archontes*] in 1 Corinthians 2:6, 8 (cf. שׂר [*sar*] in the positive sense as angelic 'Ruler/ Prince of Light' who has been appointed for Israel's defense against the Satan or the Angel of Darkness in 1QM 13:10; 1QS 3:20)." See Daniel G. Reid, "Principalities and Powers," in *Dictionary of Paul and His Letters*, ed. Gerald F. Hawthorne, Ralph P. Martin, and Daniel G. Reid (Downers Grove, IL: IVP Academic, 1993), 748.

20. O'Brien, *Ephesians*, 142.

21. Michalak, *Angels as Warriors*, 16–30, notes that the phrase *host of heaven* has a military context. Yahweh leads the host, and the host is made up of both cosmic beings and human warriors. Michalak says, "According to ancient thought, the realms of earth and heaven were closely related. Therefore it was believed that the earthly, organized military order was also found in the heavenly sphere." He draws upon Deut 33:1–5, 26–29 and follows Miller's reconstruction, noting the members of Yahweh's entourage as holy ones, warriors, and the purified ones. The purified ones likely referred to Israelite warriors who underwent purification rights and therefore are fighting alongside divine beings.

22. Clinton E. Arnold, *Ephesians*, Zondervan Exegetical Commentary on the New Testament (Grand Rapids: Zondervan Academic, 2010), 113. See 1 En 41:9; 61:10; 82:8; 3 Bar 1:8; 4 Ezra 6:6; Philo, *Spec. Laws* 2.45. Philo acknowledges the existence of powers that the gentiles have made into gods erroneously. See Philo, *The Works of Philo*, 249–50. Williams says, "This does not mean that the powers are culpable or evil, but that implication logically could have followed" (*The Spirit World in the Letters of Paul the Apostle*, 129–30). Additionally, Williams points to Matthew 24:29 where the "powers of heaven will be shaken." Again, the reference to the powers being shaken presumes a form of punishment.

the Deuteronomy 32 worldview. As we saw in previous chapters, this worldview posits the rebellion of the sons of God and their corruption of the nations that were allotted to them in the aftermath of the Babel event. Implicit as well is the "already and not yet" nature of the powers in relationship to the resurrection, ascension, and future return of Christ. These powers have been stripped of their ability to blind the nations; however, their full, future, and final defeat will take place publicly when Christ returns.[23]

The final term in Paul's list is *dominion* (*kyriotēs*). The only other place this term appears in the New Testament is Colossians 1:16, and there it refers to angelic beings. Along with the first three terms, *kyriotēs* was used frequently in Second Temple literature to refer to angelic powers.[24] It may be tempting for us to attempt to further distinguish and delineate rank, ruling authority, and other details with these terms; however, I believe Bock is right in saying: "There is no point trying to distinguish between the terms; it is Paul's way of saying 'in every conceivable category.'"[25] Instead, we should read this list as an indicator of the comprehensive, overwhelming, and all-encompassing authority and power of Christ as it is put on display in both the resurrection and ascension. While these terms may not help us delineate a taxonomy of rank and role, they do help us identify the importance of the Old Testament for Paul, as he draws

---

23. Walter Grundmann, "Δύναμαι, Δυνατός, Δυνατέω, Ἀδύνατος, Ἀδυνατέω, Δύναμις, Δυνάστης, Δυναμόω, Ἐνδυναμόω," in *Theological Dictionary of the New Testament*, ed. Gerhard Kittel, Geoffrey W. Bromiley, and Gerhard Friedrich, 10 vols. (Grand Rapids: Eerdmans, 1964–), 2:307.
24. Arnold, *Ephesians*, 114. See 1 En 61:10; 2 En 20.
25. Bock, *Ephesians*, 55.

on several Old Testament backgrounds that bring clearer definition to the nature of these *archē, exousia, dynamis,* and *kyriotēs*.[26]

This Old Testament background can be further seen in Ephesians 1:10, 20–22 with the image of a royal court, again recollecting the Deuteronomy 32 worldview divine council scenario. This could also be viewed as a conclusion to Psalm 82 where the plea for justice and righteousness is enacted through Christ, who defeats his enemies and subjects them to judgment.[27] As we noted earlier, there was an understanding within Judaism that God had delegated authority over the nations to angelic beings, specifically the sons of God.[28] The language used to describe these beings, as noted in earlier chapters, included *sons of God*, the *host of heaven*, and *Lord of hosts*. Based on Paul's language here, specifically his use of *archē, exousia, dynamis,* and *kyriotēs*, we can conclude that the powers and authorities Paul refers to are the gentile gods of the nations (the sons of God). This connection is further evident when we note the similarity of language in Deuteronomy 4:19 with the idea of the host of heaven, Old Testament examples of the host of heaven (Isa 24; 34:3–4; and Ps 82), and the shared language and positioning of the host of heaven as cosmic beings intertwined and mingling with human systems and structures through national and geopolitical means.

---

26. Barth, *Ephesians*, 172.
27. Barth, *Ephesians*, 170. Barth cites M. Dibelius, C. B. Caird, G. H. C. MacGregor, G. Rupp, and D. E. H. Whiteley as proponents of an Old Testament background for Paul's understanding of the "powers." Additionally, there is a recollection of Second Temple literature that correlates to what we've covered in chapter 5.
28. Lincoln, *Ephesians*, 63.

Tarot Cards and Psychedelic Drugs

The pursuit of tarot card readings, astral signs, symbols and projections, and energy crystals are all an overflow of the dark powers of the nations. These things are counterfeit to the true power of the Holy Spirit. What need does the believer have for tarot cards when we have the indwelling Spirit of Christ? What need does the Christian have for energy from various crystals when we have the life-sustaining and life-giving flow of the Spirit of God living within us? Why would we ever need to pursue hallucinogenic episodes through the use of drugs to gain "enlightenment" when Peter tells us to be "sober-minded" in 1 Peter 5:8? The Greek word *nēphō*, or "sober-minded," is the opposite of another word, *methuō*, which has in mind a kind of intoxication. For Paul, the most direct connection between these would been a form of intoxication induced through the use of mystic nectar to commune with the gods. The word *methuō* is used two other times in Paul's vice lists (Rom 13:12–13; Gal 5:21), where it is categorized along with "works of darkness" and "works of the flesh" (ESV).[29] All of this is Paul's way of saying, as emphatically as possible, that followers of Jesus need to stay away from anything that compromises our mental faculties and promises us clarity or ascension

---

29. Paul A. Hartog, "Drunkenness," in *Lexham Theological Wordbook*, ed. Douglas Mangum et al., Lexham Bible Reference Series (Bellingham, WA: Lexham, 2014).

of thought as a result. These are age-old tactics of the enemy and are, again, part and parcel of spiritual warfare.

As noted earlier, in Deuteronomy 4:19 astral worship connects to the host of heaven through *dynamis* in Ephesians.[30] Yahweh gives clear instruction to the Israelites that they must not worship the host of heaven (Deut 17:3).[31] Later passages make it clear that these host of heaven have an impending judgment and will face the consequences of their actions. Isaiah 24:21 (ESV) tells us, "On that day the LORD will punish the *host of heaven*, in heaven, and the kings of the earth, on the earth." Here we find the location of these cosmic beings in the heavenlies. Isaiah 34:4 (ESV) supports this too: "All the *host of heaven* shall rot away, and the skies roll up like a scroll. All their host shall fall, as leaves fall from the vine, like leaves falling from the fig tree." These passages reflect Paul's understanding that the powers and principalities are located in the heavenlies (the spiritual realm) and that they, along with the prince of the air, will eventually be subjugated under the rule and reign of Christ. In Ephesians

---

30. Betz notes, "The plur. *ṣᵉḇā'ôṯ* often refers to the heavenly hosts (Ps. 102:21 [103:21]); God is 'Yahweh Sabaoth,' i.e., the Lord of the heavenly hosts (Ps. 45:7, 11; [46:7]; 47:8 [48:8])." See O. Betz, "Might, Authority, Throne," in *New International Dictionary of New Testament Theology*, ed. Lothar Coenen, Erich Beyreuther, and Hans Bietenhard, 4 vols. (Grand Rapids: Zondervan, 1986), 2:602.
31. The concept of the stars as celestial beings was not uncommon in the ancient world. The Persians thought the *yazatas* were "protective spirits." The ancient Greeks also divinized the stars, sun, and moon. The sun was supreme for Egypt and Babylon. For more on the stars and the host of heaven see Michalak, *Angels*, 43–53.

1:20–22, he clearly places the powers and authorities in the heavenlies. Ephesians 2:1 refers to Satan as the prince of the air, which seems to place the powers there as well, though somewhere lower in rank and status. The reference to Satan as a prince in Ephesians 2:1 also recollects Daniel 10:13's reference to a *prince*, a word translated in the Septuagint as *archōn*. In Daniel, this prince is clearly an angelic being who is working in opposition to God and his angels.

As we began reflecting earlier, it is one thing to understand how Paul is connecting his own words to the Old Testament framework of an unseen cosmic battle in God's divided household—but it is another thing altogether for us to draw connections between the dark forces of the world and the various systems and structures that work within our own society to bring ongoing corruption to both humanity and the world. As an example, we are all aware of the meteoric rise of pornography consumption. Sex trafficking continues to rear its horrific presence all over the globe. Nor should we be shocked at the ongoing utilization of narcotics, fentanyl, and abuse of over-the-counter medication. And let's not forget the impact of alcoholism and the surge in dependence on hallucinogenic drugs such as DMT and Ayahuasca that promise transcendent experiences and superior hidden knowledge. As the author of Ecclesiastes reminds us, there is nothing new under the sun.

All of these corrupting tactics are familiar (if not a direct copy and paste) to what we find in 1 Enoch. There, the watchers of Genesis 6 exchanged their forbidden knowledge for the daughters of men, leading to widespread corruption of the human race and the global spread of sin leading to God's judgment in the flood of Noah. As we saw then, the improper relationship between these cosmic beings and their corrupting influence on human institutions required that Yahweh act decisively. Paul now reinforces that God's next act in his plan of judgment and redemption involves the ascension of Christ, who is placed "far above" all these cosmic beings, bringing hostile beings into subjugation through Christ (Eph 1:22). The ascension of Christ reveals the mystery of God, brings about the unification of all things, and brings the powers and principalities into subjugation.

Principalities and Powers

In *Principalities and Powers*, G. B. Caird links Paul's language back to Daniel and places it in an Old Testament context. Caird is one of the few scholars I've found who seeks to work out the Old Testament background to the powers. He helpfully writes, "Paul is using mythological language, but his language has a rational content of thought; he is working with ideas which have had a long history, but he is describing spiritual realities with which he and his fellow Christians have personal acquaintance." Caird's "long history" brings to the forefront consideration of Old Testament passages that speak directly to the origins of Paul's *powers* language. Caird also sees the pagan gods that the nations worshiped as "subordinate" and "acting under the supreme authority of Yahweh."

> Caird's contribution to the discussion of Paul's power language becomes vital when he connects Paul's understanding of the Old Testament into Paul's Greco-Roman context. Caird says, "But, in fact, Paul inherited from his Jewish forbears a very different doctrine: that the angelic guardians of pagan nations exercise a delegated authority, and that any derivative authority which sets itself up as an absolute authority, demanding absolute obedience, takes on a demonic character."[32]

THE ASCENSION OF CHRIST AND SUBJUGATION OF THE POWERS

Christ's ascension into the heavenlies and Paul's usage of "in him" (*en autō*; Eph 1:10) brings together the universal household of God centered on Christ. Christ is not a "passive observer of all that the Father was doing" but is an active participant with the Father, executing an administrative plan to overcome the obstacles caused by sin. This brings to mind the conclusion of Psalm 82 and the reclaiming of the nations alongside the execution of God's justice and judgment. Baugh notes this act of administration is "royal" and forceful" and has in mind a conquest "over all the things in heaven and things on earth in him."[33] Paul's treatment of the ascension

---

32. G. B. Caird, *Principalities and Powers: A Study in Pauline Theology: The Chancellor's Lectures for 1954 at Queen's University, Kingston Ontario* (Eugene, OR: Wipf & Stock, 2003), 17–24.

33. S. M. Baugh, *Ephesians*, Evangelical Exegetical Commentary (Bellingham, WA: Lexham, 2015), 93. The expression "in Christ" used in Eph 1:10 differs from other usages in Eph 1:7, 11. In those passages the phrase refers to the

in Ephesians draws our attention to how the influence and authority of the powers and principalities over the nations has now come to a decisive end.

The ascension also answers this question: How will Christ bring about the summation of all things in heaven and on earth? The answer: Christ constantly connects these two spheres of existence (the heavenly and earthly) together, which is a reality finalized through his ascension. For context, Paul is writing his letter to the Ephesians, an audience of gentile Christians (2:11; 3:1) living in a world inundated by the powers and the gods whom they understood to be working in and through earthly systems, structures, rulers, and authorities. New Testament scholar Frank Thielman says, "They could see signs of its strength in the political statuary, friezes, and inscriptions in the markets and on the street corners of their cities. The gods, this propaganda proclaimed, had given Rome the eternal right to rule the universe."[34] The idea of "things in heaven" and "things on earth" would not have been foreign to Paul's Ephesian audience. However, with so many competing gods and religions, the idea of unifying heaven and earth may have seemed entirely unattainable. Paul's letter is an attempt to show the Ephesian believers that unity is possible and has, in fact, already been initiated and is now being worked out. Paul does this by showing that the unification of all things "in heaven and on earth" is happening through Christ.

---

sphere of new life that is found in Christ. Here in Eph 1:10 it connotes the union and intimacy between Father and Son prior to creation.

34. Frank S. Thielman, "Ephesians," in *Commentary on the New Testament Use of the Old Testament*, ed. G. K. Beale and D. A. Carson (Grand Rapids: Baker Academic, 2007), 813.

More specifically, unification entails the ascension of Christ. As Paul declares in Ephesians 1:20–21, this happened "when he raised him from the dead *and seated him at his right hand in the heavenly places*, far above all rule and authority and power and dominion, and above every name that is named, not only in this age but also in the one to come" (ESV; emphasis added). Later, in Ephesians 3:15, Paul will remind us that every family in heaven and on earth is named after the Father. Two important connections can be drawn from Ephesians 3:15 and then applied to our understanding of Ephesians 1:20–22. First, the language of *family* (*patria*) recalls the two-family household of God, and Paul affirms this reality by stating that every being (whether human or angelic), good or evil, receives its life and being from God the Father.[35] Second, because the members of this family first belonged to God, it is only right that they return to God, and this return takes place through the ascension of Christ.

The ascension is an often-overlooked aspect of the gospel narrative. While it is not described very often in the New Testament (Mark 16:19; Luke 24:51; Acts 1:9), it is presumed in many contexts and is a significant event in the postresurrection life and ministry of Jesus. As biblical scholar Francis Foulkes says, "To Paul, and in the New Testament generally, the cross, the resurrection and the ascension are considered as three parts of one great act of God."[36] Ephesians 1:20–22 tells us that the Father acts

---

35. Clinton E. Arnold, *Powers of Darkness: Principalities and Powers in Paul's Letters* (Downers Grove, IL: IVP Academic, 1992), 100.
36. Francis Foulkes, *Ephesians: An Introduction and Commentary*, Tyndale

in both raising (*egeiras*) and enthroning/seating (*kathisas*) Christ. Note the parallel between these pairs of words in Ephesians 1:20 and 22. Paul gives a description of what God did *to* and *with* the Messiah saying, "he raised" (*egeiras*) and "seated" (*kathisas*) him, and then "he . . . put under" (*hypo*) and "gave" or "appointed" (*edōken*) all things as subject to him.[37] The Father raises and enthrones the Messiah so that the natural outcome of this ascension is the rule and reign of Christ. All things are placed under him and appointed to him in subjugation.

The raising and seating/enthroning language expresses how God brings his power into effect.[38] Christ ascends and is exalted and seated at the right hand of the Father, putting him in a position of power and authority.[39] To take one's seat instead of standing was a sign of royal enthronement and would take place after winning a great victory and exercising power over one's enemies.[40] The language Paul uses echoes Old Testament expectations, particularly recalling Psalm 110:1 (ESV): "The LORD says to my Lord, 'Sit at my right hand until I make your enemies a footstool for you.'"[41] Here we find another indication of Old Testament

---

New Testament Commentaries 10 (Downers Grove, IL: InterVarsity Press, 1989), 71.

37. Barth, *Ephesians*, 153.
38. Baugh, *Ephesians*, 124.
39. The ascension, also referred to as Christ's "heavenly session," was taught by Paul in previous letters (Rom 8:34; Phil 2:9; Col 3:1). The ascension is a consequence of the resurrection.
40. Baugh, *Ephesians*, 124.
41. Jesus refers to himself as it relates to Ps 110 during his debate with the Pharisees (Matt 22:44).

retrieval as Paul applies an Old Testament expectation of the Messiah's enthronement to the narrative of Christ.[42] The terminology of Psalm 110 also has a parallel to the ancient Near Eastern world where the king was represented as sitting next to the right hand of the deity. To be at the right hand of the deity was to exercise power and authority. It was a position of honor.[43]

In Ephesians 1:22, Paul also cites Psalm 8:2. In Psalm 8, we find the focus on God's rule over the heavens (Ps 8:3) and his sovereignty over humanity and the earth (Ps 8:4–5).[44] Paul's citation of Psalm 8 recalls the two household theme and presents God's rule and reign over both the heavens (spiritual beings) and the earth (humanity). God's two-household family is subjected to him.[45] The verb *placed under* (*hypotassō*) in Ephesians 1:22 can be translated as "to be subject," "to submit," or "to be subordinate."[46] Paul is expressing Christ's dominant position over his enemies by using the rare adverb *high above* (*hyperanō*), which is "formed on the basis of two prepositions—a term unique to Ephesians in Paul's writings."[47] In the Septuagint, *hyperanō*

---

42. Arnold, *Ephesians*, 111.
43. Lincoln, *Ephesians*, 61–62.
44. Thielman, "Ephesians," 816.
45. Best, *A Critical and Exegetical Commentary on Ephesians*, 180–81. Psalm 8:6 is also cited in 1 Cor 15:27 and Heb 2:6–8. The 1 Cor 15:27 quotation correlates to the earlier discussion of the sons of God being referred to as the host of heaven in the Old Testament and the connection to the powers and principalities that reside in the heavenlies in Ephesians.
46. Arndt et al., *A Greek-English Lexicon of the New Testament*, 1042.
47. Arnold, *Ephesians*, 111. Contra Best, *A Critical and Exegetical Commentary on Ephesians*, 172n24: "ὑπεράνω does not necessarily mean 'far above,' since in Hellenistic Greek the addition of prepositions need not affect the meaning of the basic root."

occurs twenty-two times, and in two of these occurrences (Deut 26:19; 28:1) the context refers to the nations.[48]

Paul's broader point is that the plan (*oikonimia*) of God is brought about through the subjugation of all things (in heaven and on earth) that are hostile to Yahweh.[49] This should sound familiar, as it echoes and recalls what we saw earlier in Psalm 82. The ascension of Christ in Ephesians connects to Psalm 82 in at least three ways. First, the context of Psalm 82 is a divine council scenario, and here in Ephesians 1:20 the raising and seating of Christ in the heavenlies closely resembles a divine council scenario. Second, there is continuity between Psalm 82 and Ephesians 1:20 in the language of *rising*. In the Septuagint of Psalm 82:8 (81:8), God is requested to "rise" (*anasta*), which can also have the meaning of being appointed to an office or task.[50] In Ephesians 1:20, God is also said to have "raised" (*egeiras*) Christ into the heavenly places. In the Septuagint *anasta* is used synonymously with *egeiras*[51] and in both situations there is an emphasis on the supremacy of the anointed one over the sons of God / powers and principalities. Third, the divine council and rising/ascension context leads naturally to judgment. In Psalm 82 we hear a plea to cast judgment

48. Harold W. Hoehner, *Ephesians: An Exegetical Commentary* (Grand Rapids: Baker Academic, 2002), 276.
49. Best, *A Critical and Exegetical Commentary on Ephesians*, 173.
50. L. Coenen et al., "Resurrection," in *New International Dictionary of New Testament Theology*, ed. Lothar Coenen, Erich Beyreuther, and Hans Bietenhard, 4 vols. (Grand Rapids: Zondervan, 1986), 3:259.
51. Coenen et al., "Resurrection," 279. To see the synonymous nature of these words, compare Gen 38:8 and 2 Sam 7:12, where *anistēmi* is used for man and God. In Isa 45:13, *egeirō* is used.

JESUS AND THE JUDGMENT OF THE GODS

on the sons of God. Similarly, in Ephesians 1:20–22, Christ brings these rebellious cosmic beings into right order and subjugation under the authority of Christ.

Can Angels Still Rebel, and Can Fallen Angels Be Redeemed?

It is very clear based on Psalm 82 that fallen angels *cannot* be redeemed. They have made their choice and their judgment is clear. Because of the work of Christ on the cross, they have been stripped and disarmed of their authority. However, this also makes sense logically. Angelic beings witnessed the three rebellions, they saw what happened to the serpent (*nachash*), they know that the sons of God of Genesis 6 are trapped in prison awaiting judgment, and they saw the rebellion of the sons of God who became the gods of the nations (Gen 11 and Deut 32:8–9). After all of this, why would they want to consider rebellion? The fallen angelic beings and their offspring (unclean spirits) now await the final coming of Christ and his final judgment upon them.

In earlier chapters, we established a connection between the powers and the nations. Here in Ephesians we again find the two coming together as Paul declares Christ's authority over both the powers and the nations that were allotted to them. Christ's ascension is an image of a royal household, one that has been established through Christ's military victory over his enemies.[52] We see another Old Testament echo in the ascension language of Ephesians 1:20 as we recall the motivation of the people at Babel in Genesis 11. They desired an "ascent" because they wanted their name and reputation to be exalted and lifted high. In building their ziggurat, they attempted to force God into a descent. Here in Ephesians 1:20, however, it is God who seats Christ at his right hand (ascent), and it is through Christ that redeemed humanity will experience the ascent those at Babel desired.[53] Additionally, Paul highlights the descent of those who are hostile toward God and his household, whom he refers to as the "powers and principalities."

Christ rose from the dead and was enthroned in heaven with his enemies beneath his feet (Eph 1:20–22; 4:8; cf. Pss 8:6; 68:18; 110:1). Christ's ascension puts on display his authority and subjugation of all kinds of powers. As Patrick Schreiner notes in reference to Christ's victory over the powers, "While Paul ties this action to the work on the cross, the work of the cross was only a triumph after the resurrection and ascension. Christ truly prevailed over the forces of darkness at his glorification."[54] The victory of Christ at the cross, resurrection, and the ascension brings about the exaltation of Christ, which in turn brings benefits and blessings to the

---

52. Tremper Longman III, "The Divine Warrior: The New Testament Use of an Old Testament Motif," *Westminster Theological Journal* 44 (1982): 304. Paul quotes a well-known divine warrior psalm (68:18) in Eph 4:7. His ascension therefore should be seen as a military victory.

53. This connection was triggered by Patrick Schreiner's statement: "The devil sought to ascend, to sit on the throne, and to become like God. So do the creatures under his influence." See Patrick Schreiner, *The Ascension of Christ: Recovering a Neglected Doctrine* (Bellingham, WA: Lexham, 2020), 92.

54. Schreiner, *The Ascension of Christ*, 93.

family and household of God through Christ.[55] In Christ and under his lordship, the cosmic (heavenly) and the ecclesiological (earthly) come together in proper order and function. The headship of Christ speaks to the cosmic authority of Jesus and how his authority is now put on display through the church.[56] The beginning of the end of the unseen battle is the reunification of the nations into the household of God. As we shall see, the Abrahamic promise is being fulfilled in and through the church as the nations are regathered into the household of God, back where they always belonged.

---

55. Bock, *Ephesians*, 57–58. See also Col 1:18.
56. O'Brien, *Ephesians*, 146.

EIGHT

THE CHURCH AND THE REGATHERING OF THE NATIONS

The Jew-gentile distinction was a major point of tension in the early church, one that Paul addresses in Ephesians by pointing both Jews and gentiles to their one new humanity through the Messiah, Christ (Eph 2:15). To highlight the beauty of this new multiethnic family of God, Paul recalls the separation and distinction of the gentiles from the covenant people of God, the Israelites. However, in doing this Paul is careful to avoid showing preference to Jew over gentile. He critiques both Jews and gentiles for their idolatry in following after the false gods of the nations.

In Ephesians 2:11, Paul calls on the gentiles to remember their status as disconnected and cut off from the people of Israel. He often addresses them throughout Ephesians 2 using contrasts like "far/near, foreigner/citizen, alien/member of household."[1] However, alongside his critique of the gentiles Paul criticizes the Jews for their distance from God

---

1. For more on these themes see Abraham Kuruvilla, "From 'Far' To 'Near'! A

because of idol worship. One important term Paul uses to make his critique of the Jews is *circumcision*. Paul describes the circumcision of the Jews as *so-called (legomenoi)*.[2] The term itself is not necessarily pejorative and can simply mean those "who are known as" or "are designated as."[3] However, I believe that it should be understood as pejorative or negative in this context, especially because twice in Paul's writing it is used as a slight against worshiping false gods, which matches the context in Ephesians.

In 1 Corinthians 8:5 and 2 Thessalonians 2:4, Paul uses this phrase in reference to the "gods." The larger question is how Paul understands the gods worshiped by the gentiles. The unseen battle always has the question of worship at heart. Who will humanity worship? Will they worship the one true God of heaven and earth, or the false gods of the nations? In 1 Corinthians 8:5 Paul writes, "For although there may be *so-called* gods in heaven or on earth—as indeed there are many 'gods' and many 'lords'" (ESV). Here Paul's use of *so-called (legomenoi)* is connected to the gods in heaven or on earth, and Paul agrees that the gods of the Greco-Roman world should not be placed on par with the one true God. However, he goes on to suggest that real spiritual powers lie behind these gods.[4] Paul identifies both the reality and the active presence of cosmic powers behind

---

Pericopal Theology Guide To Preaching Ephesians 2:11–22," *The Journal of the Evangelical Homiletics Society* 20 (2020): 67–86.

2. Horst Robert Balz and Gerhard Schneider, eds., *Exegetical Dictionary of the New Testament* (Grand Rapids: Eerdmans, 1990–), 346.

3. Baugh, *Ephesians*, 182.

4. Edward Adams, *Constructing the World: A Study in Paul's Cosmological Language*, Studies of the New Testament and Its World (Edinburgh: T&T Clark, 2000), 230.

the idols people worship (Gal 4:8).[5] Therefore, his use of *so-called* (*legomenoi*) should not be seen as a denial of false gods but a pejorative or insulting description of them as lesser powers. This understanding is consistent with Paul's earlier references (Eph 1:21–22, 2:1–3) to the powers and principalities and the household of God including other cosmic beings, some of which are fallen and in rebellion.[6]

We find Paul using *so-called* again in 2 Thessalonians 2:4 where he writes about the one "who opposes and exalts himself against every *so-called* god or object of worship, so that he takes his seat in the temple of God, proclaiming himself to be God" (ESV). Once again Paul uses *so-called* in reference to cosmic beings that "are really false deities and not the true God."[7] For Paul, the physical idol itself is powerless. However, what resides within, connected to the idol, is a different matter. Paul rejects sacrificial altar meat (1 Cor 10:18–22) because of its association with false gods, connecting this action to the worship of foreign gods and a pointer to Israel's failure (1 Cor 10:22; cf. Deut 32:21,

---

5. Archibald Robertson and Alfred Plummer, *A Critical and Exegetical Commentary on the First Epistle of St. Paul to the Corinthians*, International Critical Commentary (New York: T&T Clark, 1911), 167. The connection to actual existence of the gods (at least the cosmic power that the idols represent) is reinforced by passages such as Deut 10:17; Ps 136:2, 3.

6. For more on the relationship between evil powers and Paul's language of idols in 1 Cor 8:4–5, see Rohintan Keki Mody "The Relationship between Powers of Evil and Idols in 1 Corinthians 8:4–5 and 10:18–22 in the Context of the Pauline Corpus and Early Judaism," *Tyndale Bulletin* 60 (2008): 295–98. See Gay Robins, "Cult Statues in Ancient Egypt," in *Cult Image and Divine Representation in the Ancient Near East*, ed. Neal H. Walls (Boston: American Schools of Oriental Research, 2005), 1–2; Michael P. Dick, *Born in Heaven, Made on Earth: The Making of the Cult Image in the Ancient Near East* (Winona Lake, IN: Eisenbrauns, 1999), 33–34.

7. Gene L. Green, *The Letters to the Thessalonians*, Pillar New Testament Commentary (Grand Rapids: Eerdmans, 2002), 310.

contextualized by Deut 32:17) in following and worshiping the sons of God allotted to the nations.

Returning back to Ephesians, we can now see that Paul uses *so-called* in an insulting way to refer to the lesser status of beings being worshiped. He may be referring to the reality that the Jews have also forsaken Yahweh and are now worshiping false gods, the very same warning given in Deuteronomy 4:19 but subsequently ignored. In referring to them as *so-called*, Paul is reminding the Jews that they are not innocent and blameless—they are in the very same situation as the gentiles, engaged in a form of false worship. Both Jew and gentile are in need of rescue and restoration, something that can only take place when they turn away from their false gods and turn toward the one true God.

The worship of false gods and subsequent alienation from the one true God by the people of God is further reinforced when Paul in Ephesians 2:11 refers to the act of circumcision as an action *done by hand* (*cheiropoiētos*). Arnold says, "In a somewhat shocking turn, Paul denigrates the practice of circumcision by labeling it a practice 'done by hand' (χειροποίητος). This was a term well-known among Jews familiar with the Greek OT, where it was used in conjunction with the making of idols."[8] Earlier we noted the connection Paul has made between the so-called gods and the so-called Jews; now we find another insulting connection between circumcision and the forming of idols that represented gentile gods.[9]

---

8. Arnold, *Ephesians*, 153–54.
9. In the Septuagint *cheiropoiētos* is the typical word used for the Hebrew *'elil* and is used to describe the gods made by the hands of men. See Eduard Lohse, "Χείρ, Χειραγωγέω, Χειραγωγός, Χειρόγραφον, Χειροποίητος, Ἀχειροποίητος,

THE UNSEEN BATTLE

The Greek *cheiropoiētos* is a term used in the Septuagint for idols (Lev 26:1; Isa 2:18), the sanctuary (or house) of an idol (Isa 16:12), and false gods (Isa 11:9).[10] In the New Testament *cheiropoiētos* is used to describe constructing the temple (Mark 14:58; Acts 7:48; 17:24; Heb 9:11, 24).[11] Remember that gods were believed to reside in sanctuaries/temples as their houses.[12] The people at Babel built the *ziggurat* (home/temple of the deity) with their hands. The use of these two terms (*legomenoi* and *cheiropoiētos*) suggests that Paul is not simply calling out gentiles for their idolatry—he also intends to critique the idolatry of the Jews. They too have forsaken Yahweh and are serving false gods. They are so-called Jews who have only human circumcision and not spiritual circumcision. The law has become a dividing wall, as Paul will later say, that Jesus will break down so that the two families, who are both worshiping foreign gods, can together worship the one true God.

In 2 Corinthians 5:1, Paul positively affirms what he has just negatively described in Ephesians 2:11: The house(hold) of God is being built, but not with hands.[13] Throughout Ephesians 2:11, Paul has laid out the reality of Jewish idol

---

Χειροτονέω," in *Theological Dictionary of the New Testament*, ed. Gerhard Kittel, Geoffrey W. Bromiley, and Gerhard Friedrich, 10 vols. (Grand Rapids: Eerdmans, 1964–), 9:436.

10. O'Brien, *Ephesians*, 185n130.

11. There is some discussion in regard to the nature of Stephen's speech and whether it had an "antitemple" connotation. This discussion is outside the scope of the present dissertation, but for more see James P. Sweeney, "Stephen's Speech (Acts 7:2–53): Is It as 'Anti-Temple' as Is Frequently Alleged?," *Trinity Journal* 23 (2002): 199.

12. Later in this chapter we will discuss this concept in greater detail in reference to the household of God that is actually the temple of God that is growing and being built.

13. Barth, *Ephesians*, 255. See also Acts 7:48, 17:24; Mark 14:58; Heb 9:11, 24.

worship through his specific usage of *legomenoi* and *cheiro-poiētos*. He recalls a context where the Jews were influenced by false gods and idols and critiques them. But he has plenty of criticism for the gentiles as well. Jews were not the only ones who rejected Yahweh and worshiped the false gods.

It was no secret that the gentiles worshiped idols, and Paul's point is that both Jews and gentiles are engaged in idolatry and rebellion. The dark powers were explicitly identified in Ephesians 2:1–3 where the gentiles, as Arnold says, "willingly lived under the control of three forms of evil that rendered them dead to God and liable for his wrath."[14] In Ephesians 2:12, Paul refers to the gentiles as *alienated* from the covenant people of Israel. Markus Barth notes the term *alienation* has in mind a former unity. Citing Acts 17:26; Romans 5; and 1 Corinthians 15, he suggests that an "original unity is presupposed. In Ephesians 1:4–10 also the Gentiles' eternal inclusion in God's love and election is indeed affirmed."[15]

This leaves us questioning where and when this unity was originally lost. Bock gets us closer to the origin of the Jew-gentile distinction by noting the separation from God and one another occurred as a result of sin and left everyone

---

14. Arnold, *Ephesians*, 155. Arnold notes that *exclusion* (*apallotrioō*) appears twice in Ezekiel in the context of a warning to the Israelites of alienation as a result of following after idols and false gods (Ezek 14:5–7).
15. Barth, *Ephesians*, 257. Ernest Best, A Critical and Exegetical Commentary on Ephesians, International Critical Commentary (Edinburgh: T&T Clark International, 1998), 241, does not see a return to a previous unity. He says, "It was God who separated Jews and Gentiles through his choice of Abraham; neither 2:14ff nor 3:6 indicates the restoration of an original unity." However, it seems Best may go too far in making this conclusion. Genesis 11 read with Deut 32:8–9 and 4:19 makes clear that the nations were disinherited from God. This must mean that they were once included in the household of God.

estranged. Further, Bock identifies (according to Ezek 44:7, 9) that it was God's plan and intention to include the gentiles back into the covenant family of God as promised to Abraham in Genesis 12:3. The reference to Genesis 12:3 is vital in zeroing us in on both the origin of the Jew-gentile distinction and promise of a future restoration. Calvin further connects the Old Testament background of the separation of Jews and gentiles to Deuteronomy 32:8–9. He writes:

> To understand this passage, two things must be observed. The Jews were separated, for a certain time, from the Gentiles, by the appointment of God; and ceremonial observances were the open and avowed symbols of that separation. Passing by the Gentiles, God had chosen the Jews to be a peculiar people to himself. A wide distinction was thus made, when the one class were "fellow-citizens and of the household" (Eph. 2:19) of the Church, and the other were foreigners. This is stated in the Song of Moses: "When the Most High divided to the nations their inheritance, when he separated the sons of Adam, he set the bounds of the people according to the number of the children of Israel: for the Lord's portion is his people, Jacob is the lot of his inheritance" (Deut. 32:8, 9). Bounds were thus fixed by God to separate one people from the rest; and hence arose *the enmity* which is here mentioned. A separation is thus made.[16]

---

16. John Calvin, *Commentaries on the Epistles of Paul to the Galatians and Ephesians*, ed. William Pringle (Bellingham, WA: Logos Bible Software, 2010), 236. Calvin references the "sons of Israel," but as noted in earlier chapters, it is best to follow the Septuagint reading of the *sons of God*.

Calvin recollects the Old Testament background that first created the division between those who would be known as the covenant people of God, the Israelites, and those disinherited nations (Deut 32:8–9) that would come to be known as the gentiles. The disinheritance and corresponding distinction and alienation between Jews and gentiles points to an event when the gentiles were intentionally separated and removed from the household of God. Since the gentiles were not part of the household but rather under the authority of the sons of God, they were included in the rebellion of the sons of God and thus counted as members of a rebellious household, one opposed to Yahweh.[17] The alienation of the gentiles was an indication of the loss of their relationship to the true God.

Paul in Ephesians 2:12 similarly concludes that the "God-forsaken" gentiles were in fact "without God" (*atheos*). This does not mean they were "atheists" in the modern sense but that they were given over to idolatry and lesser divine beings, gods that were not the one true God.[18] In saying the gentiles were "without God," Lynn Cohick writes, "His point is that they embraced gods that were not the one true God, and thus were impious in their ignorance."[19] Paul's conclusion is that the status of gentiles being atheists (*atheoi*) prior to Christ is an indication of their estrangement from the household of God and their subjugation to "the powers." However, God

---

17. See chapter 2 and the discussion of the fallen "sons of God" and the nations of the world that worship these cosmic beings.
18. David J. MacLeod, "The Broken Wall, or: From Alienation to Reconciliation," *Emmaus Journal* 14 (2005): 141.
19. Lynn H. Cohick, *Ephesians*, New Covenant Commentary Series (Eugene, OR: Cascade, 2010), 178.

always intended to reconcile these wayward nations back into his household. The idea of being "without God" refers to the gentile allegiance to the gods of the world, whom we know to be the fallen sons of God.

In the context of the covenant promise first made to Abraham, Paul elaborates further on the estrangement of the gentiles. The alienation of the gentiles would now be overcome through the death, burial, resurrection, and ascension of Christ who, "himself is our peace, who has made us both [Jew and gentile] one and has broken down in his flesh the dividing wall of hostility" (Eph 2:14 ESV). In Christ, the gentiles who were once "far" are brought "near." In Ephesians 2:19 he reinforces the nature of the distance in order to create a juxtaposition with the nearness that comes in Christ.

EPHESIANS 2:19-22: FROM STRANGERS TO MEMBERS OF THE HOUSEHOLD

In Ephesians 2:19–22 Paul moves from the distance of the gentiles, who were once alienated and thus under the rule and reign of "powers and principalities," into the hope of reconciliation and reunion into the household of God made possible through Jesus, the head of the household. Looking back at Ephesians 2:12, Paul used specific Greco-Roman categories (excluded from citizenship and foreigners) to portray how distinctively separate gentiles once were from Israel. In Ephesians 2:19 this is further developed through the use of three familiar categories for the Ephesian audience: "foreigners" (*xenoi*), "resident aliens" (*paroikoi*), and "fellow citizens" (*sympolitai*).[20] *Xenoi* were foreigners within the city who had no guaranteed rights or privileges (see Acts 16:20–23; cf. Acts 21:39).[21] The presence of "foreigners" (*xenoi*) with "resident aliens" (*paroikoi*) accentuates the distinction of the outsider relationship.[22] Those who were *paroikoi* (resident aliens or sojourners) may have been born in and lived in a city for a generation yet still did not have the status of citizens with all the access, legal rights, and protections that came with citizenship.[23]

The idea of an "inside group versus outside group" would have been familiar to the Israelites.[24] In Hebrews 11:13 the author recalls the patriarchs referring to themselves as strangers and exiles. This seems to be an allusion to Abraham, who refers to himself as an alien and exile using the same Greek terminology in the Septuagint of Genesis 23 (*paroikos kai parepidēmos egō eime meth hymōn*) (Gen 23:4 LXX). This linguistic connection continues when Paul says in Ephesians 2:19 that gentiles are no longer aliens (*paroikoi*), a common term used in the Old Testament for gentiles living in Israel (Exod 12:45; Lev 22:10; 25:23, 35, 40, 45, 47).[25]

---

20. Baugh, *Ephesians*, 199.
21. Barth comments: "A 'stranger' could be, and sometimes was, treated as an outlaw or spy (Gen 19:1–10)." Barth, *Ephesians*, 268.
22. The terms *xenoi* and *paroikoi* are often used synonymously in the Septuagint. O'Brien notes a possible distinction where the former describes a person from another tribe or country, while the latter indicates a stranger who resides as a resident alien. Regardless, the emphasis remains in Ephesians and the Septuagint of the outsider versus insider language for gentile and Jewish readers. O'Brien, *Ephesians*, 211.
23. Baugh, *Ephesians*, 199.
24. F. F. Bruce, *The Epistles to the Colossians, to Philemon, and to the Ephesians*, The New International Commentary on the New Testament (Grand Rapids: Eerdmans, 1984), 302.
25. Arnold, *Ephesians*, 168.

Further, there is a lexical connection through the Septuagint of Genesis 11, where the people gather and say "let us build" (*oikodomēsōmen*) in verse 4 and use similar words in verses 5 and 8.[26] The presence of these words, all part of the same family group of *oik* words in the Septuagint of Genesis 11, provides a lexical connection to Babel beyond the thematic and conceptual evidence of temple, family, and household. The terms Paul employs in Ephesians 2:19 all refer back to this initial point of origin where the Jews and gentiles were first divided, namely Babel.

MEMBERS OF THE HOUSEHOLD AND FELLOW CITIZENS WITH THE SAINTS

Paul in Ephesians 2:19 now makes a pivotal transition from the gentiles' distance from God to the intimacy they now have through Christ. Paul says that once the gentiles were "outside of the house" (*paroikoi*), but now they are "within the household" (*oikeioi*). Furthermore, their former status as "foreigners" (*xenoi*) is reversed as now they are "fellow citizens" (*sympolitai*).[27]

In an important turn, Paul moves from a political

---

26. Additionally, we find *built* (*oikodomēsōmen*) in verse 5 and *building* (*oikodomountes*) in verse 8.
27. Thomas Kingsmill Abbott, *A Critical and Exegetical Commentary on the Epistles to the Ephesians and to the Colossians*, International Critical Commentary (New York: Scribner's, 1909), 68. Paul uses a play on words and creates an intentional contrast. The same word appears in 1 Tim 5:8 and has a literal sense of one's own family. Additionally, it is used in Gal 6:10 in reference to the family of believers. See Walter L. Liefeld, *Ephesians*, IVP New Testament Commentary 10 (Downers Grove, IL: InterVarsity Press, 1997), Eph 2:19–22.

metaphor (citizenship) into a familial metaphor (members of the household) pregnant with meaning. Not only are Jews and gentiles related politically now because of Christ, but their political affiliation within the kingdom of God has been strengthened through their familial bond. The familial context was normative for Greco-Roman households since these households included widows, orphans, slaves, and freedmen.[28] At the center of the household were the household gods, which played a spiritual role in the family.[29] Further, there was an understanding that the head of the house acted as a type of priest of the household.[30] Once again, central to the Greco-Roman household was an understanding of a spiritualized dimension of the family with representative activity through the head of the household and the idols within the house, such as the *Lares* and *Penates*.

Some readers may recall an iconic scene in the movie

---

28. N. T. Wright observes that Roman religion never had an exclusive focus on grand public expression over the private dimension. Wright says, "The private home was equally important, with the hearth and its 'household gods' as the focus, and the father of the family acting as priest. These 'household gods' comprise the *Lares*, small statues of two young men, and the *Penates*, the small cult statues placed at the innermost point of the home, and clearly seen as symbolic of the ultimate identity of a particular family." See N. T. Wright, *Christian Origins and the Question of God*, vol. 4, *Paul and the Faithfulness of God* (Minneapolis: Fortress, 2013), 270.

29. The same concept was present in the ANE context. Beth Alpert Nakhai shows that the home (individual and a slightly larger household based on kinship relationship) was also a kind of sacred space. Shrines were present at the hearth of the home, and she notes, "Each kind of religious act transformed the house, or some part of it, into sacred space." Here again we find the convergence of earthly and cosmic as it relates to the household that had continuity in both the ANE and Greco-Roman world. See Beth Alpert Nakhai, "The Household as Sacred Space," in *Family and Household Religion: Toward a Synthesis of OT Studies, Archaeology, Epigraphy, and Cultural Studies*, ed. Rainer Albertz (Winona Lake, IN: Eisenbrauns, 2014), 53–72.

30. David J. Williams, *Paul's Metaphors: Their Context and Character* (Peabody, MA: Hendrickson, 1999), 51.

Gladiator where Maximus (played by Russell Crowe) is holding little figurines in his hands as he prays at an altar. Those figurines are household idols. The *Lares* represented ancestors and ghosts who should receive respect.[31] The *Penates* represented a more usual household god such as what Aeneas brought with him from Troy.[32] The connection between the household as both private and public carried into the spiritual dimension. Interestingly, the *Lares* had public usage within the city that mirrored and reflected the more private familial usage. N. T. Wright says, "It was not only private houses that had *Lares*. Rome was divided into districts or wards (*compita*), each of which looked after its own *Lares compitales*, the gods of the district, and celebrated games and festivals in their honor. Augustus reorganized the districts, 265 of them, and rebuilt the main temple of the *Lares*."[33]

What About Ghosts in the Bible?

People often ask about ghosts. What are they? Are they real? The Bible often refers to something called disembodied spirits, and there are various Hebrew words to describe this. We've already covered some, like *elohim*, which refers to spirit beings. Additionally, words like *ittim*,

---

31. Alexander S. Murray, *Manual of Mythology: Greek and Roman, Norse, and Old German, Hindoo and Egyptian Mythology* (New York: Scribner's, 1881), 198. The *Lares* also had public representation beyond the household's private observance, creating another connection between the household in terms of private familial and public political.
32. Leonhard Schmitz, "PENA'TES," *Dictionary of Greek and Roman Biography and Mythology*, ed. William Smith (Boston: Little, Brown, 1870), 182.
33. Wright, *Paul and the Faithfulness of God*, 318–19.

which is related to an Akkadian term *ettemu*, is often used to refer to "ghosts" alongside the imagery of "wind" in reference to deceased ancestors (Isa 19:3).[34] Another important Hebrew word is *ob*, which refers to departed spirits (Deut 18:11; Lev 20:27).

One example of this in the Bible is found in the story of Saul and the witch of Endor. Saul asks his servants to find a "medium," which in Hebrew is *ba'alath-ov* and can be literally translated as "mistress of the spirit of the dead."[35] In 1 Samuel 28:13, the medium of Endor says that she sees an *elohim* coming up out of the earth. The idea behind this spirit (*elohim*) coming up from the earth is a reflection of the ancient Hebrew cosmology in which it was believed that Sheol (the underworld) was located under the earth with two distinct partitions. The depth of Hades was the final resting place of the unrighteous dead, and "Abraham's bosom" is where the righteous dead would reside (prior to Christ's resurrection).

The Hebrew word *elohim* generally means a disembodied spirit. But in this case, we have multiple reasons to believe this was in fact Samuel's spirit (though disembodied), which may be why the term *elohim* is used. For example, when Saul asks the medium what this being looks like, she responds that he is an "old man . . . wrapped in a robe" (1 Sam 28:14 ESV). The Hebrew word

---

34. T. Abusch, "Etemmu," *Dictionary of Deities and Demons in the Bible*, ed. Karel van der Toorn, Bob Becking, and Pieter W. van der Horst (Grand Rapids: Eerdmans, 1999), 309.
35. Michael S. Heiser, *The Bible Unfiltered: Approaching Scripture on Its Own Terms* (Bellingham, WA: Lexham, 2017), 101.

for robe here is *me'il* and refers to a "sleeveless outer garment." Why include the detail of it being sleeveless? Well, we learn elsewhere that Samuel is given a *me'il* from his mother Hannah as he was being trained and raised by Eli in the tabernacle (1 Sam 1:19). Further, we know Samuel was wearing a *me'il* when he announced that Saul was being rejected as king. Finally, when Samuel turned away from Saul as a sign of God's rejection of Saul as king, Saul grabbed him and tore off part of the *me'il* (1 Sam 15:27). The detail of the robe calls to mind Samuel's life from his early childhood to his latter days. Though this is speculative, is it possible that robe the medium sees on Samuel is the very *me'il* that Saul tore?

If a deceased person like Samuel can reappear to someone still living, can something like this still happen today? While I do not believe we can interact with the spirits of deceased people, and the Bible clearly prohibits this, I do believe it is possible for demons or evil spirits to present themselves as deceased dead in a manipulative and deceitful manner. Again, this is speculative, but we must remember that the enemy of our soul is cunning and creative in his deception. He will do whatever he can to deceive and manipulate us. So, while I do not personally believe this is something we will normally encounter, I believe there is real evil in the supernatural realm that is detrimental and destructive to our souls. As I mentioned earlier, whether or not it *can* happen, we are clearly told never to engage in this practice.

Do not turn to mediums or consult spiritists, or you will be defiled by them; I am the LORD your God. (Lev 19:31)

Whoever turns to mediums or spiritists and prostitutes himself with them, I will turn against that person and cut him off from his people. Consecrate yourselves and be holy, for I am the LORD your God. Keep my statutes and do them; I am the LORD who sets you apart. (Lev 20:6–8)

Saul died for his unfaithfulness to the LORD because he did not keep the LORD's word. He even consulted a medium for guidance, but he did not inquire of the LORD. So the LORD put him to death and turned the kingdom over to David son of Jesse. (1 Chr 10:13–14)

While the experience of Saul, Samuel, and the medium of Endor is not normative, and I believe most experiences like this today are the work of deceptive demons, my final word is simple: Let's not be like Saul. Let's take God at his word because he is trustworthy and true.

This same concept, of a household deity that brought protection and guidance, was also present within the Old Testament context. For both the Greco-Roman and Old Testament background, the household gods were connected to houses that were, in turn, linked to land and geographical locations. The land correlates to the sons of God and their geopolitical activity. We saw evidence of this earlier in the book of Daniel, which presented us with a rebellious household at war against Yahweh and his people. All of this points to of a war of households; we might even say the New Testament teaches a doctrine of *opposed households*: a household of faith, where God is the Father, and a household of Satan and those bound to him as captives (Eph 2:1–3). The idea of a household of Satan is seen in Mark 3:23–27, which presents Satan as king of a kingdom. Satan is also referred to as the head of a household, as Jesus tells the Jews, "You belong to your father, the devil, and you want to carry out your father's desire" (John 8:44 NIV).[36] This description of Satan's household is reminiscent of Paul's language here in Ephesians. Satan's household (including the powers and principalities under his rule) are referred to in both political (Satan's kingdom) and familial (Satan as father) terms.

In order for a new multiethnic household to form, there must be a transfer of citizenship and household. The transfer of citizenship can take place, as Jeffrey Jay Niehaus says, because "Christ plunders Satan's Kingdom, which is also Satan's house. The plunder is people—captive subjects. Christ populates his own Kingdom, his own house, with these liberated captives."[37] Paul, in developing this new

36. Jeffrey Jay Niehaus, *Ancient Near Eastern Themes in Biblical Theology* (Grand Rapids: Kregel Academic, 2008). For a further discussion of the "war of households," see Patrick Schreiner, *The Body of Jesus: A Spatial Analysis of the Kingdom in Matthew*, Library of New Testament Studies 555 (New York: Bloomsbury, 2016), 59–76.
37. Niehaus, *Ancient Near Eastern Themes in Biblical Theology*, 163.

reality in Christ, now identifies the gentiles as those no longer outside the family or without a homeland. Instead, they are granted new citizenship through Christ's victory and can become members of the multiethnic family and household of God.[38]

As hinted at earlier, the Greco-Roman household and the establishment of the household gods recalls the Old Testament background as well, linking the sons of God and household gods, the *teraphim*. The idols, though only physical objects, represent real cosmic forces—the powers behind the idols. These powers once enslaved and blinded the nations that were disinherited in the aftermath of Babel, and in Ephesians 2:19–20 we find a recollection of this background story and the reversal that takes place now in Christ. No longer would the gentiles be blinded by these dark powers. No longer would gentiles be cut off from the family. They are now adopted as sons and daughters and equal members with Jews, heirs and coheirs with Christ.[39] The gentiles now have a home within the household of God alongside Jews and other believers who make up the nations of the world.[40]

In this new multiethnic household, no group can claim that the house belongs singularly to their tribe. Markus Barth captures this well when he says, "The transition from one concept of 'house' to the other contains a double-edged

---

38. Lincoln, *Ephesians*, 160.
39. Baugh, *Ephesians*, 200.
40. O'Brien, *Ephesians*, 212. The progression to the household membership has been telegraphed earlier by Paul. In Eph 2:18 Paul spoke of the access to the Father. In Eph 1:5 we find gentiles being adopted into God's family as children. Finally in Eph 3:14–15 we find that all the families of earth and heaven are named by God.

warning: Jews cannot complacently claim that the house is theirs alone; Gentiles cannot presume that their arrival requires the building of a new house or an automatic completion and perfection of the old one."[41] The emphasis on a new multiethnic household revolves around sibling relationships modeled after the union found in Christ. John Stott refers to this as "the brotherhood, into which, across racial barriers, the father's children are brought. 'Brethren' (meaning 'brothers and sisters') is the commonest word for Christians in the New Testament. It expresses a close relationship of affection, care and support. *Philadelphia,* 'brotherly love,' should always be a special characteristic of God's new society."[42]

Notice that the union of this multiethnic household is due to the believers' union with the risen and ascended Christ, seated in the heavenly realm (Eph 2:4–6). Since they are now fellow "citizens with the saints" (Eph 2:19), the citizenship and fellowship that gentiles have is in conjunction with the saints (*hagiōn*). While it is possible that *saints* here refers exclusively to the Jewish people (Israel) or is a reference to the redeemed of all history, it can also refer to angels in addition to the redeemed.[43] Following Best, I believe the context suggests that *saints* should be understood as a combination of angels and the redeemed of all ages. Thus, it is better translated as "holy ones." In

---

41. Barth, *Ephesians*, 314.
42. John R. W. Stott, *God's New Society: The Message of Ephesians*, The Bible Speaks Today (Downers Grove, IL: InterVarsity Press, 1979), 106.
43. Arnold, *Ephesians*, 168.

other words, believers are now fellow citizens with the holy ones,[44] which includes the cosmic family of faithful angelic servants—the sons of God who did not rebel against their heavenly Father.

Paul has already established the context of a cosmic household of God that includes cosmic beings that reside in the heavenlies (Eph 1) and has noted that believers are raised with Christ and sit with him in the heavenlies. There is evidence the Qumran community believed the redeemed community was in the heavens with the "sons of heaven," providing us with an additional reference to this idea close to the time Paul was writing.[45] Paul refers to *hagioi* as angels elsewhere in the New Testament (cf. 1 Thess 3:13; 2 Thess 1:7, 10), and we find instances where the Septuagint also has "holy ones" (*hagioi*) understood as cosmic beings (Job 15:15; Ps 89:5, 6).[46] If correct, this subtle shift from the saints (*hagioi*) as a reference to believers' inclusion among the full household of God—including the angelic household—is yet another line of evidence reaffirming a two-household view (cosmic and earthly) of the family of God.[47]

---

44. The cloud of witnesses in Heb 12:1 should be read alongside Heb 12:22–23, where the description of the assembly includes both humans and angels. In Heb 12:22 the righteous believers "have come" into a divine council scene and take up their priestly role in the household of God, which is present also in Second Temple Judaism, especially Qumran.

45. Best, *A Critical and Exegetical Commentary on Ephesians*, 278. Angel states the "pinnacle of human experience" for Qumran was to serve in the divine assembly alongside the angels. See Joseph L. Angel, *Otherworldly and Eschatological Priesthood in the Dead Sea Scrolls*, Studies on the Texts of the Deserts of Judah 86 (Leiden: Brill, 2010), 165.

46. Lincoln, *Ephesians*, 151.

47. For more on God's two-family household, see chapter 2.

A HOUSEHOLD THAT IS A GROWING TEMPLE

Scholarship has often connected Paul's architectural imagery in Ephesians to the Greco-Roman background of the temple of Artemis.[48] Philo observes, "The temple of Artemis in Ephesus is the only house of the gods. For whoever examines it will believe that the gods exchanged the heavenly regions of immortality to have a place upon the earth."[49] However, Paul is not limited to this background, and close observation of Paul's writing shows that he is also drawing from the Old Testament, specifically the redemptive reversal of the tower of Babel as a ziggurat that served as a temple/house of deity. In Ephesians 2:20–22 Paul shifts from household and familial imagery to household and temple imagery. Far from abrupt or unexpected, however, this transition feels natural because the term for "house" can mean "household" or "temple."[50]

In contrast to pagan temples in which the inner sanctuary held the "dwelling of the god" or the Old Testament context in which the tabernacle or temple held God's dwelling in the holy of holies, Paul redefines the spiritual structure of

---

48. Baugh, *Ephesians*, 204. Baugh says, "No Ephesian could hear vv. 21–22 without thinking immediately of the great Temple of Artemis Ephesia (the Artemisium), one of the seven wonders of the ancient world and the largest building in the Greek world."
49. Gary Gromacki, "The Spiritual War for Ephesus," *Journal of Ministry and Theology* 15 (2011): 96.
50. O'Brien, *Ephesians*, 212. In the OT הֵיכָל (*hekhal*) can mean the earthly palace (household of the king), as seen in 1 Kgs 21:1; 2 Kgs 20:18; 39:7; Nah 2:7; and Amos 8:3. See Ludwig Koehler, Walter Baumgartner, M. E. J. Richardson, and Johann Jakob Stamm, *The Hebrew and Aramaic Lexicon of the Old Testament*, 5 vols. (Leiden: Brill, 1994–2000), 245.The Hebrew בַּיִת (*bayit*) can also mean a temple house, and the residence of the deity as in Gen 28:22 and 1 Sam 5:2 (124).

household in such a way that it has physical implications. God does not dwell in temples made by human hands but now indwells "in Spirit" (*en pneumati*).[51] As Abbot suggests, "The Spirit is not the means or instrument only, but the medium by virtue of which God dwells in the Church."[52] Therefore, the Greek word *en* refers to the act of "dwelling" (*katoikēsis*). The noun *to katoikētērion* (occurring only in Rev 18:2 in the New Testament) is used in the Septuagint to refer to both the temple in Jerusalem (1 Kgs 8:13) and the heavenly dwelling place.[53] There is a progression in thought here where the dwelling is no longer exclusively a physical temple or the spiritual heavenly realm; now both of these meet in space and time within the newly formed multiethnic household of God.

Again, we see the redemptive reversal of Babel. Yahweh is not forced to come down; he makes for himself a dwelling place within the multiethnic family of God. In Ephesians 2:19–22, the nations are regathered for the building project of a spiritual temple. At Babel the people used brick (Gen 11:3) to construct a temple. In Ephesians 2:20–22, the bricks and mortar that make up the temple are living stones.[54] Peter uses a similar analogy in reference to a spiritual temple in 1 Peter 2:5: "You also, like living stones, are being built

---

51. Harold W. Hoehner, Philip W. Comfort, and Peter H. Davids, *Ephesians, Philippians, Colossians, 1 and 2 Thessalonians, Philemon*, Cornerstone Biblical Commentary 16 (Carol Stream, IL: Tyndale House, 2008), 62.

52. Abbott, *A Critical and Exegetical Commentary on the Epistles to the Ephesians and to the Colossians*, 76.

53. Lincoln, *Ephesians*, 158. It is a term used in the Septuagint of God's dwelling place (Exod 15:17; 1 Kgs 8:13, 39, 43, 49; 2 Chr 30:27). See Darrell L. Bock, *Ephesians: An Introduction and Commentary*, Tyndale New Testament Commentaries 10 (London: Inter-Varsity Press, 2019), 88.

54. Barth, *Ephesians*, 320.

[*oikodomeisthe*] into a spiritual house to be a holy priesthood" (1 Pet 2:5 NIV).[55] At Babel the people gathered the building material and did the work to build the ziggurat. In Ephesians Paul tells us that God is the one doing the work of building. The material that God uses is his people, the redeemed nations of the world.

At Babel the people desired to make a name for themselves (Gen 11:4) by constructing the ziggurat. They were motivated by rebellious hearts, and the result was division and dispersion. In Ephesians, Paul presents the multiethnic household as the means by which God will make a name for himself and unify the divided family. The multiethnic household showcases unity—not division—and is a new kind of temple. As Calvin says, "All who are joined together in Christ are the temple of God. It is unity of faith that makes this possible, because for the temple to be built, those who constitute it have to be matched to one another."[56] This concept of a new multiethnic household as the prerequisite for the temple would have seemed odd and even threatening to the Greco-Roman world. Having gentiles joining the new household of God means chaos for the existing secular household that is opposed to God. The end result of this transition of households is a break with the religious customs, sacrifices, and household gods, leading to the fracture of the previously established familial household.[57]

---

55. Arnold, *Ephesians*, 172.
56. Gerald L. Bray, ed., *Galatians, Ephesians*, in *Reformation Commentary on Scripture: New Testament*, ed. Timothy George and Scott M. Manetsch, vol. 10 (Downers Grove, IL: InterVarsity Press, 2011), 301.
57. John M. Barclay, *Pauline Churches and Diaspora Jews* (Grand Rapids: Eerdmans, 2016), 24.

Paul has given us a new and powerful image: a multiethnic household of God that stands as a counterstructure to the evil systems and powers of the world.[58] The victory the multiethnic household celebrates over the world's evil powers and structures is a cosmic declaration that entails an earthly responsibility.[59] The responsibility or purpose of the multiethnic earthly household is to serve as a sign, symbol, and faithful representation of the head of the household. John Stott summarizes how the multiethnic household should showcase this to a watching world:

> I wonder if anything is more urgent today, for the honor of Christ and for the spread of the Gospel, than that the church should be, and should be seen to be, what by God's purpose and Christ's achievement it already is—a single new humanity, a model of human community, a family of reconciled brothers and sisters who love their father and love each other, the evident dwelling place of God by his Spirit. Only then will the world believe in Christ as Peacemaker. Only then will God receive the glory due to his name.[60]

We must not neglect this. The message of the gospel disrupts the activities of evil powers and authorities. The newly formed household of God, made up of Jews and gentiles, inevitably faced persecution and hatred. Though ultimately defeated, the evil powers fought back, enacting their warfare

---

58. Wright, *Paul and the Faithfulness of God*, 386–87.
59. James W. Thompson, *The Church according to Paul: Rediscovering the Community Conformed to Christ* (Grand Rapids: Baker Academic, 2014), 208.
60. Stott, *God's New Society*, 111–12.

through earthly systems and structures, as well as individual people. However, God's people were never alone in this. The new multiethnic family was sealed by the Holy Spirit, which serve as an eschatological blessing and pledge of what was to come (Eph 1:13–14).[61] A sign of this reality was the newfound unity of Jews and gentiles who were reconciled to one another through mutual forgiveness, a powerful reality that spurred further hostility and hatred toward the church by the evil powers.[62]

EPHESIANS 3:10: THE MULTIETHNIC CHURCH AS A SIGN TO THE POWERS

In Ephesians 1:22, Paul mentions the church (*ekklēsia*) for the first time within the context of Christ's two-family household.[63] In the previous chapter we noted how Christ has subjugated the powers who have been placed under his feet. As its head, Christ has been given to the church (*ekklēsia*) to bring order and direction. The term *ekklēsia* simply means "assembly." However, here we have the presence of a universal assembly of all those who belong to the household of God.[64] Witherington comments on the "universality" of the term in Ephesians, noting that *ekklēsia* "here, as elsewhere in Ephesians (3:10, 21; 5:23–32), surely has a more than

---

61. James M. Hamilton Jr., *God's Indwelling Presence: The Holy Spirit in the Old and New Testaments*, NAC Studies in Bible and Theology (Nashville: B&H, 2006), 188.
62. Best, *A Critical and Exegetical Commentary on Ephesians*, 141.
63. Kenneth L. Boles, *Galatians and Ephesians*, College Press NIV Commentary (Joplin, MO: College, 1993), Eph 1:22.
64. Bock, *Ephesians*, 58.

local sense since it is Christ's body, but it of course includes the audience of this discourse. This more universal sense of the term is in keeping with the circular nature of the document."[65] Additionally, O'Brien comments on the term and suggests a metaphorical consideration referring to the "heavenly gathering" where believers gather around Christ (Heb 12:22–24) in the heavenly realm. The church (*ekklēsia*) can be viewed metaphorically as a gathering in the heavenlies around Christ, bringing together God's two-family household in one assembly.[66]

In Ephesians 3:10, Paul adds that all of this happens, "so that through the church the manifold wisdom of God might now be made known to the rulers and authorities in the heavenly places" (ESV). God in Christ chooses to disclose and accomplish his purpose in all of this through the church.[67] As the church is faithful in this task of being God's multiethnic family, it is actively participating in the unseen battle. This is a significant part of spiritual warfare that is frequently overlooked. Christ's ascension has made possible the reunification of God's earthly family in such a way that it now serves as an active sign and symbol to the conquered powers of their impending doom and final destruction. Making known (*gnōrisas*) recalls the earlier discussion in chapter 7 of Ephesians 1:9–10 in reference to the mystery (*mystērion*) and the administration (*oikonomia*) of

---

65. Ben Witherington III, *The Letters to Philemon, the Colossians, and the Ephesians: A Socio-Rhetorical Commentary on the Captivity Epistles* (Grand Rapids: Eerdmans, 2007), 245.

66. O'Brien, *Ephesians*, 146–47. This imagery further reinforces a divine council scene as already discussed in previous chapters recalling an Old Testament background.

67. Lincoln, *Ephesians*, 184.

God. Now, in Ephesians 3:10, the mystery and administration are made known through the church and to the "rulers and authorities in the heavenly places" (ESV). The reception of gentiles into the household of God was both a tangible, visible means of putting God's wisdom on display, and it served as a sign to the powers that their stronghold over the nations was broken.[68] The gentiles are now fellow members, heirs, and sharers of the promises of God in Christ.

When and how was this wisdom made known? Because the wisdom referred to here is related to the church, it must correlate to the beginning of the church. And since the church is made up of both Jews and gentiles, and this is only possible due to the death, resurrection, and ascension of Christ, this points us to Acts 2 on the day of Pentecost. Here, as noted earlier, we find the redemptive reversal of Babel.[69] The Pentecost event is yet another example of the union of the heavenly and earthly. The Spirit (spiritual) fell upon the people (earthly) to form one new multiethnic family of God; Acts 2 is the pivotal example of Paul's cosmic ecclesiology in Ephesians (1:10, 1:20–22; 3:10). The revelation of God's wisdom to the heavenly powers is directly connected to the formation of multiethnic household of God. As Clint Arnold

---

68. John Muddiman, *The Epistle to the Ephesians*, Black's New Testament Commentary (London: Continuum, 2001), 159–60. Walter Wink suggests that the proclamation of the gospel to the gentiles was important also because the gospel would be proclaimed to angelic beings behind and associated with the nations. However, Wink goes too far in suggesting theses angelic beings could repent and be redeemed. Psalm 82 and other passages clearly speak of judgment and discipline for the angelic beings, the sons of God, and does not seem to leave room for a possible return or redemption of these cosmic beings. See Walter Wink, *Unmasking the Powers: The Invisible Forces That Determine Human Existence* (Minneapolis: Fortress, 1993), 87–127.
69. Best, *A Critical and Exegetical Commentary on Ephesians*, 324.

says, "This is consistent with Paul's emphasis throughout the letter that God has a plan that encompasses the entire heavenly sphere."[70]

The concept of God's two-family household is further clarified in Ephesians 3:15, where God places the heavenly beings in familial groupings reflecting what has been done on earth.[71] This recalls the Deuteronomy 32 worldview where the sons of God were given delegated responsibility over the nations, only to subsequently abuse and lead them astray. Now, however, the wisdom of God is seen in the church *comprised of those very same nations*, a declaration to the powers that their stranglehold has been broken. As Best says, "The existence of the church reveals to them their failure."[72]

Let's pause for a moment to consider what this means. The faithfulness of the church—in its actions, witness, and life together—is intended to be a winsome witness of the victory of Christ to the dark powers of the world. The way God confounds and puts the powers on notice is through the creation of one unified multiethnic family, bringing together people who were once at enmity in the household of God.[73] The multiethnic and diverse nature of the family of God, the church, can be seen through Paul's use of *polupoiki-los*. This term is a combination of two adjectives meaning "much" (*polus*) and "various kinds, diversified, manifold" (*poikilos*).[74] The word *polupokilos* can also mean "of many

---

70. Arnold, *Ephesians*, 196.
71. Lincoln, *Ephesians*, 186.
72. Best, *A Critical and Exegetical Commentary on Ephesians*, 326.
73. Timothy Gombis, "Ephesians 3:2–13: Pointless Digression, or Epitome of the Triumph of God in Christ?," *Westminster Theological Journal* 66 (2004): 322.
74. Arnold, *Ephesians*, 197. The word *poikilos* is used in the Septuagint to refer

colors" or "polychrome."[75] Classical Greek writers used this word to reference cloth or flowers to convey a sense of intricate beauty or an "endless variety of colors in flowers."[76] This is the type of beauty that God puts on display to the powers to present them with their downfall and demise.[77] As Timothy Gombis observes, "The powers have ordered the present evil age in such a way as to exacerbate the divisions within humanity (Eph 2:11–12). God confounds them by creating in Christ one unified, multiracial body consisting of formerly divided groups of people."[78] What an amazing and beautiful reality! The multiethnic, many-colored, and diverse people of the formerly disinherited nations of the world have been invited back and now come together to form the household of God. This revelation—of a new multiethnic family of God—is an active assault against the powers of darkness and their attempts to divide the cosmos through racial injustice or ethnic prejudices. The visible sign of the

to Joseph's coat of many colors (Gen 37:3, 23). The immediate text does not state it, but Liefeld suggests that it can be inferred from the context that the inclusion of gentiles in the family of God constitutes the display of the wisdom of God. Liefeld, *Ephesians*, 3:10–13.

75. Franco Montanari, Madeleine Goh, and Chad Schroeder, eds., *The Brill Dictionary of Ancient Greek* (Leiden: Brill, 2015), ebook.

76. Foulkes, *Ephesians*, 105.

77. In 1 Cor 6:1–3, Paul refers to the judgment of angels. Guy Williams notes the possibility that these cosmic beings are the national angels referenced in the Old Testament (Dan 7:22 LXX; Wis 3:8; Ps 149:6). Ultimately, Williams says, "The correct interpretation probably lies in Mach's suggestion that the judgment of the angels represents an *angelification* of the community." This suggests that humans take on the role of angels elsewhere with the task of judging angels. The two streams of thought need not be distinct, as the judgment done by both angels and humans may include the patron angels of the nations that are in rebellion to Yahweh. Guy Williams, *The Spirit World in the Letters of Paul the Apostle*, 117–18; following Dibelius, *Paul* (Philadelphia: Westminster, 1964), 102.

78. Timothy G. Gombis, *The Drama of Ephesians: Participating in the Triumph of God* (Downers Grove, IL: InterVarsity Press, 2010), 117.

already final and coming victory of Christ is put on full display with the formation of God's multiethnic church, a church that anticipates the future vision of Yahweh to have one restored and reconstituted household.

NINE

STRIPPED, DISARMED, AND DEFEATED

Spiritual Warfare Today

If I were to ask you what spiritual warfare is, how would you respond? Certainly, it involves battles and some kind of conflict. But what are the sides in this battle, and what are they fighting over? I hope that now you see how at the most basic level this is a war between two kingdoms, two households. The household of God is made up of his spiritual (angelic) and earthly (human) family who have bent their knee to King Jesus. The household of the enemy (both spiritual and earthly) is made up of all those who are opposed to Yahweh. The prize over which they fight is the people of the nations.

Today, the focus of much spiritual warfare seems to be on "power encounters" with malevolent spirits, exemplified by exorcisms, the casting out of demons, and various types of deliverance ministry. These efforts attempt to understand

and engage the spirit world as it breaks into and overlaps with the earthly realm. But what is often missing from these efforts is a Deuteronomy 32 worldview, which brings clarity to the chaos of modern-day spiritual warfare. This broader understanding of the unseen spiritual battle is a simple but far from simplistic lens that helps us to see and understand how the work of Christ connects with the larger cosmic narrative of the Bible. As noted earlier, every war always has a prize in mind. And the overarching narrative of the Bible clarifies that the prize in spiritual warfare is the people of the nations.

But as helpful as the Deuteronomy 32 worldview is for our understanding of spiritual warfare, several questions still remain. Yes, Jesus has been victorious over the powers. The multiethnic church is evidence of that victory. But are these powers still active today? Should we fear them? And if they are active today, what should Christians think about them?

Can Demons Read Our Minds?

I do not believe demons can read minds. Why? Because they are not omniscient. Nor are they omnipresent. As created beings they are limited within both time and space, subject to their creator. Having said that, they are very devious and have become experts on human nature from watching human beings for thousands of years. They likely have highly attuned intuition and understanding of human patterns and thought processes. Utilizing these acquired skills and knowledge at expert levels could appear as if they are reading our minds, but the truth may be far simpler. They have studied human beings—including you and me—really well for a long time.

So what exactly are demons? The Hebrew word *shedu* is the term used to describe malevolent disembodied spirits. Specifically, in Deuteronomy 32:17 they are referred to as *elohim*: "They sacrificed to demons [*shedim*], not God [*Eloah*], to gods [*elohim*] they had not known, new gods [*elohim*] that had just arrived, which your ancestors did not fear" (Deut 32:17). This verse links the demons of the Old Testament to the fallen sons of God in Deuteronomy 32:8–9. From our discussion of Jude 6, you may remember that these sons of God from Genesis 6 were punished and now await judgment in chains in Hades/Sheol.

The demons of the New Testament are related to these beings, but they have a different story. Paul uses very specific and technical terms when he refers to the sons of God in the Old Testament (e.g., powers, principalities, authorities, thrones, dominions). In the Gospels, the most common Greek term used is *daimonion*, which we commonly translate as demons. Keener importantly points out, "The Greek term δαιμόνιον had a wide range of meaning, but the negative aspects of that range made it one of the most suitable terms for hostile spirits in early

Judaism."¹ So who are these beings? And are they the same as the powers and principalities, the Old Testament sons of God? A clue to their identity can be found in the adjective commonly used to describe them. They are most often referred to as "unclean spirits" or "evil spirits."

> When evening came, they brought to him many who were *demon-possessed*. He drove out the spirits with a word and healed all who were sick. (Matt 8:16)

> When an *unclean spirit* comes out of a person, it roams through waterless places looking for rest but doesn't find any. Then it says, "I'll go back to my house that I came from." Returning, it finds the house vacant, swept, and put in order. Then it goes and brings with it seven other spirits *more evil* than itself, and they enter and settle down there. As a result, that person's last condition is worse than the first. That's how it will also be with this evil generation. (Matt 12:43–45)

> In the synagogue there was a man with an *unclean demonic spirit* who cried out with a loud voice. (Luke 4:33)

1. Craig S. Keener, *Miracles: The Credibility of the New Testament Accounts*, 2 vols. (Grand Rapids: Baker Academic, 2011), 1:769.

Additionally, in the encounters these demons have with Jesus they know who he is, and they fear the fact that he has arrived upon earth through the incarnation. The terms *unclean spirit* and *evil spirit* were closely connected to specific ideas in Second Temple Jewish thought. Writings during this time referred to unclean and evil spirits as the disembodied spirits of the Nephilim. This leads us to believe the demons of the New Testament— the unclean, evil spirits that Jesus cast out of people—are not fallen angels or sons of God but the unclean spirits of the Nephilim trapped on earth after their physical bodies perished. The following Old Testament verses support this interpretation:

> Sheol below is eager to greet your coming,
> stirring up the *spirits of the departed* for you—
> all the rulers of the earth—
> making all the kings of the nations
> rise from their thrones. (Isa 14:9, emphasis added)

> The dead do not live;
> *departed spirits* do not rise up.
> Indeed, you have punished and destroyed them;
> you have wiped out all memory of them. (Isa 26:14, emphasis added)

Given the cultural understanding of Second Temple Jewish culture and the support of these verses in Isaiah,

STRIPPED, DISARMED, AND DEFEATED

I conclude that the unclean or evil spirits of the New Testament were most likely the disembodied spirits of the Nephilim of the Old Testament. Why? Because the term *unclean* suggests an unholy mixture that hints back to the Nephilim of Genesis 6. The Nephilim were the result of an "unholy" or "unclean" union between the sons of God and the daughters of man, so the name *unclean spirit* is fitting.

In conclusion, the term *demon* can be used broadly to refer to a supernatural or semidivine being, but as we examine the context, we should consider if it is a reference to the fallen, angelic sons of God (powers, principalities, etc.) or to their unclean offspring, the disembodied spirits of the Nephilim (unclean or evil spirit).

Yes, the powers and principalities are still active today. But they are not to be feared. And our response to them is to do exactly what Jesus told us to do. Nothing more and nothing less.

It may be helpful to look at the framework in which Paul's use of *powers and principalities* is rooted. Sometimes called an "inaugurated eschatological framework," a simpler way to describe it is the "already but not yet."[2] In this "already but not yet" reality—in which Christ has defeated our enemy, but there are still ongoing battles—we

---

2. Michael S. Heiser, "Principalities and Powers," *Dictionary of Paul and His Letters: A Compendium of Contemporary Biblical Scholarship*, ed. Scot McKnight (Downers Grove, IL: IVP Academic, 2023), 865.

find multiple instances where our enemy and his malevolent supernatural beings are still actively at work against Yahweh and his people.

> Put on the full armor of God so that you can stand against the schemes of the devil. For our struggle is not against flesh and blood, but against the rulers, against the authorities, against the cosmic powers of this darkness, against evil, spiritual forces in the heavens. For this reason take up the full armor of God, so that you may be able to resist in the evil day, and having prepared everything, to take your stand. (Eph 6:11–13)

> For I am persuaded that neither death nor life, nor angels nor rulers, nor things present nor things to come, nor powers, nor height nor depth, nor any other created thing will be able to separate us from the love of God that is in Christ Jesus our Lord. (Rom 8:38–39)

> Now the Spirit explicitly says that in later times some will depart from the faith, paying attention to deceitful spirits and the teachings of demons, through the hypocrisy of liars whose consciences are seared. (1 Tim 4:1–2)[3]

> And no wonder! For Satan disguises himself as an angel of light. So it is no great surprise if his servants also disguise themselves as servants of righteousness. Their end will be according to their works. (2 Cor 11:14–15)

---

3. See Heiser, "Principalities and Powers," 865.

So we wanted to come to you—even I, Paul, time and
again—but Satan hindered us. (1 Thess 2:18)

These verses are just a sample of what the New Testament
says about the evil beings still active in the world. We learn
they are still trying to oppress the people of God to keep
them blinded from the truth of the gospel. And while the
powers are still active today, their activity has been severely
limited from what it was in the world prior to the death,
resurrection, and ascension of Christ. In a legal sense, their
power was nullified when the perfect and unique Son of
God willingly submitted himself to death on a cross, was
resurrected from the grave after a period of three days, and
after forty days ascended to the heavens to take his rightful
place at the right hand of the Father.

At the cross Jesus defeated, disarmed, and stripped the
powers, principalities, and authorities and in so doing erased
the certificate of debt against humanity. Colossians 2:14–15
spells this out clearly: "He erased the certificate of debt, with
its obligations, that was against us and opposed to us, and
has taken it away by nailing it to the cross. He disarmed
the rulers and authorities and disgraced them publicly; he
triumphed over them in him" (Col 2:14–15). There are two
truths to pay close attention to here. First, the "certificate of
debt" or "legal demands" (*dogmata*) have been cleared. These
are the legal claims and demands the enemy was able to use
to divide and separate Yahweh from his people. Because God
is a perfect and just judge, the sin and idolatry of humanity
demanded a consequence. There was a legal requirement
that any breach of covenant loyalty must be punished and

179

accounted for. At the cross Jesus satisfied the legal debt of sin through the penal substitutionary atonement of Christ (propitiation), resulting in his victory (*Christus Victor*) over the dark powers of the world. The victory of Christ dealt with the legal demand our enemy could bring against us as well as the accompanying indebtedness of humanity. These accusations and debts owed were weapons wielded against humanity by the enemy in the unseen battle.[4] Through the cross, Christ erases (*exaleiphō*) the certificate of debt. This Greek verb also carries with it the meaning of "rooting out" (Ps 14; 50[51]:11; 108[109]; Isa 43:25; Jer 18:23; 2 Macc 12:42; Acts 3:19),[5] a poetic play on the impact of sin and the resolution the gospel brings. Because sin digs deep into the core of our humanity, creating corruption and chaos, the dark beings of the world seek to deeply entrench their hold over enslaved humanity and keep them separated from Christ by utilizing the power of sin. However, Christ on the cross roots out sin at its core. Christ sets us free from the entrapment of the enemy by freeing us from the power of sin and its henchman, death. This is why being freed from the legal demands of the law and the corresponding consequences of the law is "good news" (*euangelion*) or gospel. Through Christ, our relationship to our Father fundamentally changes from one of legal obedience to the free gift of adoption into his family. The legal requirements are fully met, and the accusations of our enemies no longer have the power they once did.

4. Garwood P. Anderson, "Law," in McKnight, *Dictionary of Paul and His Letters*, 617.
5. Markus Barth, Helmut Blanke, and Astrid B. Beck, *Colossians: A New Translation with Introduction and Commentary*, Anchor Yale Bible 34B (New Haven, CT: Yale University Press, 2008), 328.

Thus, a direct consequence of the victory of Christ on the cross is the "disarming and defeat" of the powers. However, we might still wonder how we can consider the powers disarmed and defeated if they are still active in the world. Once again, a retrieval of the Deuteronomy 32 worldview helps us make sense of this tension. On the surface, what seems to be a problem is very congruent within a worldview that sees spiritual warfare as a battle over the nations and peoples (*ethnos*) of the world. In Deuteronomy 32:8–9, Yahweh allotted the gods (*elohim*) to the nations as stewards to guard, protect, and guide them until such a time that he would reclaim them as his possession. However, these *elohim* failed in their task and entered into rebellion (Deut 4:19–20) by taking advantage of their delegated authority. They have been blinding the nations ever since. And because nations are made up of people, these powers have been taking people captive and blinding them to the truth about God. At the cross, Jesus disarms these powers. But what, more specifically, are they being disarmed from?

The Greek compound verb *apekdyomai* in Colossians 2:15 is found only one other time in the New Testament, in Colossians 3:9 in reference to "putt[ing] off the old self." The corresponding cognate noun *apekdysei* is used in Colossians 2:11 in connection with circumcision and putting off the old self. These instances make sense when we consider the context of the Jew-gentile distinction. But interpreters must still decide which English word is most appropriate for Colossians 2:15. Here I agree with G. K. Beale that the primary rendering of "stripped" or "unclothed" is closest to the meaning Paul intends, with a secondary idea of "disarmed" a close second. It seems likely that Paul is drawing on a Roman militaristic background where it was common for the Romans to strip their conquered enemies of clothing and parade them through the city in a procession that would often end with their death.[6]

So again, we ask, what have the powers been stripped and disarmed of? The answer is that the powers have been stripped and disarmed of *their ability to blind the nations from the good news of the gospel*. In other words, they have no legal right over the nations as their stewards any longer, which means they have no legal claim over the people in those nations. Christ on the cross nullifies the original stewardship granted to the sons of God (*bene elohim*) of the nations. Christ on the cross declares these powers illegitimate because he has fulfilled the judgment of Psalm 82:8. All the earth now belongs to him, the powers are judged, and the nations are reclaimed.

As we noted, the imagery behind this idea comes from the Roman world, where an enemy was stripped, disarmed, defeated, and paraded through the city toward their death. In our context today, we can say that our spiritual enemies have been stripped of their authority (the nations are no longer under their stewardship) and disarmed of any credible and legal rights (they can no longer bring a legal accusation against sinners where forgiveness has been offered and received). However, their eventual defeat is not yet final. It is still in process. They are stripped and naked yet *still on the march towards their impending death*. On this final march

---

6. G. K. Beale, *Colossians and Philemon*, Baker Exegetical Commentary on the New Testament (Grand Rapids: Baker Academic, 2019), 201.

our spiritual enemies are bent on engaging in the unseen battle by shouting insults, condemnations, and sowing doubts, yet the fact remains that they are being marched toward their doom.

I once heard a story about lions that had been fatally wounded. These wounded animals were even more dangerous during their final moments because they knew they had nothing left to lose. Perhaps the same is true of our spiritual enemies as they are on the way to their final defeat. They have nothing left to lose, so they will do whatever they can to sow discord and destruction, bringing as many as they can with them. Their powers are still formidable and at play, though severely limited.

The powers and principalities are at work in our individual lives and through the systems and structures in our society—including government and politics. To some extent I agree with N. T. Wright and Michael Bird's assessment of the powers as including "both what we might call any 'earthly' or 'political' rulers and what we might call any 'non-human' or 'supernatural' quasi-personal 'forces' that stand behind the 'earthly' rulers."[7] This fits well with the evidence we have reviewed in earlier chapters dealing with Daniel 7, as well as Isaiah 14 and the origin story of Satan. However, I would caution against any view of the powers today that sees them lacking agency, intellect, strategy, or personhood, as could be suggested with terms like "quasi-personal or subpersonal forces."[8] To the contrary, these are real, spiritual

---

7. N. T. Wright and Michael F. Bird, *Jesus and the Powers: Christian Political Witness in an Age of Totalitarian Terror and Dysfunctional Democracies* (Grand Rapids: Zondervan, 2024), 51.
8. In reading Wright and Bird we are left wondering what they believe the powers

beings with personality and a certain degree of agency. One needs only reflect on the words spoken by the demons of the New Testament to see this:

> What do you have to do with us, Jesus of Nazareth? Have you come to destroy us? I know who you are—the Holy One of God! (Mark 1:24)

> And he cried out with a loud voice, "What do you have to do with me, Jesus, Son of the Most High God? I beg you before God, don't torment me!" (Mark 5:7)

> In the synagogue there was a man with an unclean demonic spirit who cried out with a loud voice, "Leave us alone! What do you have to do with us, Jesus of Nazareth? Have you come to destroy us? I know who you are—the Holy One of God!" (Luke 4:33–34)

Perhaps one of the most important passages on this, 1 Corinthians 2:8, portrays the powers and rulers as strategically (i.e., intentionally, intellectually, and purposefully) working to crucify Christ.

> None of the rulers of this age knew this wisdom, because if they had known it, they would not have crucified the Lord of glory. (1 Cor 2:8)

---

are ontologically. The language of "creatures, quasi-personal, shadowy sub-personal, and quasi-personal forces of evil" leads the reader to question where Wright and Bird land on the connection of the powers to the *elohim* of the Old Testament, specifically Deut 32:9.

These powers are stripped and disarmed, both defeated and in the process of experiencing their final defeat. The powers are working within earthly political systems to undermine the spread of the gospel and the kingdom of God. This battle, while spiritual, is real and earthly, and it encompasses issues of justice, racism, the mass production of drugs used to exploit humanity, and the promotion of greed and wealth as a means of power and control.

What About Demon Exorcism?

In today's culture, there is a fascination with demon exorcism. Podcasts are conducting deep dives into the topic. TikTok and Instagram reels are going viral based on possible scenarios that require an exorcism or by documenting exorcisms. Yet there is nothing new under the sun. Exorcisms were not new or novel in church history, but they did have a starting point.

You may be surprised to learn that there is one thing Jesus does in his earthly ministry that we don't find prophets perform in the Old Testament: Jesus deals with demons through exorcism. Craig Keener rightly points out, "Exorcism is connected closely with the gospel of the kingdom, as a concrete manifestation of the deliverance it brings."[9] In fact, this is exactly what Jesus says during a exorcism in Luke 4.

Jesus enters a synagogue and the text says:

---

9. Keener, *Miracles*, 1:785.

> The scroll of the prophet Isaiah was given to him, and unrolling the scroll, he found the place where it was written: The Spirit of the Lord is on me, because he has anointed me to preach good news to the poor. He has sent me to proclaim release to the captives and recovery of sight to the blind, to set free the oppressed, to proclaim the year of the Lord's favor. (Luke 4:17–19)

In this moment, Jesus telegraphs why he is on earth and what he is about to do. He will indeed release the captives and set the oppressed free. He does so in the next two scenes, both of which take place in a house—first, the house of God, and second, Simon's house. These two houses remind us that nothing in the cosmos is outside the supremacy of Christ. And Jesus proves this.

First, Jesus casts out (exorcises) a demon from a man with authority (Luke 4:31–32). The Greek word *exousia* (ἐξουσία) has in mind authoritative power. In other words, Jesus isn't all bark and no bite. He does exactly what he says.

Authority without the power to enact that authority is weakness. Power without the authority to enact those actions is tyranny. Jesus isn't weak, and he isn't a tyrant. He is the king of the cosmos. Demon exorcism proves this fact.

When Jesus speaks, the demon is in shock. Why? The demons know who Jesus is and what he's about. When he walks into the room, everything changes for everyone, whether you are for or against him.

The demons know who Jesus is. The supernatural realm is fully aware of Jesus. Are you?

Eventually, Jesus has had enough of the interaction and "rebukes" the demon, silences it, and then commands it to come out of the person. Jesus has both authority *and* power.

The demon throws the man down and then comes out of him without hurting him at all.

The second scene takes place at Simon's house. This story must be placed in its original context. Simon's mother-in-law was suffering from a high fever. Fevers, sickness, disability, and hurts of all kinds are always the result of living in a broken world. But sometimes these things can be a result of affliction by supernatural malevolent forces that are bent on our destruction. The ancient view of the ancient Near East and the Greco-Roman world was that those people who "have a demon" and suffer from sickness are being oppressed by diabolical forces and need "release and rescue."

There are two significant hints that it is, in fact, an exorcism scene. First, the detail of the high fever, which in this cultural context could have been associated with demonic oppression or possession.[10] Luke notes that

---

10. James H. Charlesworth, *The Old Testament Pseudepigrapha*, vol. 1 (New Haven, CT: Yale University Press, 1983), 980. The Testament of Solomon says, "The nineteenth said, 'I am called Mardero. I inflict incurable fevers; write my name in some such way in the house, and I retreat immediately.'"

Simon's mother was suffering (*synechomenē*). We could also translate this Greek word as "held fast" or "in the grip" of the fever.[11] The second is the presence of the word *rebuked* (*epitiman*) in Greek, which is often used as a technical term for exorcisms.[12]

With this understanding, we have Simon's mother-in-law who has been "taken captive" by this fever. What does Jesus do? He rebukes the fever and releases her from its grip. Jesus is setting the captives free. As he sets captives free, he is announcing the inbreaking of the kingdom of God, saying, "If I drive out demons by the finger of God, then the kingdom of God has come upon you." (Luke 11:20 CSB)

What about us today? Are we called to participate in fighting demons and actively seek them out?[13] No, there does not seem to be any indication throughout the Scriptures that there is an imperative to actively pursue this practice. However, this also doesn't mean there isn't a need for it. Keener makes the interesting observation, "Missiologists show, however, that power encounters often occur when worldviews that depend on spiritual power come into conflict."[14] Therefore, this seems to be a nuanced discussion that requires wisdom, care, and most

11. David E. Garland, *Luke*, Zondervan Exegetical Commentary on the New Testament (Grand Rapids: Zondervan, 2012), 217.
12. Joseph A. Fitzmyer, *The Gospel According to Luke I–IX: Introduction, Translation, and Notes*, vol. 28, Anchor Yale Bible (New Haven, CT: Yale University Press, 2008), 546.
13. For a full treatment on demon exorcism, see Keener, *Miracles*, appendix B, 1:788–856.
14. Keener, *Miracles*, 1:856.

importantly, a calling and grace from the Lord personally to participate in it.

The powers don't need new ideas. They have been fighting this battle for a very long time and understand our weaknesses, working to exploit them by repackaging ancient, tried-and-true ideas in new ways. The powers entice us to return to the ways of the flesh and create new ways that prompt our inclination to engage in evil. They do this in several ways.

First, they encourage false worship and idolatry (Lev 17:7; Deut 32:15–17; Ps 106:35–37). Their goal is for us to give our worship and glory to anything other than Yahweh. The battle against idolatry is spiritual warfare, and while it can be extremely subtle, it can have devastating consequences. How does false worship and idolatry present itself in a twenty-first century context? Ask yourself or others what provides satisfaction, stability, and a sense of control in this world. Your answers may vary—money, vocation, education, family, hobbies, food, and so on. Now, ask yourself: How would I react if that thing was threatened, removed, or restricted? Your reaction, if evidence of a deep addiction to that object or a fear of it being taken away, may be an indication you have a functional idol. G. K. Beale puts it this way: "What we revere we will reflect, either to our ruin or restoration."[15] So one evidence of spiritual warfare in our lives is the objects of our reverence, and whether we love

---

15. G. K. Beale, *Union with the Resurrected Christ: Eschatological New Creation*

anything greater than God. The enemy wants our reverence (our affection, love, ambitions, desires) pointed toward anything other than the only one worthy of it. When we love something other than God in this way, we are engaged in spiritual adultery and working with the enemy to produce our own ruin. But when we turn our affection, love, and loyalty toward King Jesus, we are stepping firmly into the restoration and renewal that only Christ can give us through the power of the Holy Spirit.

The enemy also attempts to oppress the people of God. I agree with New Testament scholar Clint Arnold, who makes an important and clarifying distinction between oppression and possession in reference to spiritual warfare and the demonic. Those who now belong to the household of God can be oppressed, but they cannot be possessed. Arnold puts it this way: "Christians cannot be demon-possessed if one means by that expression ownership of a believer by Satan or demons. Believers are the property of God and belong exclusively to him."[16] Part of the challenge we have in this discussion is loss of nuance in translating from Greek to English. For instance, the English words *possessed* and *possession* imply a level of ownership. So when translating from the Greek we are faced with a question: Can Christians, those who are said to be "in Christ" (Gal 3:26) and have been delivered from the dominion of darkness (death and dark powers) into the kingdom of light (the household of God, Col 1:13), be "owned" by Satan? The answer is a resounding no. We

---

and New Testament Biblical Theology (Grand Rapids: Baker Academic, 2023), 281.
16. Clinton E. Arnold, *3 Crucial Questions About Spiritual Warfare* (Grand Rapids: Baker Academic, 1998), 138.

cannot find any place in the New Testament where believers are said to be possessed or owned by Satan or malevolent spirits. There are specific Greek words for ownership (*echō, hyparchō, peripoieō*), but these are not used to describe the instances in the New Testament that depict demonic activity.

Instead, the Greek word describing demonic presence and activity is *daimonizomai*. Perhaps the best translation of this word is "demonized" in English—to avoid the implication of being demon-possessed. Arnold points out one instance that comes close to "possession" but notes, "the expression 'he has a demon' (*echei daimonion*) does appear in the Gospels (e.g., Luke 4:33; 8:27), but the inverse, 'a demon has him,' never occurs."[17] For Christians who wish to be faithful to the text of Scripture, it is important to reframe the question of possession to that of influence. Arnold poses it this way: "We might ask, 'Can Christians come under a high degree of influence by a demonic spirit?' or, 'Is it possible for Christians to yield control of their bodies to a demonic spirit in the same way that they yield to the power of sin?'"[18]

The answer to this reframing from possession to demonic oppression and influence over the believer is yes. This also helps us make sense of people's experiences when they say they feel like they have been "under the control" of evil spirits yet identify as Christians. In fact, Tertullian comments on a situation where a known believer enters a theater and comes home with a demon. Through exorcism (the demon being cast out), the demon was asked how it was possible that a believer could come under such influence. The demon

---

17. Arnold, *3 Crucial Questions About Spiritual Warfare*, 79n10.
18. Arnold, *3 Crucial Questions About Spiritual Warfare*, 80.

simply replied, "And in truth I did it most righteously, for I found her in my domain."[19] So what do we do with these examples? I suggest that we seek to be clear with our language, nuancing between possession, control, ownership, influence, and oppression.

While "ownership" of a believer by dark forces is not possible, the possibility of demonic influence and, in my view, a higher degree of influence that approximates a type of control is possible. But it is only possible as the enemy creates a foothold within the life of a believer. Even in situations where this dual dwelling within the believer occurs (as they open themselves up to sin, dark arts, addictions, and the like) there is still opportunity for a believer to resist and fight back. Some would deny this concept of "dual dwelling" because believers are the temple of God and thus could not share a dwelling with the enemy (1 Cor 6:19). But the image of the believer who is the temple of God is about ownership. This still leaves open the issue of oppression and influence, even from within.

We have evidence of this aspect of the unseen battle in both the Old Testament and New Testament. In the Old Testament, the people of God desecrated the temple by bringing in idols and false worship within the physical geography of the temple. An example of this is found in 2 Kings 23 after the Torah was rediscovered at the beginning of King Josiah's reign. Part of the renewal and restoration of the temple involved the removal of objects of idolatry and the

---

19. Tertullian, "The Shows, or De Spectaculis," in *Latin Christianity: Its Founder, Tertullian*, ed. Alexander Roberts, James Donaldson, and A. Cleveland Coxe, trans. S. Thelwall, The Ante-Nicene Fathers, vol. 3 (Buffalo, NY: Christian Literature Company, 1885), 90.

false gods they represented from their current dwelling place in the temple of God, placing them outside of the temple. The issue wasn't whether they could or could not be physically present but that these idols and the spirits they represent do not "belong." Their presence compromises the holiness of the temple. In the New Testament, Paul is comfortable saying the power of sin and death can be so strong and influential in the life of the believer that it could "reign" (*basileuetō*) over them (Rom 5:17; 6:12). The sense of *basileueto* he has in mind is that of a ruling king, and spiritual conflict involves sin's attempt to reign as a counterfeit king over us. Paul warns us not to let this happen.

But how can this happen if a person belongs to Jesus? Paul warns us in Ephesians 4:27 not to give the enemy a foothold in our lives. As believers, we should take these warnings seriously. A foothold suggests an entry point that allows the potential of dual dwelling by an evil spiritual being, one that compromises the holiness of the temple of God, namely you and me. The purpose of a foothold is to work deeper in, not remain on the outside or periphery. Arnold puts it well when he comments that "demons will take as much room as we will give to them."[20]

This is precisely why the marching orders Paul gives us in Ephesians 6 are all about how we take a stand and fight this unseen battle. As a point of clarity, the people of God are never called to seek out a fight with the powers. They are not even called to preach at the powers. They are called to bear witness to the victory of Christ simply through their existence as the multiethnic family of God. N. T. Wright

---

20. Arnold, *3 Crucial Questions about Spiritual Warfare*, 82.

sums it up well: "The church, thus united through the grace of God in the death of Jesus, *is the sign to the principalities and powers that their time is up.*"[21] Their preaching is aimed instead toward those *human* family members who are alienated from the household of God and in active rebellion against Yahweh through their disbelief. The language Paul uses for how we engage against the powers is, however, worth further exploration.

First, Paul calls us to "stand" (*stenai*), which has in mind endurance and perseverance through struggle and hardship. The divine armor of God and the power of the Spirit enable us to do this simple but significant action in the presence of the onslaught of the enemy's tactics. We stand in the power of Christ. Our ability to stand is strictly through the empowerment of the Spirit. The believer is strengthened, equipped, and enabled to put on the armor of God precisely because of the empowerment of the Spirit. In other words, we are the passive recipients of a divine action, and as we receive the power of the Spirit, we are called to put on the armor of God.

Entire books have been written on the armor of God and the believer, and though I will not go into detail on every piece of armor, I will highlight a few things we should note about it and how it is to be used. First, we should note that the elements of the armor are not arbitrary or randomly chosen. For several, in fact, there seems to be an echo back to the Old Testament. In the story of David and Saul, for example, Saul desired David to adorn his armor, to wear the armor of the king. However, David was uncomfortable with it as

---

21. Tom Wright, *Justification: God's Plan and Paul's Vision* (London: SPCK, 2009), 149.

he had no training in it and frankly wasn't strong enough to wear it (1 Sam 17:38–39). However, in Ephesians 6 we are enabled and equipped to adorn the armor of the king because of the Spirit of God within us. What an incredible gift when we realize that Ephesians 6 isn't speaking of old rusty armor hidden away in a closet. Paul says we have been given the very armor of God—what God uses to equip himself for the battle. The echoes of this are found in Isaiah 59:16–17:

> He [the LORD] saw that there was no man—
> he was amazed that there was no one interceding;
> so his own arm brought salvation,
> and his own righteousness supported him.
>
> He put on righteousness as body armor,
> and a helmet of salvation on his head;
> he put on garments of vengeance for clothing,
> and he wrapped himself in zeal as in a cloak.
> (Isa 59:16–17)

When we adorn this divine armor we should have in mind Isaiah 59 and marvel that the armor we have is the armor of the King of kings and Lord of lords, Yahweh's very own armor. What better way to equip us to stand against the schemes of the enemy!

To discern the schemes and plans of our enemy, we must know the truth of God, which is why the entire armor is built around the belt of truth. Some New Testament commentators draw on the specific details of the Roman military outfit of Paul's time, and it is possible Paul has this in mind.

However, we should not neglect the Old Testament focus on the messianic warrior of Isaiah 11:5, "Righteousness will be a belt around his hips; faithfulness will be a belt around his waist." The truth spoken of here is the enactment of righteousness through faithfulness to the ethics of the King and his kingdom.[22] This is how we "stand" against the powers in defiance of their illegitimate claims upon humanity and creation: We daily put on the armor of the messianic warrior as we faithfully proclaim the ministry of reconciliation (2 Cor 5). Our efforts, by God's grace, will lead to the expansion of the gospel, the return of the lost, and their welcome into the household of God. The "already" victory of the unseen battle will be made visible through the formation of God's multiethnic church. The unity of God's family demonstrates that the powers have been stripped and disarmed, and their ultimate defeat is at hand as we await the day of the Lord.

---

22. Ernest Best, *A Critical and Exegetical Commentary on Ephesians*, International Critical Commentary (Edinburgh: T&T Clark International, 1998), 598.

CONCLUSION

A s you've read through the pages of this book, you've undoubtedly come across some theological ideas that may be new to you. The fundamental context for understanding this book and the narrative of the Bible is that God is a good Father who has a two-family household: an earthly, human family and a supernatural, angelic family. We've seen how that narrative unfolds with rebellions that take place in *both* spheres of this family, leading to division in the family of God. The supernatural family entices the human family into deep rebellion against Yahweh and then creates a competing household led by Satan, who eventually takes his place as head over other malevolent cosmic rulers. This unseen battle, the story behind the reality we commonly call spiritual warfare, is fought over the outcome of the human family. God desires to redeem and restore people to his household; Satan wishes to enslave, kill, and destroy them.

We could come to the end of this book and be tempted to feel anxious and concerned about this unseen battle. Yes, there is spiritual warfare taking place all around us, all the time, every day. However, giving in to anxiety would be a tragic mistake. As we reflect and meditate on the victory of

Jesus Christ over the powers and principalities, our perspective on the unseen battle should instead be one of victory and hope. We have the advantage of looking back to the past and seeing this unfolding battle from the vantage point of the cross, the resurrection, and ascension of Christ as King of kings and Lord of lords. Throughout the pages of this book we've talked about the gospel—the good news of the victory of Christ over the dark powers. In fact, the Greek word *euangelion* has a very particular context. It was often associated with a military battle.

For a moment, imagine with me that a battle is taking place. Kings wage war against one another; powerful princes muster abilities and knowledge far beyond our own. What happens on this battlefield will determine the result of the war. If our king wins, the war is won. Numerous skirmishes are being fought throughout the land. Then, suddenly, there is great news: Our king has won the decisive battle. What does he do? In the ancient world, there was no Instagram Live or YouTube, and he could not appear on Fox, CNN, or MSNBC to announce his victory. So what does he do instead? He takes his fastest horse and assigns his fastest rider to race as quickly as that rider can go to each of the battlefields to proclaim the good news (*euangelion*) that the war is won. Victory has been achieved. The enemy is defeated.

This task is of essential importance. The longer the wait for the arrival of the good news, the more deaths that can occur on the battlefield because the people have not yet heard of the king's decisive victory. Friend, we *are* in this battle, and we *have* been tasked with a great commission—to proclaim the news that the King of the cosmos has won! We have an urgent task at hand because you and I are witnesses to the victory of Christ. We proclaim his good news, and as such we should be filled with joy and urgency in our proclamation.

In the previous chapters we dove into the theology of Ephesians and traced several connections to the Old Testament and the larger context of the household of God. We touched on the temple of Artemis, which formed the conceptual background for the temple imagery that Paul brilliantly puts on display in Ephesians 2:18–20. The temple of Artemis, the household of the patron goddess of the city of Ephesus, was once considered one of the seven wonders of the world. In its prime the Artemision Temple was four times larger than the Parthenon in the Athenian Acropolis and had 127 pillars, each representing a different king, a reminder of the connection between the spiritual and the earthly. First constructed around 550 BCE, Pliny reports that it took 120 years to build, though that number is debated and it could have taken as long as 220 years.[1] At the center of the temple was an image of the goddess Artemis, whom we now understand to be one of the gods of the nations, a rebel *elohim* given stewardship over some of humanity. In 356 BCE, the temple of Artemis burned down, and many were discouraged, trying to understand how something like this could happen to the house of a powerful goddess. Plutarch sarcastically suggests that when the fire took place, Artemis (who was the goddess of

---

1. James M. Freeman and Harold J. Chadwick, *Manners and Customs of the Bible* (North Brunswick, NJ: Bridge-Logos, 1998), 531.

midwifery) was busy aiding in the birth of Alexander the Great and couldn't protect her own house.[2]

Sounds wild, huh?

From this point on, the temple is destroyed and rebuilt several times. The house of the goddess was built on marshy land and over time began to fall apart. The Goths end up destroying it around 263 BCE. It was rebuilt again, only to be destroyed 600 years later. Those 127 pillars representing once-famous kings were slowly pillaged for other architecture projects, and the temple was looted.

The home of the once-great goddess Artemis is nothing but ruins today. Only one pillar is still standing, and that pillar is home to a family of storks. In contrast to such ruin, however, the multiethnic family of God—a temple built with spiritual stones—is alive and well and growing bigger each passing day. The church advances the kingdom of God as the restored household of God and the visible representation of God's victory in the unseen battle.

Friends, at one point each of us lived under the rule of a wicked king, the Father of Lies, Satan. But through the work of Jesus, all who repent of their sins are forgiven and reclaimed and adopted back into the family of God. We are elevated from the earthly to the heavenly family, and we take our appropriate place in the divine council, that royal throne room where God holds court with his sons and daughters. The rebel sons of God, once stewards of the nations, have been rejected and replaced by adopted sons and daughters of God who have been raised with Christ and seated with

---

2. W. S. Lasor, "Artemis," in *The International Standard Bible Encyclopedia*, rev. ed., Geoffrey W. Bromiley, 4 vols. (Grand Rapids: Eerdmans, 1979–88), 1:307.

him in the heavens. And one day that heavenly court—where Jesus rules and reigns today at the right hand of the Father— will be reunited with the earth in a new Eden, as the garden city of God, the capital of a restored and renewed creation.

This is not just good news—it is the best news! For us it includes an invitation that every person, no matter their background or ethnicity, no matter what sin or wrong they have committed, can turn from sin to receive pardon and acceptance into God's family. The Father's arms are open wide to all people as he awaits the return of his wayward children. And best of all, we are not alone on this journey home. No, we are brought home by the "better" elder son, a good shepherd who seeks out his lost sheep, who finds his lost coin at any cost. We continue to fight alongside our King, for our foe is defeated but not yet fully conquered, and there are many yet to be saved from his power. But we fight knowing that God has defeated the enemy, won the battle, and united heaven and earth under one family (the *ekklēsia* of Jesus) and under one king (King Jesus), who sits now at the right hand of the Father. And that is good news.

Friends, let's rejoice! Christ is victorious, and that victory is ours today and forevermore.

Come quickly, Lord Jesus! We await your return when all things are made new and death, our enemy, will be swallowed up in victory, all to the glory of God the Father.

ACKNOWLEDGMENTS

I've always believed that theology should always be done in the context of community. This is why I am so grateful for the community that God has gifted me with throughout the journey of this project which started as my PhD dissertation. There are so many to thank.

To my Doktoravtor, Patrick Schreiner: You were literally a godsend. I had no clue who I would seek out as a PhD advisor as I was nearing the end of my coursework. Then you came to Midwestern, and I knew after I read your work on the ascension and saw you wearing Jordan 1s that I had to seek you out. Thank you for accepting me as your PhD student. You were never easy on me, and you always made me fight for clarity and cohesion in my argumentation. This is something I will take with me into every project I work on. Thank you for your encouragement and support. It truly is an honor to not only be counted among your PhD students but to be the first one you minted with a PhD!

To the Heiser Family: On behalf of so many, thank you. Thank you for continuing Mike's legacy through the Heiser Foundation. And thank you for championing those of us that continue to work through the implications of the Deuteronomy

32 worldview in the area of biblical theology. In many ways this is the book I always wanted to coauthor with Mike.

Lysa TerKeurst-Adams, your fingerprints are all over this book. For an academic leaning book, I found myself always asking the question you taught me: Where is the humanity in the text? Thank you for your years of mentorship, encouragement, and belief in me. You are a gift to me and my family, and I am forever indebted. Theology study days are the best days, and you helped me clarify so many thoughts and ideas during my random theology ADHD moments in our study sessions. Thank you!

Leah and Shae, thank you for always pushing me to fight for the everyday average Bible reader. I found that even more important in this project, and I often imagined you both raising your hand saying, "Joel, hold up. Just raising my hand and asking this question for the average everyday Bible reader." You stopped me dead in my tracks to clarify and explain so many times, and I know those that read this book will be able to make sense of the theological substance because of your influence.

Meredith, thank you for believing in me as an author. You are the best agent, and Britt, the kids, and I truly love you and your family. What a joy to do ministry and life together. Thank you for pushing me to always fight for the reader and helping me hone my thoughts and ideas.

Luke, Nate, thanks for asking me about Bigfoot and creating a space with *Blurry Creatures* where I can "speculate" with theology friends. Grateful for your friendship!

Mom, thank you for covering me in prayer as I wrote on such a significant topic like spiritual warfare. I'm so grateful for how you've always called us to follow Jesus with all of our hearts and minds.

Britt, I could never have done this without you. Thank you for creating space for me to research and write, holding things down with the kids, and enduring my random thoughts about the unseen realm and spiritual beings in our world today. You've always believed in me and encouraged me. I wouldn't be who I am today without you.

Liam, Levi, Lucas, and EmJ, I long for you to be captivated by Jesus, the one true God of heaven and earth. May you never be deceived by the false gods of the nations and always be enamored by the goodness of Yahweh.

APPENDIX

Teraphim and the Household Gods

Scholars have worked to identify the *teraphim* that are depicted in Scripture. The generally accepted view is that these *teraphim* were ancestor deities. But there may be much more to them within the backdrop of the Deuteronomy 32 worldview. For instance, K. van der Toorn says, "There have been innumerable attempts to explain the etymology of *tᵉrāpîm*."[1] The word *teraphim* functions metonymically as a term for "idolatry and divination in general at 1 Sam 15:23 (RSV 'idolatry')."[2] The *teraphim* were common in Syria, in

---

1. K. van der Toorn and T. J. Lewis, "תְּרוּעָה and תְּרָפִים," in *Theological Dictionary of the Old Testament*, ed. G. Johannes Botterweck, Helmer Ringgren, and Heinz-Josef Fabry, trans. David E. Green, 17 vols. (Grand Rapids: Eerdmans, 2006), 15:778. Hamilton presents four possibilities: (1) old rags, (2) interpreters, (3) demon/spirit, in connection to the Hittite *tarpis*, and (4) healers, based on the Septuagint connection to *therapeuō*, indicating that the *teraphim* are ancient ancestors who provide healing. Hamilton ultimately says, "The third and fourth options seem most likely, but none is convincing." See Victor P. Hamilton, *The Book of Genesis, Chapters 18–50*, The New International Commentary on the Old Testament (Grand Rapids: Eerdmans, 1995), 293.
2. Allen C. Myers, ed., *The Eerdmans Bible Dictionary* (Grand Rapids: Eerdmans, 1987), 994. The etymology of the word is debated and ultimately lost. Earlier Jewish commentaries suggested a connection with *toreph*, which means "foulness." However, if this was true, the meaning was eventually

Palestine, and among the Israelites throughout the preexilic period.[3] The *teraphim* are most commonly interpreted and translated as household deities (Gen 31:19; 1 Sam 19:13; 16).[4] An important clue into the nature of the *teraphim* may be found in its linguistic and cultural similarity to the Hittite "*tarpiš*, a spirit that can be either protective or malevolent."[5] In 1966 the German Hittitologist H. Otten noted that *shedu* in a Babylonian column was defined in Hittite as *tarpis*.[6] We should recall that the *shedu* are connected to the *shed* and refer to the sons of God. Therefore, the establishment of a relation between *tarpis* and *shedu* connects all these terms. Hoffner, commenting on the connection between *tarpis* and *shedu*, says:

---

substituted and the original lost. A later possibility, suggested by Schwally, is a connection with *raphah*, which relates to *rephaim*, or shades, in Isa 14. Ultimately, the origin of the word cannot be explicitly stated; however, the possibility of a connection with shades follows the larger setting of the household gods and their relationship to the sons of God and disinheritance of the nations. See Adam C. Welch, "תְּרָפִים," in *A Dictionary of the Bible: Dealing with Its Language, Literature, and Contents Including the Biblical Theology*, ed. James Hastings et al. (New York: Scribner's, 1911–12), 718.

3. Paul J. Achtemeier, ed., *Harper's Bible Dictionary* (San Francisco: Harper & Row, 1985), 1035. See also 2 Kgs 23:24.

4. Welch, "תְּרָפִים," 718. Hoffmann (1905) followed by G. von Rad and A. Alt understand the תְּרָפִים to be a form of cultic mask. See Harry A. Hoffner Jr., "The Linguistic Origins of תְּרָפִים," *Bibliotheca Sacra* 124 (1967): 231. Van Der Toorn understands the *teraphim* to be figurines of dead ancestors. He makes this appeal through observation that *teraphim* are called in Gen 31:30. Also, since *elohim* refers to spirits and not gods in 1 Sam 28:13; Isa 8:19, the *teraphim* could be spirits and not deities. This may be true, but *elohim* is connected to *lashedim* in Deut 32:17, and therefore this argumentation seems to be weakened. See Shawn W. Flynn, "The Teraphim in Light of Mesopotamian and Egyptian Evidence," *Catholic Biblical Quarterly* 74 (2012): 694–711. Additionally, there could be a comparison drawn between the *teraphim* and the *Lares* and *Penates* in Roman times.

5. Myers, *The Eerdmans Bible Dictionary*, 994.

6. Cited in Hoffner, "Linguistic Origins," 235.

Shēdu has two different but related meanings, depend-
ing upon its context. When it is grouped with another
word, *lamassu*, the two words denote protective deities
or guardian spirits, which supervise the personal safety of
the person under their charge. When *shēdu* occurs alone
(without *lamassu*), it often denotes an evil spirit or demon
whose presence is undesirable and who must be confined
in the depths of the netherworld by means of spells and
incantations. If the Hittite scribe used his word, *tarpis*, to
define Babylonian *shēdu*, did it also have the same range
of meanings? A study of the other occurrences of *tarpis*
in Hittite texts reveals that it had.[7]

This discovery has a vital implication on how we understand the meaning of *teraphim*. If the *teraphim* are in fact
understood as the same type of spirits as the *tarpis*, and the
tarpis are referred to as *shedu*, then the household gods of
Terah, Nahor, and Laban that Rachel steals are *bene ha
elohim* and are conceptually related to *shed*, the two terms
found in Deuteronomy 32:17. Furthering this possibility is
that the lexical lists that include *tarpis* often have the term,
"represented by the Akkadogram *ŠĒDU*, '(protective) spirit,'
a meaning that could in many respects be associated with
Heb. *t°rāpîm*."[8] K. van der Toorn and Lewis say, "Since the
Hebrew lexicons do not provide a convincing etymology
for *t°rāpîm*, Hoffner's suggestion has found considerable

7. Hoffner, "Linguistic Origins," 236. For a technical discussion of the relationship of *tarpis* and *teraphim*, see H. A. Hoffner Jr., "Hittite *Tarpiš* and Hebrew
Terāphîm," *Journal of Near Eastern Studies* 27 (1968): 61–68.
8. van der Toorn and Lewis, "תְּרוּעָה and תְּרָפִים," 778.

support."[9] Additionally, as noted earlier, the *shedu* were territorial sprits that had a protecting or guarding function. The Hittite temples were considered houses, and the Hittite *tarpis* can now be understood as a territorial type of spirit that protects a temple or the dwelling place of the deity. In other words, the Hittite temples are houses of the deity. These houses were territorial (and at times national) and were occupied and protected by the *teraphim* (*shed*). Therefore, the *teraphim* and *shed* have an overlapping conceptual meaning.

The linguistic support behind the household gods being understood as the *shed* of Deuteronomy 32:17 is accompanied by functional support. In other words, the nature and function of the household gods is similar in terms of protection (territorial) and inheritance rights (familial/national). The function of the household gods can be understood by questioning the motive and desire for Rachel to steal her father's *teraphim*.[10] Chrysostom makes an important observation in regard to the effort and desire of Rachel to steal the household gods, saying, "Consider how [Rachel] went to so much trouble as to steal nothing else of her father's than the household gods alone and did it without her husband

9. van der Toorn and Lewis, "תְּרוּעָה and תְּרָפִים," 778.
10. The presence of the household gods is well established in the Mesopotamian households. Vreugdenhil notes that these household deities played an important role in the domestic life of the people within the household as the deity was responsible for health, wealth, and the reputation of the family. Vreugdenhil says, "Every self-respecting Mesopotamian household possessed such household gods. These familial deities were daily lavished with food-offerings and prayers." As a direct connection to the situation of Rachel, Vreugdenhil comments on the ancient Near Eastern context, "Whoever leaves the house, however, puts himself beyond the sphere of influence of the familial gods and ancestors and is thus even more vulnerable." See Gerrit C. Vreugdenhil, *Psalm 91 and Demonic Menace*, Old Testament Studies 77 (Leiden: Brill, 2020), 33–107.

noticing; Jacob would not have allowed it to happen, you see."[11] This leads us to question the motivation of Rachel's actions, longings, and desires, and why they would be aimed toward these *teraphim*. Rachel takes the *teraphim* that represent ancestor *elohim* who guarded the house. In doing so, she retains an attachment to her family in the land of Haran.

Myers notes the connection of Rachel's theft of the *teraphim* (Gen 31:19) in relation to the texts from Nuzi that were associated with inheritance rights and the possession of the "household gods." Myers claims, "Although direct Nuzi influence has been challenged, in early Israelite practice also the תְּרָפִים [*teraphim*] may have been tokens of clan or family status, with implications for inheritance and/or succession."[12] The household gods clearly have a connection with both inheritance and familial lineage.[13] Sarna comments on the practice of the Nuzi to connect the birthright or clan

---

11. Mark Sheridan, ed., *Genesis 12–50*, Ancient Christian Commentary on Scripture (Downers Grove, IL: InterVarsity Press, 2002), 207.
12. Myers, *The Eerdmans Bible Dictionary*, 994. Greenberg rejects the inheritance or entitlement motive. Rather, he posits the motivation for Rachel is tied into who would succeed as the head of the household. See M. Greenberg, "Another Look at Rachel's Theft of the תְּרָפִים," *Journal Biblical Literature* 81 (1962): 239–48. This may be true, but the sharp distinction may be unnecessary. Further, the purpose of this dissertation and the argument that familial motivation is present within the context of the *teraphim*, both possibilities may be seen to correlate to each other. In other words, inheritance and entitlement seem to flow logically to the inheritance of the head of the household or an heir to an estate.
13. Some scholars have seen a correlation with the *teraphim* and the "*ilānī* of the northern Mesopotamian cultures, which in particular at the ancient city of Nuzi were passed on by the father to his chief heir." See Hoffner, "Linguistic Origins," 232. Speiser says, "According to the Nuzi documents, which have been found to reflect time and again the social customs of Haran . . . , possession of the house gods could signify legal title to a given estate, particularly in cases out of the ordinary, involving daughters, sons-in-law, or adopted sons." See E. A. Speiser, *Genesis: Introduction, Translation, and Notes*, Anchor Yale Bible 1 (New Haven, CT: Yale University Press, 2008), 250.

leadership status based on possession of the household gods. A Nuzi contract stipulates, "If Nashwi has a son of his own, he shall divide [the estate] equally with Wullu, but the son of Nashwi shall take the gods of Nashwi. However, if Nashwi does not have a son of his own, then Wullu shall take the gods of Nashwi."[14] The point being made here is that the household gods were intimately connected to birthrights and inheritance. In other words, there was a cost to abandon these gods. There was a risk associated with putting your faith in Yahweh. Not much is different today. We have various gods and idols that are vying for our attention and affection; to deny them and turn to Yahweh comes with a cost, something that Rachel herself had to deal with.

14. Nahum M. Sarna, *Genesis*, JPS Torah Commentary (Philadelphia: Jewish Publication Society, 1989), 216.

BIBLIOGRAPHY

Abbott, Thomas Kingsmill. *A Critical and Exegetical Commentary on the Epistles to the Ephesians and to the Colossians.* International Critical Commentary. New York: Scribner's, 1909.

Achtemeier, Paul J., ed. *Harper's Bible Dictionary.* San Francisco: Harper & Row, 1985.

Adams, Edward. *Constructing the World: A Study in Paul's Cosmological Language.* Studies of the New Testament and Its World. Edinburgh: T&T Clark, 2000.

Alexander, T. Desmond, and David W. Baker, eds. *Dictionary of the Old Testament: Pentateuch.* Downers Grove, IL: IVP Academic, 2003.

Allis, Oswald T. "The Blessing of Abraham." *The Princeton Theological Review* 25 (1927): 263–98.

Alpert Nakhai, Beth. "The Household as Sacred Space." In *Family and Household Religion: Toward a Synthesis of OT Studies, Archaeology, Epigraphy, and Cultural Studies,* 53–72. Winona Lake, IN: Eisenbrauns, 2014.

Arndt, William, Frederick W. Danker, Walter Bauer, and F. Wilbur Gingrich. *A Greek-English Lexicon of the New Testament and Other Early Christian Literature.* Chicago: University of Chicago Press, 2000.

Arnold, Bill T., and Brent A. Strawn, eds. *The World around the*

Old Testament: The People and Places of the Ancient Near East. Grand Rapids: Baker Academic, 2016.

Arnold, Clinton E. Power and Magic: The Concept of Power in Ephesians in Light of Its Historical Setting. Eugene: Wipf & Stock, 1989.

———. Ephesians. Zondervan Exegetical Commentary on the New Testament. Grand Rapids: Zondervan Academic, 2010.

———. Powers of Darkness: Principalities and Powers in Paul's Letters. Downers Grove, IL: IVP Academic, 1992.

Athenagoras. Ante-Nicene Fathers. Vol. 2, Fathers of the Second Century: Hermas, Tatian, Athenagoras, Theophilus, and Clement of Alexandria. Edited by Alexander Roberts, James Donaldson, and A. Cleveland Coxe. Buffalo: Christian Literature Company, 1885.

August, Jared M. "The Messianic Hope of Genesis: The Protoevangelium and Patriarchal Promises." Themelios 42 (2017): 46–62.

Balz, Horst Robert, and Gerhard Schneider. Exegetical Dictionary of the New Testament. Grand Rapids: Eerdmans, 1990–93.

Barry, John D., et al., eds. The Lexham Bible Dictionary. Bellingham, WA: Lexham, 2016.

Barth, Markus. Ephesians: Introduction, Translation, and Commentary on Chapters 1–3. Anchor Yale Bible 34. New Haven, CT: Yale University Press, 2008.

Baugh, S. M. Ephesians. Evangelical Exegetical Commentary. Bellingham, WA: Lexham, 2015.

Beale, G. K. The Temple and the Church's Mission: A Biblical Theology of the Dwelling Place of God. New Studies in Biblical Theology 17. Downers Grove, IL: IVP Academic, 2004.

Beale, G. K., and D. A. Carson. Commentary on the New Testament Use of the Old Testament. Grand Rapids: Baker Academic, 2007.

Beckwith, Roger. "The Creation and Fall of the Angels." The Churchman 124 (2010): 37–42.

Best, Ernest. *A Critical and Exegetical Commentary on Ephesians.* International Critical Commentary. Edinburgh: T&T Clark, 1998.

Block, Daniel I. *The Book of Ezekiel, Chapters 25–48.* The New International Commentary on the Old Testament. Grand Rapids: Eerdmans, 1997.

———. *The Gods of the Nations: Studies in Ancient Near Eastern National Theology. Second Edition.* Eugene, OR: Wipf & Stock, 1988.

Bock, Darrell L. *Ephesians: An Introduction and Commentary.* Tyndale New Testament Commentaries 10. London: Inter-Varsity Press, 2019.

Bodel, John P., and Saul M. Olyan. *Household and Family Religion in Antiquity.* Malden: Wiley, 2008.

Boles, Kenneth L. *Galatians and Ephesians.* College Press NIV Commentary. Joplin, MO: College, 1993.

Botterweck, G. Johannes, Helmer Ringgren, and Heinz-Josef Fabry, eds. *Theological Dictionary of the Old Testament.* Translated by John T. Willis, Geoffrey W. Bromiley, David E. Green, and Douglas W. Stott. Grand Rapids: Eerdmans, 1977–2012.

Brannan, Rick, Ken M. Penner, Israel Loken, Michael Aubrey, and Isaiah Hoogendyk, eds. *The Lexham English Septuagint.* Bellingham, WA: Lexham, 2012.

Briggs, Charles A., and Emilie Grace Briggs. *A Critical and Exegetical Commentary on the Book of Psalms.* International Critical Commentary. New York: Scribner's, 1906–7.

Bromiley, Geoffrey W., ed. *The International Standard Bible Encyclopedia, Revised.* Grand Rapids: Eerdmans, 1979–88.

Brown, Colin, ed. *New International Dictionary of New Testament Theology.* Grand Rapids: Zondervan, 1986.

Bruce, F. F. *The Epistles to the Colossians, to Philemon, and to the Ephesians.* The New International Commentary on the New Testament. Grand Rapids: Eerdmans, 1984.

Burke, Trevor J. *Adopted into God's Family: Exploring a Pauline Metaphor*. New Studies in Biblical Theology 22. Downers Grove, IL: IVP Academic, 2006.

Burnside, Jonathan P. *The Signs of Sin: Seriousness of Offence in Biblical Law*. Journal for the Study of the Old Testament Supplement Series 364. Sheffield: Sheffield Academic Press, 2003.

Caird, G. B. *Principalities and Powers: A Study in Pauline Theology: The Chancellor's Lectures for 1954 at Queen's University, Kingston Ontario*. Eugene, OR: Wipf & Stock, 2003.

Calvin, John. *Commentaries on the Epistles of Paul to the Galatians and Ephesians*. Edited by William Pringle. Bellingham, WA: Logos Bible Software, 2010.

Carr, Wesley. *Angels and Principalities: The Background, Meaning and Development of the Pauline Phrase Hai Archai Kai Hai Exousiai*. New York: Cambridge University Press, 2005.

Carson, D. A., R. T. France, J. A. Motyer, and G. J. Wenham, eds. *New Bible Commentary: 21st Century Edition*. 4th ed. Leicester: Inter-Varsity Press, 1994.

Carroll, M. Daniel R. "Blessing the Nations: Toward a Biblical Theology of Mission from Genesis." *Bulletin for Biblical Research* 10 (2000): 17–33.

Charlesworth, James H. *The Old Testament Pseudepigrapha and the New Testament: Expansions of the "Old Testament" and Legends, Wisdom, and Philosophical Literature, Prayers, Psalms and Odes, Fragments of Lost Judeo-Hellenistic Works*. 2 vols. New Haven, CT: Yale University Press, 1983–85.

Clines, D. J. A. "The Image of God in Man." *Tyndale Bulletin* 19 (1968): 53–103.

Cockerill, Gareth Lee. "Hebrews 1:6: Source and Significance." *Bulletin for Biblical Research* 9 (1999): 51–65.

Cohick, Lynn H. *Ephesians*. New Covenant Commentary Series. Eugene, OR: Cascade, 2010.

Cole, Graham A. *Against the Darkness: The Doctrine of Angels,*

Satan, and Demons. Foundations of Evangelical Theology. Wheaton, IL: Crossway, 2019.

Dean, David Andrew. "Covenant, Conditionality, and Consequence: New Terminology and a Case Study in the Abrahamic Covenant." *Journal of the Evangelical Theological Society* 57 (2014): 281–308.

DeRouchie, Jason S. "From Condemnation to Righteousness: A Christian Reading of Deuteronomy." *The Southern Baptist Journal of Theology* 18 (2014): 87–113.

DeWitt, Dale S. "The Historical Background of Genesis 11:1–9: Babel or Ur?" *Journal of the Evangelical Theological Society* 22 (1979): 15–26.

Di Berardino, Angelo, and James Hoover, eds. *Encyclopedia of Ancient Christianity.* Translated by Joseph T. Papa, Erik A. Koenke, and Eric E. Hewett. Downers Grove, IL: IVP Academic, 2014.

Driver, S. R. *The Book of Daniel with Introduction and Notes.* The Cambridge Bible for Schools and Colleges. Cambridge: Cambridge University Press, 1900.

Driver, Samuel Rolles, and George Buchanan Gray. *A Critical and Exegetical Commentary on the Book of Job.* International Critical Commentary. Edinburgh: T&T Clark, 1921.

Evans, Craig A. "Inaugurating the Kingdom of God and Defeating the Kingdom of Satan." *Bulletin for Biblical Research* 15 (2005): 49–77.

Flynn, Shawn W. "The Teraphim in Light of Mesopotamian and Egyptian Evidence." *Catholic Biblical Quarterly* 74 (2012): 694–711.

Foulkes, Francis. *Ephesians: An Introduction and Commentary.* Tyndale New Testament Commentaries 10. Downers Grove, IL: InterVarsity Press, 1989.

Freedman, David Noel, et al., eds. *The Anchor Yale Bible Dictionary.* New York: Doubleday, 1992.

García Martínez, Florentino, and Eibert J. C. Tigchelaar, eds. *The*

Dead Sea Scrolls Study Edition (Translations). Leiden: Brill, 1997–98.

Gesenius, Friedrich Wilhelm. *Gesenius' Hebrew Grammar*. Edited by E. Kautzsch and Sir Arthur Ernest Cowley. 2nd English ed. Oxford: Clarendon, 1910.

Gianoulis, George C. "Is Sonship in Romans 8:14–17 a Link with Romans 9?" *Bibliotheca Sacra* 166 (2009): 70–83.

Goldingay, John E. *Daniel*. Word Biblical Commentary 30. Dallas: Word, 1989.

Gombis, Timothy G. *The Drama of Ephesians: Participating in the Triumph of God*. Downers Grove, IL: IVP Academic, 2010.

———. "Ephesians 3:2–13: Pointless Digression, or Epitome of the Triumph of God in Christ?" *Westminster Theological Journal* 66 (2004): 313–23.

Green, Gene L. *The Letters to the Thessalonians*. The Pillar New Testament Commentary. Grand Rapids: Eerdmans, 2002.

Greenberg, Moshe. *Ezekiel 21–37: A New Translation with Introduction and Commentary*. Anchor Yale Bible 22A. New Haven, CT: Yale University Press, 2008.

Gromacki, Gary. "The Spiritual War for Ephesus." *Journal of Ministry and Theology Volume* 15 (2011): 77–130.

Gupta, Nijay K. "'They Are Not Gods!' Jewish and Christian Idol Polemic and Greco-Roman Use of Cult Statues." *Catholic Biblical Quarterly* 76 (2014): 704–19.

Hagner, Donald A. *The New Testament: A Historical and Theological Introduction*. Grand Rapids: Baker Academic, 2012.

Hamilton, Victor P. *The Book of Genesis, Chapters 1–17*. New International Commentary on the Old Testament. Grand Rapids: Eerdmans, 1990.

———. *The Book of Genesis, Chapters 18–50*. New International Commentary on the Old Testament. Grand Rapids: Eerdmans, 1995.

Hannah, Darrell D. "Guardian Angels and Angelic National Patrons in Second Temple Judaism and Early Christianity."

In *Angels: The Concept of Celestial Beings—Origins, Development and Reception*, edited by Friedrich Vinzenz Reiterer, Tobias Nicklas, and Karin Schöpflin, 413–36. Berlin: de Gruyter, 2007.

Harris, R. Laird, Gleason L. Archer Jr., and Bruce K. Waltke, eds. *Theological Wordbook of the Old Testament*. Chicago: Moody, 1999.

Harris, W. Hall III. "'The Heavenlies' Reconsidered: Οὐρανός and =Ἐπουράνιος in Ephesians." *Bibliotheca Sacra* 148 (1991): 72–89.

Hartley, John E. *The Book of Job*. New International Commentary on the Old Testament. Grand Rapids: Eerdmans, 1988.

Hastings, James, et al., eds. *A Dictionary of the Bible: Dealing with Its Language, Literature, and Contents Including the Biblical Theology*. New York: T&T Clark, 1911–12.

Hastings, James, John A. Selbie, and Louis H. Gray, eds. *Encyclopædia of Religion and Ethics*. Edinburgh: T&T Clark, 1908–26.

Hastings, James, John A. Selbie, John C. Lambert, and Shailer Mathews, eds. *Dictionary of the Bible*. New York: Scribner's, 1909.

Hawthorne, Gerald F., Ralph P. Martin, and Daniel G. Reid, eds. *Dictionary of Paul and His Letters*. Downers Grove, IL: IVP Academic, 1993.

Heiser, Michael S. "Monotheism, Polytheism, Monolatry, or Henotheism? Toward an Assessment of Divine Plurality in the Hebrew Bible." *Bulletin for Biblical Research* 18 (2008): 1–30.

———. *Demons: What the Bible Really Says about the Powers of Darkness*. Bellingham, WA: Lexham, 2020.

———. *The Unseen Realm: Recovering the Supernatural Worldview of the Bible*. Bellingham, WA: Lexham, 2015.

Hiebert, Theodore. "The Tower of Babel and the Origin of the World's Cultures." *Journal of Biblical Literature* 126 (2007): 29–58. https://doi.org/10.2307/27638419.

Hobbins, John F. "Critical Biblical Theology in a New Key a Review Article." *Journal for the Evangelical Study of the Old Testament* 1 (2011–12): 81–102.

Hoehner, Harold W. *Ephesians: An Exegetical Commentary.* Grand Rapids: Baker Academic, 2002.

Hoehner, Harold W., Philip W. Comfort, and Peter H. Davids. *Ephesians, Philippians, Colossians, 1 and 2 Thessalonians, Philemon.* Cornerstone Biblical Commentary 16. Carol Stream, IL: Tyndale, 2008.

Hoffner, Harry A., Jr. "The Linguistic Origins of תְּרָפִים." *Bibliotheca Sacra* 124 (1967): 230–37.

Jabini, Frank. "Sons of God Marrying Daughters of Man: An Exercise in Integrated Theology." *Conspectus* 14 (2012): 81–122.

Jastrow, Morris, Jr. *The Religion of Babylonia and Assyria.* Boston: Ginn, 1898.

Jeon, Jeong Koo. "The Abrahamic Covenant and the Kingdom of God." *The Confessional Presbyterian* 7 (2011): 123–38.

Josephus, Flavius. *The Works of Josephus: Complete and Unabridged.* Edited by William Whiston. Peabody, MA: Hendrickson, 1987.

Joüon, Paul, and T. Muraoka. *A Grammar of Biblical Hebrew.* Rome: Pontificio Istituto Biblico, 2006.

Keil, Carl Friedrich, and Franz Delitzsch. *Commentary on the Old Testament.* Peabody, MA: Hendrickson, 1996.

Kidner, Derek. *Genesis: An Introduction and Commentary.* Tyndale Old Testament Commentaries 1. Downers Grove, IL: InterVarsity Press, 1967.

Kittel, Gerhard, Geoffrey W. Bromiley, and Gerhard Friedrich, eds. *Theological Dictionary of the New Testament.* Grand Rapids: Eerdmans, 1964–.

Kline, Meredith G. "Divine Kingship and Genesis 6:1–4." *Westminster Theological Journal* 24 (1961): 187–204.

Koehler, Ludwig, Walter Baumgartner, M. E. J. Richardson, and

BIBLIOGRAPHY

Johann Jakob Stamm. *The Hebrew and Aramaic Lexicon of the Old Testament*. Leiden: Brill, 1994–2000.

Kuruvilla, Abraham. "From 'Far' to 'Near'! A Pericopal Theology Guide to Preaching Ephesians 2:11–22." *The Journal of the Evangelical Homiletics Society* 20 (2020): 67–86.

Lee, Chee-Chiew. "גיר in Genesis 35:11 and the Abrahamic Promise of Blessings for the Nations." *Journal of the Evangelical Theological Society* 52 (2009): 467–82.

Liefeld, Walter L. *Ephesians*. IVP New Testament Commentary 10. Downers Grove, IL: InterVarsity Press, 1997.

Lincoln, Andrew T. *Ephesians*. Word Biblical Commentary 42. Dallas: Word, 1990.

Lioy, Daniel T. "A Comparative Analysis of the Song of Moses and Paul's Speech to the Athenians." *Conspectus* 16 (2014): 1–46.

———. "The Garden of Eden as a Primordial Temple or Sacred Space for Humankind." *Conspectus* 10 (2010): 25–57.

Longman, Tremper, III, and Peter Enns, eds. *Dictionary of the Old Testament: Wisdom, Poetry, and Writings*. Downers Grove, IL: IVP Academic, 2008.

Longman, Tremper, III. "The Divine Warrior: The New Testament Use of an Old Testament Motif." *Westminster Theological Journal* 44 (1982): 290–307.

MacLeod, David J. "The Broken Wall, or: From Alienation to Reconciliation." *Emmaus Journal* 14 (2005): 135–66.

Macmillan, Kerr D. "Exegetical Theology. Review of Light on the Old Testament from Babel by Albert T. Clay." *Princeton Theological Review* 6 (1908): 662–65.

Martin, Oren R. *Bound for the Promised Land: The Land Promise in God's Redemptive Plan*. New Studies in Biblical Theology 34. Downers Grove, IL: IVP Academic, 2015.

Martin, Ralph P., and Peter H. Davids, eds. *Dictionary of the Later New Testament and Its Developments*. Downers Grove, IL: IVP Academic, 1997.

McClellan, Daniel. "The Gods-Complaint: Psalm 82 as a Psalm of Complaint." *Journal of Biblical Literature* 137 (2018): 833–51.

Merrill, Eugene H. "Rashi, Nicholas de Lyra, and Christian Exegesis." *Westminster Theological Journal* 38 (1975): 66–79.

Michalak, Aleksander R. *Angels as Warriors in Late Second Temple Jewish Literature*. Wissenschaftliche Untersuchungen Zum Neuen Testament 2/330. Tübingen: Mohr Siebeck, 2012.

Mody, Rohintan Keki. "The Relationship between Powers of Evil and Idols in 1 Corinthians 8:4–5 and 10:18–22 in the Context of the Pauline Corpus and Early Judaism." *Tyndale Bulletin* 60 (2008): 295–98.

Montanari, Franco, Madeleine Goh, and Chad Schroeder, eds. *The Brill Dictionary of Ancient Greek*. Leiden: Brill, 2015.

Morales, L. Michael. *Who Shall Ascend the Mountain of the Lord? A Biblical Theology of the Book of Leviticus*. New Studies in Biblical Theology 37. Downers Grove, IL: IVP Academic, 2015.

Muddiman, John. *The Epistle to the Ephesians*. Black's New Testament Commentary. London: Continuum, 2001.

Myers, Allen C., ed. *The Eerdmans Bible Dictionary*. Grand Rapids: Eerdmans, 1987.

Neyrey, Jerome H. Neyrey. "'I Said: You Are Gods': Psalm 82:6 and John 10." *Journal of Biblical Literature* 108 (1989): 647–64.

Noel, Ted, and Ken Noel. "A Scientific Paradigm for the Genesis Flood." *Journal of the Adventist Theological Society* 12 (2001): 106–38.

Noll, K. L. *Canaan and Israel in Antiquity: An Introduction*. Biblical Seminar 83. New York: Sheffield Academic, 2001.

Noll, Stephen F. *Angels of Light, Powers of Darkness: Thinking Biblically About Angels, Satan and Principalities*. Eugene, OR: Wipf & Stock, 1998.

Noonan, Benjamin J. "Abraham, Blessing, and the Nations: A Reexamination of the *Niphal* and *Hitpael* of ברך in the Patriarchal Narratives." *Hebrew Studies* 51 (2010): 73–93.

O'Brien, Peter Thomas. *The Letter to the Ephesians*. Pillar New Testament Commentary. Grand Rapids: Eerdmans, 1999.

Parker, Simon B. "The Beginning of the Reign of God—Psalm 82 as Myth and Liturgy." *Revue Biblique* 102 (1995): 532–59.

Penley, Paul T. "A Historical Reading of Genesis 11:1–9: The Sumerian Demise and Dispersion Under the Ur III Dynasty." *Journal of the Evangelical Theological Society* 50 (2007): 693–714.

Philo of Alexandria. *The Works of Philo: Complete and Unabridged*. Edited by Charles Duke Yonge. Peabody, MA: Hendrickson, 1995.

Pope, Marvin H. *Job: Introduction, Translation, and Notes*. Anchor Yale Bible 15. New Haven, CT: Yale University Press, 2008.

Pritchard, James Bennett, ed. *The Ancient Near Eastern Texts Relating to the Old Testament*. 3rd ed. with Supplement. Princeton: Princeton University Press, 1969.

Putthoff, Tyson L. *Gods and Humans in the Ancient Near East*. New York: Cambridge University Press, 2020.

Reed, Annette Yoshiko. *Demons, Angels, and Writing in Ancient Judaism*. New York: Cambridge University Press, 2020.

Reid, Daniel G. "Principalities and Powers." In *Dictionary of Paul and His Letters*, edited by Gerald F. Hawthorne, Ralph P. Martin, and Daniel G. Reid, 746–52. Downers Grove, IL: IVP Academic, 1993.

Robertson, Archibald, and Alfred Plummer. *A Critical and Exegetical Commentary on the First Epistle of St. Paul to the Corinthians*. International Critical Commentary. New York: T&T Clark, 1911.

Sarna, Nahum M. *Genesis*. JPS Torah Commentary. Philadelphia: Jewish Publication Society, 1989.

Schaff, Philip, ed. *A Dictionary of the Bible: Including Biography, Natural History, Geography, Topography, Archæology, and Literature*. Philadelphia: American Sunday-School Union, 1880.

Schreiner, Patrick. *The Ascension of Christ: Recovering a Neglected Doctrine.* Bellingham, WA: Lexham, 2020.

Sheridan, Mark, ed. *Genesis 12–50.* Ancient Christian Commentary on Scripture. Downers Grove, IL: InterVarsity Press, 2002.

Skehan, Patrick W. "A Fragment of the 'Song of Moses' (Deut. 32) from Qumran." *Bulletin of the American Schools of Oriental Research* 136 (1954): 12–15. https://doi.org/10.2307/3218997.

Skehan, Patrick W., and Alexander A. Di Lella. *The Wisdom of Ben Sira: A New Translation with Notes, Introduction and Commentary.* Anchor Yale Bible 39. New Haven, CT: Yale University Press, 2008.

Skinner, John. *A Critical and Exegetical Commentary on Genesis.* International Critical Commentary. New York: Scribner's, 1910.

Smith, Gary V. "Structure and Purpose in Genesis 1–11." *Journal of the Evangelical Theological Society* 20 (1977): 307–19.

Speiser, E. A. *Genesis: Introduction, Translation, and Notes.* Anchor Yale Bible 1. New Haven, CT: Yale University Press, 2008.

Steinmann, Andrew E. *Genesis: An Introduction and Commentary.* The Tyndale Commentary 1. Downers Grove, IL: InterVarsity Press, 2019.

Stevens, David E. "Daniel 10 and the Notion of Territorial Spirits." *Bibliotheca Sacra* 157 (2000): 410–31.

Stott, John R. W. *God's New Society: The Message of Ephesians.* The Bible Speaks Today. Downers Grove, IL: InterVarsity Press, 1979.

Sweeney, James P. "Stephen's Speech (Acts 7:2–53): Is It as 'Anti-Temple' as Is Frequently Alleged?" *Trinity Journal* 23 (2002): 185–210.

Stuckenbruck, T. Loren. *The Myth of Rebellious Angels.* Grand Rapids: Eerdmans, 2017.

Tanner, J. Paul. *Daniel.* Evangelical Exegetical Commentary. Bellingham, WA: Lexham, 2020.

Thiessen, Matthew. "The Form and Function of the Song of Moses (Deuteronomy 32:1–43)." *Journal of Biblical Literature* 123 (2004): 401–24. https://doi.org/10.2307/3268040.

Thompson, James W. *The Church According to Paul: Rediscovering the Community Conformed to Christ.* Grand Rapids: Baker Academic, 2014.

Tigay, Jeffrey H. *Deuteronomy.* JPS Torah Commentary. Philadelphia: Jewish Publication Society, 1996.

VanDrunen, David. *Divine Covenants and Moral Order: A Biblical Theology of Natural Law.* Emory University Studies in Law and Religion. Grand Rapids: Eerdmans, 2014.

Vangemeren, Willem A. "The Sons of God in Genesis 6:1–4: An Example of Evangelical Demythologization?" *Westminster Theological Journal* 43 (1980): 320–48.

Walton, John H. *Ancient Near Eastern Thought and the Old Testament: Introducing the Conceptual World of the Hebrew Bible.* Grand Rapids: Baker Academic, 2006.

Wenham, Gordon J. *Genesis 1–15.* Word Biblical Commentary 1. Dallas: Word, 1987.

Westermann, Claus. *Genesis 1–11.* Continental Commentary. Minneapolis: Fortress, 1994.

Widyapranawa, S. H. *The Lord Is Savior: Faith in National Crisis: A Commentary on the Book of Isaiah 1–39.* International Theological Commentary. Grand Rapids: Eerdmans, 1990.

Williams, David J. *Paul's Metaphors: Their Context and Character.* Peabody, MA: Hendrickson, 1999.

Williams, Guy. *The Spirit World in the Letters of Paul the Apostle: A Critical Examination of the Role of Spiritual Beings in the Authentic Pauline Epistles.* Forschungen zur Religion und Literatur des Alten und Neuen Testaments 231. Göttingen: Vandenhoeck & Ruprecht, 2009.

Wilson, Robert Dick. "The Names of God in the Old Testament." *Princeton Theological Review* 18 (1920): 460–92.

Witherington, Ben, III. *The Letters to Philemon, the Colossians,* and the *Ephesians: A Socio-Rhetorical Commentary on the Captivity Epistles.* Grand Rapids: Eerdmans, 2007.

Woods, Edward J. *Deuteronomy: An Introduction and Commentary.* Tyndale Old Testament Commentaries 5. Nottingham: Inter-Varsity Press, 2011.

Woudstra, Marten H. *The Book of Joshua.* New International Commentary on the Old Testament. Grand Rapids: Eerdmans, 1981.

Wright, N. T. *Christian Origins and the Question of God.* Vol. 4, *Paul and the Faithfulness of God.* Minneapolis: Fortress, 2013.

———. *Justification: God's Plan and Paul's Vision.* London: Society for Promoting Christian Knowledge, 2009.

Young, Edward J. "The God of the Fathers." *Westminster Theological Journal* 3 (1940): 25–40.

SUBJECT INDEX

Abbot, Thomas Kingsmill, 163
Abraham. *See also* Laban; Rachel
  blessing of, 30, 72–73
  Christ Jesus and, 115, 117–18,
    150
  father, 80–81
  gentile inclusion and, 83–87
  idolatry and, 10–11n26,
    73–79, 88, 89n1
  promise to, 30, 65, 78–83, 98,
    141, 148
  significance of Ur, 74–77
Abrahamic Covenant, 57,
  79–80, 81
Acts 2 and Pentecost, 47, 56–57,
  85, 168
Adam, 2–5, 24–30, 41, 50, 51–52
aliens, 53–55
Ancient Near Eastern (ANE)
  context and Bible, 3–4, 10, 28,
    33, 49n7, 90n5, 106, 110
  myths and, 34–35, 104n30
  sons of God, 15–16, 41
  temples, 111n44, 153n29
  viewpoint, 6, 33–34, 77,
    125n14
angels. See also *nachash;*
  rebellions
  elohim as, 31

creation and, 13–14
fallen, 31, 41, 139
humans after death, 10
humanity and, 32–33, 38
punishment of, 42–44
sons of God and, 18–19, 22
worship of, 130–31
Arnold, Bill, 7, 145, 147
Arnold, Clint, 190–91, 193
Babel. *See also* Deuteronomy 32
  worldview
  Abraham and, 74–76
  background, 46–47
  God's response to, 55–58
  one language, 47–50
  redemptive reversal of, 81–82
  return to Eden, 50–52
  tower of, 52–53
Barth, Markus, 147, 159
Baugh, S. M., 133
Beale, G. K., 181, 189
Best, Ernest, 160, 169
blessing of the nations. *See*
  Abraham
Bock, Darrell L., 127, 147–48
Caird, G. B., 132–33
Calvin, John, 148–49, 164
Christ
  ascension of, 113, 123, 133–41

SCRIPTURE INDEX

SCRIPTURE INDEX